ICT and Innovation in the Public Sector

TECHNOLOGY, WORK AND GLOBALIZATION

The Technology, Work and Globalization series was developed to provide policy makers, workers, managers, academics and students with a deeper understanding of the complex interlinks and influences between technological developments, including information and communication technologies, work organizations and patterns of globalization. The mission of the series is to disseminate rich knowledge based on deep research about relevant issues surrounding the globalization of work that is spawned by technology.

Also in this series:

GLOBAL SOURCING OF BUSINESS AND IT SERVICES
Leslie P. Willcocks and Mary C. Lacity

KNOWLEDGE PROCESSES IN GLOBALLY DISTRIBUTED CONTEXTS
Julia Kotlarsky, Ilan Oshri and Paul C. van Fenema

OFFSHORE OUTSOURCING OF IT WORK
Mary C. Lacity and Joseph W. Rottman

EXPLORING VIRTUALITY WITHIN AND BEYOND ORGANIZATIONS
Niki Panteli and Mike Chiasson

OUTSOURCING GLOBAL SERVICES
Ilan Oshri, Julia Kotlarsy and Leslie P. Willcocks

ICT and Innovation in the Public Sector

European Studies in the Making of E-Government

Edited by

Francesco Contini

and

Giovan Francesco Lanzara

First published 2009 by
PALGRAVE MACMILLAN

Palgrave Macmillan in the UK is an imprint of Macmillan Publishers Limited, registered in England, company number 785998, of Houndmills, Basingstoke, Hampshire RG21 6XS.

Palgrave Macmillan in the US is a division of St Martin's Press LLC, 175 Fifth Avenue, New York, NY 10010.

Palgrave Macmillan is the global academic imprint of the above companies and has companies and representatives throughout the world.

Palgrave® and Macmillan® are registered trademarks in the United States, the United Kingdom, Europe and other countries.

ISBN-13: 978–0–230–22489–6
ISBN-10: 0–230–22489–X

This book is printed on paper suitable for recycling and made from fully managed and sustained forest sources. Logging, pulping and manufacturing processes are expected to conform to the environmental regulations of the country of origin.

A catalogue record for this book is available from the British Library.

A catalog record for this book is available from the Library of Congress.

10 9 8 7 6 5 4 3 2 1
18 17 16 15 14 13 12 11 10 09

Printed and bound in Great Britain by
Cromwell Press Ltd, Trowbridge, Wiltshire

For Claudio Ciborra
ad memoriam

CONTENTS

TABLES

Figures

Acronyms

ADV	*Automatisierte Datenverarbeitung* (Ger.): Electronic data processing
AEV	*Abbuchungs- und Einziehungsverordnung* (Ger.): Regulation for debit entries
AFV	*ADV-Form Verordnung* (Ger.): Regulation for ADV
AIPA	*Autorità per l'Informatica nella Pubblica Amministrazione* (Ita.): Authority for Information Technology in Public Administration
AIX	Advanced Interactive eXecutive (Unix operating system)
ANT	Actor Network Theory
ASCII	American Standard Code for Information Interchange
ASVG	*Allgemeines Sozialversicherungsgesetz* (Ger): Social security law
ATM	Automatic Teller Machine
BGBlG	*Bundesgesetzblattgesetz* (Ger.): Federal Law Gazette
BRZ	*Bundesrechenzentrum* (Ger.): Federal Computing Centre
BSD Licence	Berkeley Software Distribution Licence (Open Source/ Free Software Licence)
B-VG	*Bundes-Verfassungsgesetz* (Ger.): Constitutional law
CCBC	County Court Bulk Centre
CELEX	Communitatis Europeae Lex
CESROG	*Centro Studi e Ricerche sull'Ordinamento Giudiziario dell'Università di Bologna* (Ita.): Research Centre for Judicial Studies of the University of Bologna
Cineca	Interuniversity Consortium for the development and managing of ICT
CMS	Case Management System
CNIPA	*Centro Nazionale per l'Informatica nella Pubblica Amministrazione* (Ita.): National center for information technology in the Italian public administration
CPL	Callable Personal Librarian

D&M	Delone and McLean model for IS success
DB2	Data Base 2
DCA	Department of Constitutional Affairs
DGSIA	Direzione Generale Sistemi Informativi Automatizzati del Ministero della Giustizia (Ita.): ICT Department of the Italian Ministry of Justice
DIN A4	International paper page standard
DTD	Document Type Definition
EDI	Electronic Data Interchange
EDP	Electronic Data Processing
EDS	Electronic Data System (Company)
EFTA	European Free Trade Association
EG	*Europäische Gemeinschaft* (Ger.): European Community
ELC	Electronic Legal Communication (English transation of ERV *Elektronischer Rechtsverkehr*)
EPS	Electronic Posting Service
ERP	Enterprise Resource Planning
ERV	*Elektronischer Rechtsverkehr* (Ger.): Communication channel with the judicial system; See ELC
ES	Entreprise System
FinStrG	*Finanzstrafgesetz* (Ger.): Penal law governing finance and taxes
G2B	Government to businesses
G2C	Government to citizens
G2G	Government to government
HGB	*Handelsgesetzbuch* (Ger.): civil law
HTML	Hypertext Markup Language
IBM	International Business Machines (Corporation)
ICT	Information and Communication Technologies
ICT	Information and Communication Technology
ID	IDentification
IEE	Internal efficiency and effectiveness
IMS	*Information Management System*, database and transaction manager from IBM
IR	Inland Revenue
IRSIG-CNR	*Istituto di Ricerca sui Sistemi Giudiziari Consiglio Nazionale delle Ricerche* (Ita.): Research Institute on Judicial Systems of the Italian National Research Council
IS	Information Systems

IWG	*Informationsweiterverwendungsgesetz* (Ger.): law on reusing information
JOP	Justice of the Peace Office *(Ufficio del giudice di Pace)*
LAN	Local Area Network
LIS	Legal Information System (English translation of RIS: *Rechtsinformationssystem des Bundes*)
MCOL	Money Claim Online
MS	Microsoft (Corporation)
NGO	Non-Governmental Organisation
NHS	National Health Service
NPM	New Public Management
PA	Public Administration
PDA	*Punto Di Accesso* (Ita.): Access Point to the RUG or to the SPC
pdf	Portable Document Format
PEC	*Posta Elettronica Certificata* (Ita.): Certified electronic mail
PFI	Private Finance Initiative
PKI	Public Key Infrastructure
PL/1	Programming Language One
PSBR	Public Sector Borrowing Requirement
PSI	Public Sector Information
RDB	*Rechtsdatenbank* (Ger.): Legal database
Re.Ge.	*Registro Generale* (Ita.): Case tracking system for criminal procedures
RIS	*Rechtsinformationssystem des Bundes* (Ger.): see LIS
RUG	*Rete Unitaria Giustizia* (Ita.): Virtual private network of the Italian Ministry of Justice
RUPA	*Rete Unitaria della Pubblica Amministrazione* (Ita.): Public administration unified network
SICC	*Sistema Informativo Contenzioso Civile* (Ita.): CMS for civil procedures developed for the Italian Courts of General Jurisdiction
SIDDA	*Sistema Informativo Direzione Distrettuale Antimafia* (Ita.): Information system for the italian District anti-mafia bureau
SIDNA	*Sistema Informativo Direzione Nazionale Antimafia* (Ita.): Information system for the Italian national anti-mafia bureau
SIGP	*Sistema Informativo del Giudice di Pace* (Ita.): CMS for civil procedures developed for the Italian Justice of the Peace Offices

SINTEF	*Selskapet for INdustriell og TEknisk Torskning ved Norges tekniske høgskole* (Nor.): The Foundation for Scientific and Industrial Research at the Norwegian Institute of Technology
SPC	*Sistema Pubblico di Connettività* (Ita.): Public system of connectivity
SQL	Standard Query Language
SSH2	Secure SHell 2
SSL	Secure Socket Layer
SSL2	Secure Sockets Layer 3
SSL3	Secure Sockets Layer 3
STAIRS	STorage And Information Retrieval System
StPO	*Strafprozessordnung* (Ger.): Law governing trials
TOL	Civil Trial OnLine (English translation of *Processo Civile Telematico – PCT*)
V	Volt
VoIP	Voice over the Internet Protocol
XML	Extended Markup Language
Y2K	Year 2000

ACKNOWLEDGEMENTS

The four year research project that led to this book was financed by the Italian Ministry of University and Research (FIRB Project 2001, grant nr. RBNE01KJTP). We are indebted to many colleagues and institutions, both academic and non academic, that gave us substantial support and advice. In particular, we wish to thank Giuseppe Di Federico, Director of IRSIG-CNR, the Research Institute on Judicial Systems of the Italian National Research Council, for intellectual stimulation and unfailing encouragement over the years. We also want to thank Francesca Zannotti, Director of CeSROG, the Centre for Judicial Studies of the University of Bologna, for her support in the early phases of designing the project proposal. Marilena Cerati and Battistina Fini, court administrators of the Justice of the Peace Office in Bologna, Kari Kujanen, Chief Information Officer of the Finnish Ministry of Justice, and Perry Timms of the British Department of Constitutional Affairs all provided support and access to information necessary for conducting the case study research. Stefano Aprile, Deputy ICT Director of the Italian Ministry of Justice and Marco Fabri, Senior Researcher at IRSIG-CNR gave us great assistance throughout the FIRB project. We warmly thank all of them.

Francesco Contini would like to thank colleagues of the IRSIG-CNR for the support and the help received during the preparation of the book. Special thanks go to Davide Carnevali, who shared ideas and many steps of the project. He would also like to express his gratitude to Antonio Cordella for his constructive collaboration from the first stages of the research project.

Giovan Francesco Lanzara wishes to mention the University of Bologna, who granted him sabbatical leave in the academic year 2006–2007. In this period both the London School of Economics and Political Science, where he was a visiting professor in the Information Systems and Innovation Group of the Department of Management, and the European University Institute in Florence, where he spent the spring semester of 2007 as a visiting scholar in the Department of Social and Political Sciences, provided perfect environments for carrying out the research and completing the book. Warm thanks go to all these institutions.

The ideas and the research findings presented here have been discussed in a number of seminars and workshops held at the London School of Economics, at the Gothenburg Research Institute of Gothenburg University, at the Libera Università degli Studi Sociali 'Guido Carli' in Rome, and at several international conferences. We are indebted to many colleagues who, on these occasions, have provided helpful criticism and advice. In particular, we want to thank Ole Hanseth of the University of Oslo, Adrienne Hèritier of the European University Institute in Florence and Geoffrey Walsham of the University of Cambridge , UK for their valuable remarks on critical research issues.

Alexandra Dawe and Vidhya Jayaprakash have carefully and skillfully coached us in the editing process and we are very grateful to them.

Finally each one of us wishes to thank his own and the co-editor's wife – Claudia and Grazia – for their patience and support, which greatly facilitated our collaboration and the successful completion of this book.

SERIES PREFACE

Technology is all too often positioned as the welcome driver of globalization. The popular press neatly packages technology's influence on globalisation with snappy sound bites, such as "any work that can be digitized, will be globally sourced." Cover stories report Indians doing US tax returns, Moroccans developing software for the French, Filipinos answering UK customer service calls, and the Chinese doing everything for everybody. Most glossy cover stories assume that all globalisation is progressive, seamless, intractable, and leads to unmitigated good. But what we are experiencing in the twenty first century in terms of the inter-relationships between technology, work and globalisation is both profound and highly complex.

We launched this series to provide policy makers, workers, managers, academics, and students with a deeper understanding of the complex interlinks and influences between technological developments, including in information and communication technologies, work organisations and patterns of globalisation. The mission of this series is to disseminate rich knowledge based on deep research about relevant issues surrounding the globalisation of work that is spawned by technology. To us, substantial research on globalisation considers multiple perspectives and levels of analyses. We seek to publish research based on in-depth study of developments in technology, work and globalisation and their impacts on and relationships with individuals, organisations, industries, and countries. We welcome perspectives from business, economics, sociology, public policy, cultural studies, law, and other disciplines that contemplate both larger trends and micro-developments from Asian, African, Australia, and Latin American, as well as North American and European viewpoints.

The first book in the series, *Global Sourcing of Business and IT Services* by Leslie P. Willcocks and Mary Lacity is based on over 1,000 interviews with clients, suppliers, and advisors and 15 years of study. The specific focus is on developments in outsourcing, offshoring, and mixed sourcing practices from client and supplier perspectives in a globalising world. We found many organisations struggling. We also found other practitioners adeptly creating global sourcing networks that are agile, effective, and cost efficient. But they did so only after a tremendous amount of trial-and-error and close attention to details. All our participant organisations acted in a context of fast moving technology, rapid development of supply side offerings, and ever changing economic conditions.

Knowledge Processes in Globally Distributed Contexts by Julia Kotlarsky, Ilan Oshri, and Paul van Fenema, examines the management of knowledge processes of global knowledge workers. Based on substantial case studies and interviews, the authors – along with their network of co-authors – provide frameworks, practices, and tools that consider how to develop, coordinate, and manage knowledge processes in order to create synergetic value in globally distributed contexts. Chapters address knowledge sharing, social ties, transactive memory, imperative learning, work division and many other social and organisational practices to ensure successful collaboration in globally distributed teams.

Offshore Outsourcing of IT Work by Mary Lacity and Joseph Rottman examines the practices for successfully outsourcing IT work from Western clients to offshore suppliers. Based on over 200 interviews with 26 Western clients and their offshore suppliers in India, China, and Canada, the book details client-side roles of chief information officers, programme management officers, and project managers and identifies project characteristics that differentiated successful from unsuccessful projects. The authors examine ten engagement models for moving IT work offshore and describe proven practices to ensure that offshore outsourcing is successful for both client and supplier organisations.

Exploring Virtuality within and Beyond Organizations by Niki Panteli and Mike Chiasson argues that there has been a limited conceptualisation of virtuality and its implications on the management of organisations. Based on illustrative cases, empirical studies and theorising on virtuality, this book goes beyond the simple comparison between the virtual and the traditional to explore the different types, dimensions and perspectives of virtuality. Almost all organisations are virtual, but they differ theoretically and substantively in their virtuality. By exploring and understanding these differences, researchers and practitioners gain a deeper understanding of the past, present and future possibilities of virtuality. The collection is designed to be indicative of current thinking and approaches, and provides a rich basis for further research and reflection in this important area of management and information systems research and practice.

ICT and Innovation in the Public Sector by Francesco Contini and Giovan Franceso Lanzara examines the theoretical and practical issues of implementing innovative ICT solutions in the public sector. The book is based on a major research project sponsored and funded by the Italian government (Ministry of University and Research) and coordinated by Italy's National Research Council and the University of Bologna during the years 2002–2006. The authors, along with a number of co-authors, explore the complex interplay between technology and institutions, drawing on multiple theoretical traditions such as institutional analysis, actor network theory, social systems theory, organisation theory and transaction costs economics. Detailed case studies offer realistic and rich lessons. These case studies include e-justice in Italy and Finland, e-bureaucracy in Austria, and Money Claim On-Line in England and Wales.

In addition to these first five books, several other manuscripts are under development. These forthcoming books cover topics of ICT in developing countries, global ICT standards, and identity protection. Each book uniquely meets the mission of the series.

We encourage other researchers to submit proposals to the series, as we envision a protracted need for scholars to deeply and richly analyse and conceptualise the complex relationships among technology, work and globalisation.

LESLIE P. WILLCOCKS
MARY C. LACITY
November 2007

Edward Bernroider is Senior Lecturer at the Royal Holloway University of London. In 2005 he received the Habilitation from the Vienna University of Economics and Business Administration. His current research interests include governance, risk and compliance with active model support applied to IT service management and other service systems. Output from his research activities has been presented in over 50 international publications including various refereed journals, conferences and books.

Francesco Contini has been a researcher at the Research Institute on Judicial Systems, National Research Council (IRSIG-CNR), Bologna, Italy, since 1996. His main research interests are the processes of institutional and technological change in justice systems and the analysis of policies designed to improve and assess the quality of justice. He has written extensively on these topics and has edited various books, among which is *Technology and Justice in Europe* (Kluwer, 2001, with Marco Fabri). He has served as a consultant for institutions such as the Council of Europe, the World Bank, and the United Nations Office on Drugs and Crime.

Antonio Cordella is Lecturer in Information Systems at the London School of Economics and Political Science. His research interests cover the areas of E-government, Economic Theories of Information Systems, and the Social Studies of Information Systems. His most recent publications in the e-government area are: 'E-government: towards the e-bureaucratic form?' *Journal of Information Technology* (2007), and Contini, F. and A. Cordella. 'Information System and Information Infrastructure Deployment: the Challenge of the Italian e-Justice Approach' *Electronic Journal of E-Government* (2007).

Barbara Czarniawska holds a Chair in Management Studies at GRI, School of Business, Economics and Law at the University of Gothenburg, Sweden. Her research takes a constructionist perspective on organising, most recently exploring the connections between popular culture and the practice of management. She is interested in methodology, especially in field studies and in the application of narratology to organisation studies. Recent books in English: *A Tale of Three Cities* (Oxford University

Press 2002), *Narratives in Social Science Research*, (Sage 2004), *Actor-Network Theory and Organizing* (edited with Tor Hernes, Liber 2005), *Global Ideas* (edited with Guje Sevón, Liber 2005), *Management Education and Humanities* (edited with Pasquale Gagliardi, Edward Elgar 2006), *Shadowing and Other Techniques of Doing Fieldwork in Modern Societies*, (Liber 2007).

Marco Fabri has been a senior researcher at the Research Institute on Judicial Systems, National Research Council (IRSIG-CNR), Bologna, Italy, since 1996, and adjunct professor at the Faculty of Political Science of the University of Bologna. His main research interests, and the focus of his publications, are in the areas of judicial administration, justice reform, court management, information and communication technology in the justice system, where he takes a comparative perspective. He has coordinated several European research projects on the administration of justice, and he has served as a consultant for institutions such as the Council of Europe, the World Bank, the Italian Ministry of Justice.

Jannis Kallinikos is Professor and Research Chair in the Information Systems and Innovation Group, Department of Management, London School of Economics. Major research interests include the study of the practices, technologies and formal languages by which organisations are rendered predictable and manageable and the modes by which current institutional and technological developments challenge the organisational forms that have dominated modernity. Some of these themes are analysed in detail in his recent book *The Consequences of Information: Institutional Implications of Technological Change,* Edward Elgar, 2006.

Stefan Koch is Associate Professor of Information Business at the Vienna University of Economics and Business Administration. His research interests include cost estimation for software projects, the open source development model, software process improvement, the evaluation of benefits from information systems and ERP systems. He edited a book entitled 'Free/Open Source Software Development' for an international publisher in 2004, and has published over ten papers in peer-reviewed journals and over 30 in international conference proceedings and book collections.

Giovan Francesco Lanzara is professor of Organisation Theory and Political Science at the University of Bologna and, since 2006, a visiting professor at the London School of Economics and Political Science in the Information Systems and Innovation Group, Department of Management. His research interests concern ICT and organisational innovation, learning processes in organisations and institutions, and organisational knowledge and design. His work has been published in a number of books and in major international journals such as the *Journal of Management Studies, Organization Studies, Accounting Management and Information Technology, the Journal of Strategic Information Systems, American Behavioral Scientist, and the European Journal of Political Research.*

Marco Velicogna has worked as a researcher at the Research Institute on Judicial Systems of the Italian National Research Council since 2003. His main fields of interest are judicial administration, comparative judicial systems, court technology, and the evaluation and management of innovation. He is currently a PhD candidate at the University of Utrecht, Faculty of Law with a thesis on "ICT evaluation in the Judiciary". He has participated in a number of national and international research projects. He has also served as a consultant for the Italian Ministry of Justice and as a scientific expert for the European Commission on the Efficiency of Justice of the Council of Europe (Cepej).

Leslie P. Willcocks is Professor of Technology Work and Globalisation at the London School of Economics and Political Science, head of the Information Systems and Innovation group and director of The Outsourcing Unit there. He is known for his work on global sourcing, information management, IT evaluation, e-business, organisational transformation as well as for his practitioner contributions to many corporations and government agencies. He holds visiting chairs at Erasmus, Melbourne and Sydney universities, is Associate Fellow at Templeton, University of Oxford, and has been for the last 18 years Editor-in-Chief of the *Journal of Information Technology,* He has co-authored 29 books, including most recently *Major Currents in the IS Field* (Sage, London 2008), and *Global Sourcing of Business and IT Services* (Palgrave, London, 2006) He has published over 180 refereed papers in journals such as *Harvard Business Review, Sloan Management Review, MIS Quarterly, MISQ Executive, Journal of Management Studies, Communications of the ACM, and Journal of Strategic Information Systems.*

Introduction

Francesco Contini and
Giovan Francesco Lanzara

This book takes issue, both empirically and theoretically, with the problem of building e-government systems for the delivery of public services. In its contributing chapters it variously explores a range of phenomena that appear when Information and Communication Technologies (ICT) encounter the current administrative routines and the established institutional and normative frameworks of the public sector.

It is commonplace that the rise of the Internet offers the public sector a great deal of opportunity for change, and visible changes have indeed taken place in recent years. If we take even a cursory look at the public services delivered by governments to citizens in most Western democracies, we are likely to be surprised at the extent to which the production and delivery of such services are now dependent on ICT. Technology reaches out everywhere across an increasing range of public sectors, affecting the performance of core government functions and having an influence on the very legitimacy of public institutions. Nowadays the presence and operations of ICT in the public sector are visible (though perhaps not obvious) to any citizen who happens to engage in transactions with a state agency through a computer and the Internet – paying a tax or a fine, registering a vehicle, requesting a birth certificate, or applying for planning permission.

Yet, despite the rapid diffusion of ICT-based innovation and the perceived 'visibility' of the ongoing changes in the delivery channels of public services, the rate of failure of e-government development projects is high. Problems and pitfalls in implementation make the 'Online One-Stop Government' model still a distant ideal (Wimmer and Traunmuller, 2002). In practice the design of e-government systems is a difficult endeavour. The depth and magnitude of the changes have often been underestimated. The construction of a new electronic channel for the delivery of public services requires the establishment of a composite architecture, not only technological but also – and perhaps mainly – institutional. But bureaucratic procedures and institutional frameworks exhibit pervasive institutional inertia, which renders transformation difficult.

The generally accepted model for building e-government systems is 'the electronic public service delivery model'. Design focuses on specific functional applications, software programs, virtual interfaces and the output of services. The design problem is usually defined as 'putting public services online'. Solutions are mainly imported from e-commerce and e-business environments, where 'the public' does not exist as a category and users are seen as customers buying and selling on the market, not citizens with rights and obligations. Yet, e-government is not only or simply e-service provision or putting online what is currently traded and delivered offline; it involves much more – the design of sound and effective ICT infrastructures and the creation of institutionally embedded communication systems. This entails nothing less than a reconfiguration of the existing institutional frameworks.[1]

At the present stage, not much is yet known about the underlying infrastructures that support the smooth running of software programs and functional applications that are critical for the deployment of electronic services in the public domain. Only sparse knowledge is available on the processes by which such infrastructures are assembled. And even less is known about the implications that they have for the overall architecture and viability of public institutions and for effective government-to-citizen computer-mediated communication. The need for the design of integrated e-government architectures has been recurrently evoked, but has not yet taken the centre stage in the research and development agenda. This gap is partly pardonable because these infrastructures are complex, elusive, unbounded and evolving. They defy empirical definition and have ambiguous 'location' in space and time. Besides, research so far has largely focused on the 'performance' of e-government (Dunleavy, Margetts, Bastow and Tinkler, 2006), and less on the ICT-enabled 'architectures' that support and make the delivery of public services possible. Practical concern has been on information systems, conceived as autonomous and self-contained software applications embodying specialised functionalities, while only mild interest has been shown in the emerging problems of interoperability of systems, programs or codes that were to be integrated in order to support more complex functionalities (Hanseth and Lundberg, 2001). Indeed, the early experience of e-service development in the public sector shows that interoperability extends beyond the problem of technical standards, involving critical issues of integration and compatibility between technologies and institutions (Hanseth and Monteiro, 1998).

Given these premises, the purpose of this book is to contribute to a deeper understanding of the emergent technical and institutional architectures for e-government. Its major source has been a multiple-year research project on ICT for justice in four European countries. The project was sponsored by Italy's Ministry of University and Research and jointly coordinated by the Research Institute on Judicial Systems of the Italian National Research Council (IRSIG – CNR) and the Research Centre for Judicial Studies of the University of Bologna (CESROG) during the years 2002–06. Among the project's main objectives was the development of new methodologies for supporting ICT-based innovation in the judiciary and in public administration at large. As a critical public sector in contemporary democracies, justice exhibits specific characteristics that make it quite an interesting field for studying ICT development for e-government and the electronic delivery of public services. The judiciary is a normatively thick public domain, with a heavy regulative status and a bulky legacy system that make it quite recalcitrant to innovation (Di Federico, 2001). Problems of authority, autonomy, control, territorial jurisdiction, legal validity and legitimacy make all efforts at introducing ICT to the judiciary rather cumbersome. The interactions of 'new' technical procedures and requirements with engrained institutional practices often produce rigidities that obstruct the processes of innovation and the long-term evolution of the emerging ICT-mediated institutional ecology. Given the institutional conditions, the design of an integrated ICT-enabled institutional framework is difficult.

Yet at the same time, because of the very same characteristics mentioned above, the judiciary constitutes a field of phenomena and problems that can also offer broader insights into ICT-based innovation in the public sector and the dynamic interplay of ICT and institutions. The encounter – at times cooperative, at times competitive – between two powerful regimes of regulation – technology and the law – generates problems of accountability, effectiveness, legitimacy, fairness, authority and agency, which, at any rate, are shared by all government sectors where the delivery of public services to the citizen is the critical mission. But in the judiciary, perhaps due to its peculiar normative 'thickness', problems and tensions tend to manifest themselves in a magnified manner.

The argument running across the chapters is two-fold: on the one hand ICT and the networked information infrastructures that support the public sector's bureaucratic procedures help to build new institutional architectures and administrative processes; on the other hand the institutional and legal order channels and shapes ICT, treating it as a new object of codification. In this framework, the electronic delivery of public services is regulated by a mixed regime of technical and normative rules and entrusted to public-private networks, where private companies play an increasingly important role.

When an e-service is implemented two major changes occur:

1. ICT becomes a constitutive element of the public sector and the government's overall institutional fabric, not simply an instrument or a means to an end. ICT technical standards and software codes tend to assume regulatory functions, adding to, complementing or displacing traditional legal norms and regulations. Therefore two different regulative regimes emerge, which work in parallel and in competition and whose interactions often generate adverse side effects.

2. Public administration must increasingly rely on private companies, often multinational corporations, providing technical infrastructure, software applications, skilled personnel, and a range of critical functionalities such as identity certification, payment systems, technical maintenance and the like. Consequently, new institutional arrangements emerge that are increasingly based on private-public partnerships and extensive outsourcing, which in turn demand new forms of regulation and management, sophisticated contracting and new procedures for accountability.

A variety of institutional configurations result from the encounter and the entanglement of different elements: the technology, the law, the bureaucracy and the market. These elements have limited mutual compatibility and, when they come together, they generate frictions and tensions. The chapters of this book explore, each in its own way, the varied phenomenology and the practical implications of such encounters, with a specific focus on the limited compatibility and the tensions that arise in the process of building e-government systems and architectures.[2] The four chapters of Part I contribute in different ways to opening and articulating the emerging conceptual space at the intersection of ICT and institutions. To begin with, Giovan Francesco Lanzara describes the emerging landscape of digital institutions as an 'assembled mix' of technical and institutional components that are in part an evolutionary outcome and in part a product of human intervention and design. In an 'assemblage', administrative action tends to be 'dislocated' to technical devices and administrative capabilities are increasingly enabled and mediated by the technical infrastructure. Taking the case of the Internet, in the second chapter Barbara Czarniawska reviews the idea that institutions and the legal order in general are inscribed in machines and technical norms and the implications of this for e-government and e-justice. She discusses how the Internet and its norms may become mechanisms for social control, thus performing critical institutional functions, but at the same time she points at the boundaries of such control. Jannis Kallinikos' ideas about the regulative power of technology and its implications for bureaucracy are presented in the third chapter. The author points out that, due to limited compatibility, effective translation or reduction of bureaucratic procedures to technological devices and media require 'functional simplification' and 'system closure', without which e-government systems and the operations of e-bureaucracy will be seriously impaired. Antonio Cordella and Leslie Willcocks broadly examine the mutual relationships between bureaucracy and the market in the making of e-government systems, going beyond the unsatisfactory experience of New Public Management. Based on an appraisal of the UK public sector they assess the possibilities and the limitations of outsourcing in the provision of government e-services and stress the need for a new balance between the private sector and the market on the one hand and, on the other, the crucial mission of public bureaucracies in modern democracies.

The five chapters of Part II deal with experiences of ICT development in four European countries. In the fifth Chapter Marco Fabri compares two very divergent examples in Europe, Italy and Finland, leading to what he calls the constraining and the enabling models for e-justice development. Whilst in Finland the procedural law is seen as an enabler of technology, in Italy technology is regarded as an enabler of the exact application of procedural law, with the two models yielding quite different outcomes as to the effective development of e-services for the citizens. Stefan Koch and Edward Bernroider's study of the Austria's ICT projects in Chapter 6 illustrates the transition from traditional ICT development based on mainframe, proprietary logic to the open logic of the Internet. As the design focus shifts from in-house software applications to interfaces and communication infrastructures, the new systems, in order to be developed and operated, require the collaboration of multiple private and public actors within a changed institutional configuration that crosses the boundaries of traditional bureaucratic organisations. In Chapter 7, based on a rich case study of a web-based electronic system for money claims in England and Wales, Jannis Kallinikos illustrates how the technical components of the pre-existing installed base can be resourcefully exploited and smartly combined with institutional and normative components to the purpose of designing the new services. Kallinikos argues that complex administrative procedures undergo a process of functional simplification to fit technological requirements, while offline procedures are occasionally activated to back up the online system. Next, Marco Velicogna and Francesco Contini tell the story of the painstaking and controversial effort to develop a web-based portal and e-services for the Justice of the Peace Office in Bologna, Italy. Tracking the ongoing process of development as participant observers and project facilitators for more than two years, the authors describe the subtle dynamics of the installed base, technical and institutional, and, most crucially, discover that the achievement of a satisfactory alignment of technical and institutional infrastructures requires a continuous activity of bargaining, brokerage, coordination, cultivation and *bricolage* within the project. Finally, the last Chapter by Francesco Contini pulls the research threads together drawing the major lessons from the case studies. Using the theoretical concepts illustrated in the first part of the book, Contini assesses and compares the different development experiences in terms of the multiple mediations that need to be enacted between the technology and the institutional framework both in the design and in the contextual use of e-services. Such mediations are shown to play a critical role in the making of assemblages and in dealing with the issue of the fair accessibility and usability of e-government services in contemporary democracies.

Notes

1. The scale of the institutional changes entailed by ICT and government is stressed in several studies and reports to the European Commission. See for example Leitner (2003).
2. Giovan Francesco Lanzara was responsible for editing Part I of this volume and Francesco Contini for Part II.

References

Di Federico, G. (2001), *Foreword.* In Fabri, M. and F. Contini (eds), *Justice and Technology in Europe: How ICT is Changing Judicial Business.* The Hague: Kluwer (v–viii).

Dunleavy, P., Margetts, H., Bastow S. and J. Tinkler (2006), *Digital Era Governance.* London: Oxford University Press.

Hanseth, O. and E. Monteiro (1998), 'Changing Irreversible Networks: Institutionalization and Infrastructure'. *Proceedings of the IRIS Conference.* Retrieved at heim.ifi.uio.no/-oleha/Publications/nordunet.pdf. Visited 7 November 2007.

Hanseth, O. and N. Lundberg (2001), 'Designing Work Oriented Infrastructures'. *Computer Supported Cooperative Work*, 10, 347–372.

Leitner, C. (2003) (ed.), *eGovernment in Europe: the State of Affairs.* Report presented at eGovernment 2003 conference. Como, Italy, 7–8 July. European Institute of Public Administration, Maastricht, NL.

Wimmer, M. and R. Traunmuller (2002), 'Towards an Integrated Platform for Online One-Stop Government'. *ERCIM News, Special Theme: e-Government*, Issue 48, January, 14–15.

PART I

Perspectives: ICT, institutions and e-government

CHAPTER 1

Building digital institutions: ICT and the rise of assemblages in government

Giovan Francesco Lanzara

Mapping the emerging landscape

The encounter between Information and Communication Technology (ICT) and institutions generates phenomena that invite us to reframe our ways of looking at the organisational structures and at the overall institutional fabric of our society. Markets, corporate firms, public agencies and governments increasingly rely upon technology for collecting, producing, processing, and exchanging information (Benkler, 2006; Kallinikos, 2006). In many public domains, similarly to what has occurred in markets, it has become more and more difficult to do without technology in the production and delivery of services to the citizens. Public sector providers, from healthcare to education and justice, increasingly depend on large information infrastructures for their operations (Hanseth, 2000; Hanseth and Lundberg, 2001), and larger and larger components of the public sector are regulated by ICT standards and protocols. Although in the public sector we do not yet have the equivalent, for example, of the computer trading systems of the financial markets or the corporate Enterprise Resource Planning (ERP) systems of industry, ICT produces specific structural changes and arrangements in the public domain. What an institution or administration can do depends more and more on the technical and architectural choices that are made at the level of the technology. Technology is gaining a new centrality in the configuration of political and economic space at the local and global level, becoming itself a political object (Barry, 2001).[1] The phenomenon does not only affect single organisations and institutions, or single countries or regions, but spreads across political, functional and geographical spaces by re-scaling traditional hierarchies and connecting single and self-contained administrative agencies into multiple networks. The nature of the agencies is changed, as they become more and more entangled in a variety of crosscutting arrangements, and once well established organisational and administrative boundaries are blurred. As students of globalisation have noticed (Duffield, 2001; Walsham, 2001; Avgerou, 2002; Sassen, 2006), local changes may be inconspicuous but over time the overall outcome is not.

For example, consider the following:

- In the health care sector hospitals, health centres, diagnostic laboratories, pharmaceutical firms, social insurance offices, suppliers, and the general practitioners themselves are all connected to a technical infrastructure, structured in multiple layers, that allows for the transmission of social, medical and diagnostic data enabling therapeutic work, supporting inter-organisational coordination, and giving rise to a wide array of institutional practices and arrangements. Without such infrastructure what we perceive today to be a health care system and its services would collapse.
- In taxation fiscal agencies, accountants, professional service firms and tax payers are wired to a computer-based system through which, nowadays, only the government can extract taxes from the citizen and citizens can fulfil their fiscal obligations. The technical system connects multiple agencies into a network where demographic, income, corporate and fiscal data circulate and support basic operations of inspection and cross-checking, management, accountability, and enforcement of sanctions.
- Judicial procedures are increasingly supported by network infrastructures that allow the exchange of data and judicial documents between the courts and the parties, and also connect banks, bailiffs, postal services and other public or private bodies that play a part in the administration of justice. With the growth of such infrastructures, the companies that develop and administer the systems can assume key public functions in the same administration of justice. Moreover, in criminal justice, effective crime prevention and the due process of law are strictly dependent on the imbrications of the information infrastructure with the new institutional arrangements and the legal codifications that take shape around such infrastructures.

These examples suggest that large sectors of government and administrative operations are becoming increasingly 'wired'. However, while recent research has documented the dynamics of large-scale ICT infrastructures in the corporate sector (Weill and Broadbent, 1998; Broadbent and Weill, 1999; Monteiro and Hanseth, 1999; Ciborra, 2000), comparatively less attention has been dedicated to the institutional effects and implications of large ICT-based systems in the field of public administration. Information Systems Research and Science Technology and Society studies (Bijker, Hughes and Pinch, 1987; Hughes, 1987; Joerges, 1998) have mainly focused on technological components and capabilities, but the complex imbrications of the latter with existing institutional frameworks have been little explored so far. Particularly, it is as yet unclear whether the lessons learned in the corporate sector can be directly transposed to the public domain. For example, it is doubtful whether public administration will ever achieve a degree of organisational agility and responsiveness comparable to that of firms and other corporate actors in ways that are adequate enough for the effective deployment and management of electronic services. More critically, and differently from corporate firms, in the area of governmental institutions only scant and fragmented knowledge is available on the restructuring of entrenched administrative practices and institutional configurations occasioned by the technology (Barley, 1986; Dunleavy, Margetts, Bastow, and Tinkler, 2006).

In this chapter I move away from issues concerning technology proper or e-government performance and shift my focus of attention to the institutional dynamics triggered by the appearance of ICT within institutional settings.[2] I am interested in shedding some light upon the multiple mediations that take place between ICT and existing institutions in their encounters. My leading questions are: What is involved in building online institutions? What kind of institutional dynamics is enacted as a consequence of the adoption and use of ICT in the institutional environment? What kind of technical and institutional landscape emerges from the interplay of ICT and public bureaucracy? Specifically, I try to capture the core features of the emerging landscape by discussing the rise and implications of new configurations that I will call 'assemblages'.[3] Assemblages result from the encounter and the multiple mediations between large ICT systems and the existing institutional frameworks and codes of the society. They are made up of heterogeneous components displaying multiple logics which cannot be easily reduced to one another. Hence, assemblages are not 'hybrid' entities, but rather 'composites' – collection of components which tend to maintain their specificity. Within such assemblages technical objects and systems come to play an increasingly important role, to the point of gaining an institutional, constitutive valence. In this perspective, technical components cannot be simply considered as 'instruments' or tools to execute administrative tasks. Rather, they are themselves 'formative' of the cognitive and institutional context within which tasks and routines are executed and gain their meaning (Ciborra and Lanzara, 1994, 1999).[4] Technology becomes thus equally critical for execution as well as for sensemaking and legitimacy. However, at the same time technology needs to be standardised and aligned by issuing standards and designing interfaces, and that can only be done by and within existing institutions. This is how the normative, institutional dimension finds its way down into the technical component. We can reasonably speak of ICT-mediated and supported institutional arrangements. In sum, as institutions become more 'wired' into technological circuits, so at the same time ICT becomes increasingly regulated, both legally and institutionally. More often than not a competitive field is generated, where technology and the law strive to 'civilise' one another, each trying to reduce the other to its own precepts or requirements (Lessig, 1999, 2007).

Assemblages comprise in various mixes and connections a plethora of actors such as political authorities, technical agencies, bureaucratic organisations, ICT providers, professional service firms, regulatory bodies, software engineering companies, research centres, together with the technical, functional and normative components with which they run their transactions. Taken as a whole, an assemblage constitutes a loosely structured, ever evolving institutional ecology of heterogeneous elements, where boundaries and linkages among administrative bodies cannot be unequivocally fixed, because they tend to shift and drift in time. Assemblages are always *ad hoc* and change all the time, thereby needing constant re-conceptualisation. What seems to emerge as a distinctive feature of this institutional ecology is that coordination and execution of administrative tasks are equally dependent on formal, normatively based authority structures *and* on functional linkages and communication standards and protocols. The overall functioning of assemblages and the viability of the ecology itself are based as much upon communications and functional relations as upon authority and norms. The regulatory and enforcing capabilities of public administration are thus likely to be equally embodied into formal laws and regulations *and* into technical standards and devices brought about by the technology, while the share of the latter is constantly growing. The combination of technical standards and software codes with bureaucratic procedures and legal codes gives rise to novel institutional arrangements and practices, where ICT increasingly provides the implicit context for the performance of such practices and the overall operation of administrative agencies. One of the visible consequences is that normativity gets disaggregated into specialised sub-assemblages (Sassen, 2006, pp. 421–422).

Theoretical perspectives: inscription-delegation and functional simplification

The encounter and the mediations between ICT and institutions can be explored and framed along two different but not necessarily incompatible perspectives. In either perspective a specific view of the phenomena that mark the rise of an assemblage is advanced. In one perspective ICT is regarded as an analogue or a functional equivalent of a traditional institution, that is, a sort of code that, vicariously, *does* what the institution did. This means that the technology *works as* an institution in its own right, by producing cognitive, normative and regulative effects in specific administrative domains or in society at large (see Kallinikos, in Chapter 3). Instead of formulating laws and norms, and threatening with sanctions or rewarding with incentives, technological artefacts enforce certain practices that become institutionalised along with the recurrent use of the artefacts.[5] The fundamental problem of channelling and regulating social and administrative behaviour is thus taken care of by the technology – be it artefacts, tools, media, or other ('taken care of' is by no means equivalent to 'resolved'). In this sense, the institutional component is absorbed within/by the technological machinery. As the cases reported in this book show, administrative, judicial and legal procedures, together with the agency that comes with them, are *inscribed*, although not entirely, into technical procedures and objects. Basically, the institutional authority for enforcing rules and regulating social conduct is increasingly *delegated* to the technology.[6] Compliance and appropriate conduct are obtained *by technology*, which appears to be more 'objective' or at least less questionable than formal authority, legal rule or direct human supervision. The technical artefact with its pre-programmed uses tells us what to do and how to do it, often in a more compelling manner than the law does.[7] Fine-grained distributed systems and pervasive software codes make possible ubiquitous and effective law enforcement, a phenomenon that Lawrence Lessig has expressed in synthetic and non-equivocal terms: 'Code is law' (Lessig, 1999, 2007).

In a second perspective institutions become more technical inasmuch as they have to adapt to the possibilities and constraints brought about by new technologies for the electronic processing and exchange of administrative data and the delivery of products and services. Institutional codes, practices, and administrative procedures need to be *functionally simplified* (or *reduced*) in order for the technology to be able to manipulate and sustain them.[8] Technology is a self-contained code itself, but of a different kind than the normative and regulative codes supporting existing institutions: it has its own self-referential language and works as a regime based on standards, to which traditional institutions must adapt or be made compatible with. It follows that, within its own functional domain, technology can only recognise institutional objects, relations and procedures which are streamlined and standardised to the extent that they can be properly handled.[9] When the complexity of the administrative or legal procedure is too high, bits and segments of it may be left out by the technology, discarded, or arranged so that they can eventually be enacted as offline back ups when necessary.[10] At the same time, and as a distinctive effect of the interaction, ICT also transforms and remoulds institutional configurations, boundaries and linkages by pushing them either towards increased connectivity and network-like forms or, alternatively, towards poor integration and high fragmentation.

The two ways of accounting for the emergence of an assemblage seem to capture complementary aspects of the same broad phenomenon, but in fact, although the processes occasionally converge to the same outcome, they point to two distinctive theoretical frameworks through which the emergence and the dynamics of such assemblages can be accounted for. One is based on Actor Network Theory (ANT) and the sociology of translation (Callon, 1980, 1986; Joerges and Czarniawska, 1998; Latour, 2005; Law and Hassard, 1999), while the other draws on social systems theory (Luhmann, 1990, 1996) and old and new institutional analysis (Weber 1978; Powell and DiMaggio, 1991). The first perspective stresses the *inscription-delegation* of institutional and administrative agency to technological objects or systems which assume authority on behalf of institutional agents and produce the very same effect of enforcement (Czarniawska and Hernes, 2005; Lanzara and Patriotta, 2007). Specifically, it points to the emergence of complexly entangled networks of human agents and technical artefacts (or 'action nets', in Czarniawska's variation) (Czarniawska, 2004), where, symmetrically, technology is regarded as having the same 'active' ordering properties of institutional and administrative agents. The second perspective instead focuses on what the technology *does* to institutional and normative frameworks. Here a different phenomenon is predicated, namely the *reduction* of the institutional to the technological (objects, rules, practices, domains, languages). The critical point at issue is how and to what extent complex administrative agency can be transformed and eventually 'simplified', in order to be harnessed within the functional circuits of technology, and what is lost or gained in such reduction. In this view not all the complexities of human agency can be fully inscribed into the technology, but only what technological codes admit (Kallinikos, 2005, 2006).[11]

Whereas in the former perspective ICT is regarded as producing institutional effects and enforcing institutional practices, hence coming to gain an institutional valence, in the latter an institution or normative code is regarded as responding and eventually adapting to technological features, requirements and standards, hence becoming itself a technology of regulation. However, no matter which perspective we take, what is of more substantive interest for our purposes is that new mediations are enacted and a new institutional environment takes shape where administrative action and regulation assume new features. As a consequence of multiple mediations, new composite entities emerge.

Assemblages and information infrastructures

In order to explore the descriptive and interpretive potential of the notion of assemblage for institutional analysis, it is important to distinguish it from the notion of information infrastructure (Hanseth, 1996; Star and Ruhleder, 1996; Weill and Broadbent, 1998; Ciborra, 2000; Hanseth and Lyytinen, 2004). The idea of an assemblage, in the sense intended here, captures the peculiar nature of the emerging institutional configurations that unfold from (and because of) the encounter of existing institutional frameworks with ICT infrastructures.

The 'assemblage-like' configuration essentially emerges for two different sets of reasons. First, multiple conflicting logics are simultaneously at work when ICT-based systems enter established institutional domains. For example, technical and, in general, cost-effectiveness requirements may be at odds with existing bureaucratic or legal constraints, or with principles of democracy and fairness. Moreover, economic, legal and political forms of accountability interact with one another and all have repercussions on institutional and technical innovation. It is therefore difficult to obtain, in the design of both technical and institutional systems, fully formalised and well-integrated configurations. What come out instead are incomplete, semi-formalised components that must be connected and made compatible with one another; in other words they need to be 'mediated'. Second, technical implements and institutional components, which were set in place in the past but are now obsolete or unusable, cannot be easily 'discarded' or 'erased' and replaced by brand new ones. They remain there, sometimes one on top of the other, even if they do not quite fit coherently. Assemblages tend to grow 'by accretion' and 'in layers'. They are always in the process of being assembled, but seldom worked out into a final state. Their components are best captured in the ongoing transformation (Lanzara, 1999). From this perhaps stems the difficulty of studying assemblages: they are made of mutable elements and relations, and are always in the process of becoming. As Cooper has underlined, what counts in an assemblage is what falls 'in-between' – the mediations (Cooper, 1998, 168).

Although assemblages need to be conceptually and empirically distinguished from information infrastructures, many features of the underlying information infrastructures filter into the fabric of assemblages. Thus, similar to information infrastructures, assemblages tend to be heterogeneous, loosely structured (although some parts can be tightly coupled), patchwork-like, open-ended, modular and often functionally redundant. Assembled technical and institutional components gain the character of 'hook-ups', connected through interfaces, linkages and gateways (David and Bunn, 1988). Thus, the technical infrastructure is just the shared, multilayered platform supporting the administrative operations and transactions taking place within and across the assemblages. The point we want to make is that the nature and the relative mix of the infrastructural base upon which current institutions rely are changing, and as a consequence the shape of the institutions themselves is also changing.

Consider for example a university library system. At the national and international level, a library system increasingly depends for its basic services upon a web of connections and communications linking other libraries, staffing services, publishing companies, bookstores, dotcom sales companies, brokers, telecom companies, call centres, and so on. All such connections are regulated by shared standards and protocols. The management and delivery of library services are performed through software applications which are 'plugged in' to the larger infrastructural web. Large components of the agency of the library system are now part of (and dependent on) a standardised ICT infrastructure, without which the service would be unthinkable. For the library user the visible outcome of the change are new frames, procedures and linkages accessible through the computer, supporting inter-library enquiries and exchanges, requests, controls, check points and other daily operations. As a result we come to confer an institutional status to software artefacts and devices that on the one hand allow us to do things that we could not do before and on the other hand channel our behaviour apparently without formal enforcement.[12] We experience a shift in the common perception of what a library is and what it means to have dealings with a library. The library becomes less a *holder* where books are physically contained or a place one goes to, and more a *hub* to which one hooks up electronically, thus gaining access to a wide range of inter-library transactions. However, together with improved accessibility and informativity new forms of regulation are brought about.

Organisations and institutions of the public sector, as they accommodate the pervasive pressure of technological developments and learn to exploit the powerful connective properties of ICT, change their configurations, through a process that has been described, perhaps too simplistically, as a transition from the hierarchical to the network form (Rhodes, 1997; Benkler, 2006; Kallinikos, 2006; Sassen, 2006). But there is more than that: in the process old forms are disassembled and their components are transformed, re-assembled and re-utilised according to a different logic. New functional linkages and communication channels are established. As a consequence, new technical and administrative things can now be done that could not be done before, but have become possible thanks to the features of the new ICT-based infrastructure.[13]

Adding to the complexity of the picture, the studies collected in this book show that the institution-specific normative logic has an influence, too, on the overall dynamics. Authorities, legal frameworks, rules of law, territorial and functional jurisdictions, security and privacy requirements, established administrative capabilities and the daily practices of local offices all contribute to the shaping of the assemblages. As a result, technical infrastructures will not work effectively unless they are carefully hosted and integrated in the institutional settings and somehow dressed in legal clothes and 'domesticated'. A struggle for dominance and compatibility ensues, where at times convergent and at times divergent movements and pressures lead to patchy, makeshift arrangements that can emerge in different combinations. In the process of change, not all routines and skills specific to pre-existing institutional structures can be smoothly and non-problematically transposed into the new institutional environment. As Sassen (2006) illustrates in her socio-historical study on globalisation, the change is never linear and straightforward, it happens along multiple dimensions, affecting a broad range of features.[14]

The dynamics of the installed base: technical and institutional components

The above discussion leads us to the observation that assemblages do not come out of the blue, nor can they be designed in a conventional sense. They result from the bringing together and adapting of pre-existing technical and institutional materials. But the character of the available components to be assembled and the configurations in which they come *do* make a difference for the kinds of assemblages that are put together and come into being. All technical and institutional innovations face a conversion problem. Materials and components that were designed and utilised for specific functions or tasks in the past can be either discarded or converted to new uses.

However, not everything can be converted or, alternatively, discarded. Recent studies of the dynamics of large ICT infrastructures have underlined the critical role of the *installed base*, that is, the standing elements and systems that are already in place when a development project starts and are largely irreversible (Chae and Lanzara, 2006; Ciborra, 2000; Ciborra and Hanseth, 1998; Hanseth and Lundberg, 2001).[15] These studies, though, only consider the technical dimension of the installed base, that is, the standards imposed by the ICT, even if they confer a socio-technical character to it.[16] Our research shows, however, that the technical infrastructure can only in part account for the emerging configurations of assemblages in the domain of government institutions. In order to fully account for the complex dynamic patterns of ICT-based innovation in the public sector we must also consider the institutional and organisational components of the installed base, which comprise the existing institutional arrangements, the organisational routines and capabilities *and* the established legal codes and frameworks. Depending on the specific characteristics of the institutional installed base, new organisational configurations and capabilities and new ICT solutions can be fostered or hindered. Therefore both the technical and the institutional components of the installed base have 'enframing' properties, to use Heidegger's terminology (Heidegger, 1977). In other words, the dynamics behind the rise of assemblages result from the complex interaction of the ICT standards and protocols with the bureaucratic machinery and the established normative order. Indeed our cases show that, in different conditions, such interaction can produce both enabling and hindering effects on technical and institutional innovation, occasioning assemblages of very different kinds.[17]

The emergence of assemblages is in itself neither a desirable nor an undesirable occurrence, but can of course be characterised by positive or negative externalities. The self-propelling or, alternatively, self-defeating consequences of techno-institutional change have been highlighted by Yochai Benkler in his book *The Wealth of Networks* (Benkler, 2006). In a healthy dynamics, certain institutional changes will enable innovative uses of ICT that in turn will enable further institutional changes that expand the range of opportunities for a wider number of people, for example extended access to services, fairness, time and cost savings, higher quality of services, more freedom, and so on, while at the same time increasing administrative effectiveness. Here a virtuous circle is set in place. In Finland, for example, new opportunities provided by the technology have been exploited to redesign judicial procedures so as to improve citizens' access to judicial services. Developers have started from the concrete judicial practices to implement the ICT. As a consequence, a new family of ICT-mediated legal practices has emerged. Alternatively, less favourable dynamics will unfold where existing institutions enforce certain uses of ICT, which hinder changes and innovations in institutional practices, thus leading to a vicious circle. In Italy, for example, information technology has been used by central administration as a tool to enforce the proper functioning of existing formal procedures – basically to automate formal legal transactions – according to a strict logic of bureaucratic control. Although the objective may have been 'rational' in principle and the project guided by good intentions, the unwanted consequence has been an increased rigidity brought about by the further layer of ICT-based regulation. A second-order unwanted consequence has been that while in the old system actors had learned to design smart and flexible ways of getting around the rigidities of the 'law on the book' to get things accomplished, with the new system they have to start all over again, and this is even more difficult due to the accumulation of rigidities. In both cases new institutional and technical arrangements are produced, but while in the former case the new institutional configuration is assembled from the informal practices already in place and by amending the legal code accordingly, in the latter case it is generated within the existing bureaucratic logic of control and formality, thus embedding all the negative features of the previous system. Consequently innovation cannot happen or lags behind.[18]

The installed base always exhibits a dual character. It can be a resource for creative design and innovation or a trap from which it is difficult to escape. On the one hand the installed base constitutes a pool of available resources that can be turned into convertible and usable materials for the development of new configurations. In this sense it is a nurture ground for innovation and a platform for change. On the other hand it is a source of inertia, limiting the scope of innovation and hindering the development of new configurations. More subtly, the dynamics of the installed base is such that the larger it becomes, thus generating increasing returns on adoption, the more likely it is that it will eventually turn into an ever bigger trap by irreversibly excluding alternative choices and paths of action, or by making the learning costs of change too high. In many an instance the installed base can be unfavourable and obtrusive to the point of becoming hostile to the desired change. Indeed new configurations can sometimes be obtained only by destroying the extant installed base or by struggling hard to neutralise its inertial influence. In contrast, in other instances the installed base can reveal surprising generative and adaptive properties that greatly facilitate evolutionary change and the diffusion of innovation. In either case the installed base is something that we cannot avoid confronting in a process of innovation. Because of its duality, when one engages in the development of ICT-based institutional and administrative innovation, as Hanseth (2000) has put it, one must design at the same time *with* and *against* the installed base. In order to effectively face up to such a challenge what is required is both 'resourcefulness', that is the ability to creatively use or re-use the available resources, and a 'balancing capability', that is the ability to live and play with the dilemmas inherent in the dynamics of the installed base. As we have experienced in our research, the actors' capability of understanding and playing with the dual nature of the installed base can vary widely, depending on culture, on the design logic and on the intrinsic characteristics of the existing infrastructure.

If we look at the case studies in Part II of this volume, both the Money Claim Online development project in the United Kingdom (MCOL, Chapter 7) and the design of e-services for the Justice of the Peace Office in Italy (JOP, Chapter 8) provide vivid illustrations of such twofold dynamics. MCOL provides an example of resourceful use and conversion of the available installed base, both technological and institutional, by pragmatically enacting a strategy of functional simplification. Administrative rules and routines are adapted to the requirements of the technology, and ICT components are modified so as to make them compatible with the existing legal and administrative procedures. By contrast, the Justice of the Peace case in Italy reveals the persistent obtrusiveness of the available installed base, particularly of its normative components, in the design of e-services. Most of the JOP project is a story of the painstaking efforts to find ways to detour the bureaucratic obstacles and technical constraints repeatedly and unexpectedly emerging at different stages in the process. The ongoing prototyping and experimental activity goes hand in hand with the 'political' activity of coordinating, negotiating and building consensus among the partners of the project, in order to make things happen and get the project going.

On the other hand, in Italy's Civil Trial OnLine (TOL, known as *Processo civile telematico or PCT* in Italian, see Chapter 5), the existing normative and organisational framework is taken as given and untouchable – it is the formal code of civil procedure and its associated back office procedures – and the bulk of the design effort resides in aligning the information technology with the institutional installed base. Here there is very little mutual adaptation and learning, and no attempt at converting and exploiting what there is for purposes of innovation. The underlying philosophy is to design the new technical system from scratch, only looking at the formal rules of procedure and plainly ignoring all considerations regarding organisational constraints or practical effectiveness. In comparison to Civil TOL, Finland's online legal services (*Tuomas* and *Santra*, in Chapter 5) epitomise the obverse case of smart exploitation of both the technical and institutional installed base: developers look first at the practices of concrete agents and amend formal rules so as to adapt them creatively to the opportunities offered by the ICT. This may be said to be a virtuous case of 'plastic design'. Finally, the Austrian innovation story (Chapter 6) instructively shows in the clearest form the passage between the in-house, hierarchical, top-down development logic of a traditional information system such as Legal Information Services (LIS) and the open logic of the web-based Electronic Legal Communication (ELC). While in the development of LIS there is very little consideration of the installed base, in the case of ELC installed base considerations become paramount. Indeed, no development would be possible without relying on the available technical and institutional infrastructure.

What emerges distinctively from our case studies is the context-specific and history-dependent character of the installed base in its technical and institutional dimensions. In this connection, it is important to stress once more that the installed base is not only an inertial entity that prevents or slows down innovation; it is also a potential, a platform, a reservoir (or a *standing reserve*, again to use Heidegger's formulation) of possibilities for action that need to be enacted. In this sense, it gains a much more dynamic connotation. As it does things, produces effects and makes things happen (or prevents them from happening), the installed base can be viewed as an actor in its own right, having a life of its own (Hanseth, 2002). This adds to the ambivalence of the installed base, as in some respects it can be conceptualised as a *material* that must be shaped, while in other important respects it is an independent actor or *actant* that cannot be fully controlled, but can nevertheless shape the course of future ICT and institutional innovation.[19]

The tension between innovation and conservation

The ambivalent nature of the installed base is at the root of the dynamic tension between innovation and conservation. With different emphasis this tension is revealed by our studies.

Whenever one sets out to initiate a process of innovation and engages in developing new ICT-based systems and applications, dilemmas emerge which are intrinsic to the structural dynamics of allocative processes. We must distinguish between inter-group and inter-temporal problems of resource allocation. All efforts at innovation require the mobilisation of collective resources, which must be (re)allocated across groups and across time. Resources are material and cognitive. Large components of these resources are embodied in the installed base, technological and institutional, and can condition the future paths of innovation to a large extent. In the simplest possible terms, innovation amounts to learning how to do new things that could not be done before, or to do the same things more effectively or efficiently than before. In many an instance innovation entails being able to creatively convert available resources to different purposes and uses. In most efforts at innovation a dilemma arises as to what extent one should exploit what is already there or should instead discard it and start all over again from scratch by exploring brand new possibilities, which make little or no use of what there is (March, 1991).[20]

Any innovation – technical, organisational, socio-cultural, even a political innovation – brings about a change in the set of possibilities that define what can be done and how. All processes of innovation involve transformations of artefacts, practices and cognitive frameworks. Innovation entails both making and breaking patterns of agency, de-structuring as well as re-structuring, and the emergence of new repertoires of routines and capabilities. In a broader sense, innovation involves the making of a world different from what came before, that is, the production of a world that no longer conforms to (and no longer confirms) the one that has been experienced so far. However, and this is whence dilemmas find their nurturing ground, at the outset the new world appears at the same time to be an offspring and a negation of the old world. It is intended to transcend it, but is being built on top of it and is supported by it. In turn the old world, while it makes resources available for building up and going beyond, at the same time generates incentives and pressures to conservation that make the *status quo* hard to relinquish (Genschel, 1997). A consequence of such dynamics is that in processes of innovation much of the old world percolates into the new one, sometimes to an extent that paradoxically it seems that the innovative endeavour itself becomes a means to reproduce the *status quo* (Schon, 1971).[21] Thus in the end conservation wins. But at the opposite extreme we may find a dynamic that does not admit any 'carrying over' from the old to the new, as when for instance the departure from the old order is so radical and abrupt that nothing of what we have is compatible with the new order, or admitted by it. The obvious consequence of the latter dynamics is that the new world, because of the high transformation and compatibility costs, is unattainable or unsustainable: it will never generate the critical mass that will make it desirable to an increasing number of potential adopters. Indeed, the greater the design efforts spent in the creation of a different world, the stronger the neutralising or counteracting pressures that hinder change and push back to the old tend to be.[22] Hence, again, conservation wins.

All processes of innovation and change involving the mobilisation and allocation of critical resources are apparently affected by a contrasting dynamics. If change must be obtained, the durability of old practices and structures must be suspended and new tentative arrangements must be designed and tried out. However, such change produces instability, and old practices and structures suddenly become more salient, in order to hold on to something solid and reliable and to mitigate the uncertainty associated with instability. Therefore contrasting pressures develop: on the one hand durability is rejected and transiency is produced by a variety of designs, experiments and explorative moves; on the other hand, simultaneously, transience is contested and durability is searched for by tentatively casting some kind of structure on indeterminate, shifting situations. Yet, enduring stabilisation is not produced overnight: most often it requires time, patience and endurance. Low tolerance for uncertainty, both at the individual and organisational level, will impede the process of innovation and make it roll back to the safer territory of familiar routines. But too high a tolerance for uncertainty, or even fascination with it, may lead nowhere or to disaster. Both fear and fascination simultaneously drive agents' behaviour when faced with novelty and uncertainty, thus enacting a complex dynamics and pushing them into dilemmas of action (Schon, 1982).

Our analytical difficulties in accounting for the emergence of assemblages stem precisely from having to deal with an array of objects and phenomena that retain an ambivalent, dual character: they are at the same time 'other' and 'the same', different and alike, novel and familiar, 'moving' and 'still', so that it is difficult to assign them a non-ambiguous ontological status.[23]

In different modalities and with varying degrees of visibility and drama the dilemma of innovation and conservation emerges in all the contributions to this book. In the efforts at developing new ICT-based configurations and services in different institutional settings we observe an ongoing tension between simultaneous and opposing pressures of innovation and conservation. Both the technical systems and the institutional frameworks tend to offer selective incentives to forms of agency that reproduce the system or are at least compatible with its operations. In a way, systems only recognise and admit forms of agency or even types of agents that are compatible with their own logic. Therefore, long established repertoires of capabilities and patterns of agency tend to become embedded, sometimes deeply engrained, in self-reproducing structures and to become system or structure-specific. Reinforcing a particular kind of selectivity produces the opportunity and the learning costs of change, that is of switching to new competencies. This makes innovation difficult.

Can assemblages be designed?

A recurrent *leit-motif* of the innovation stories reported in this book is the ongoing struggle between the dynamics of the installed base and human design. All the studies reveal a tension between the deliberate, purposeful efforts at designing new ICT-based institutional configurations and the shifting and drifting phenomena resulting from inertial, evolutionary forces or from contingent and unpredictable events. In their dealings actors are caught between the shadow of the past and the image of the future (Kuran, 1988). In the midst of these complexities it is critical to assess the place of design. If the installed base is so autonomous and dominant that it seems to have a life of its own and behave as a 'nonhuman actant', to use the language of ANT (Latour, 1991), what is the meaning and the scope of design? How can the properties of the installed base be harnessed to the purpose of ICT development and innovation? If human agency is to play a role, how can it be made compatible with the quasi-autonomous logic of the installed base? More generally, what kind of design is compatible with evolution? The underlying question is whether the complex configurations that we have called 'assemblages' can be designed at all, and, if they can, what meaning should be given to the term 'design', what should the design process look like, and what exactly is it that is designed.

In the recent research literature there is a growing awareness that information infrastructures exhibit features that make them quite different objects from traditional information systems based on stand-alone software applications (Hanseth, 1996; Hanseth and Monteiro, 1997; Hanseth and Lyytinen, 2004). Specifically, it is acknowledged that large-scale ICT infrastructures are too complex to be designed according to given technical and functional specifications that can be fixed *ex ante* and enforced by a single authoritative designer. Indeed, if we closely look at real life design and implementation we notice that a great deal of design activity amounts to *bricolage*, that is, the creative recombination and conversion of available materials so that they *make do* for new purposes (Ciborra, 2002). User needs and system specifications shift over time. Systems evolve in the course of the development process, sometimes in directions and ways that defeat the very same requirements and conditions the original design was supposed to meet. Other times instead, endogenous processes, which cannot be easily anticipated or understood, lead the system to paths and configurations that were not expected but may nevertheless contain interesting and surprising opportunities for further development. Structured, grid-like development methodologies, traditionally applied to in-house software applications and systems development, are ineffective in design settings characterised by multiple actors with shifting or indeterminate objectives, specialised skills, divergent views and stakes, limited learning capabilities, and partial authority over the design process and the outcomes of it. In addition, actors must cope with the features of the installed base, which may heavily influence the feasible solutions or the design paths that can possibly be taken, thereby becoming a 'critical design factor' (Hanseth and Lyytinen, 2004). Design situations of this kind demand a great deal of experimental and improvisational skill.

In such situations one of the critical challenges for the design of innovation becomes how to meet two opposing sets of requirements: *evolvability* and *robustness* (Wagner, 2005). On the one hand *evolvability* must be allowed, that is the ability of a system or infrastructure to undergo adaptive changes and evolve easily in the face of changing environments, which pose novel and ever shifting requirements. The problem here is that one must design for possibilities, for what is *not yet there*. Designs and configurations must be open and loose enough so as to be future-proof or extendible. Indeed, as we have observed in our cases, many components are designed to be part of something else, which is as yet unknown. On the other hand *robustness* must also be ensured, that is the ability of a system or infrastructure to quickly achieve a stable structure and produce increasing returns on adoption and use. This involves some kind of systemic *closure* and lock-in, channelling the system into selected paths to the exclusion of others, so that it can become profitably usable in a relatively short space of time. But, as robustness and evolvability seem to be at odds with one another, how can this apparent dilemma be tackled? How can design produce openness and closure at the same time? The cases show that a tentative answer to the question may reside precisely in the way systems and their components are assembled and linked together in loose *composites*. Gateways, linkages and interfaces help to lock the system into closed circuits of functional operations, but at the same time, by reaching out to an increasing number of potential users, open up evolutionary possibilities for change and innovation.

In the attempt to deal with such complexities, a fruitful perspective on the design of information infrastructures, based on the metaphor of *cultivation*, has been proposed by Dahlbom and Janlert (1996) and further developed by Hanseth (1996) and Hanseth and Lyytinen (2004). In this view processes of technical and institutional innovation are seen as similar to organic processes in nature and agriculture, whose natural evolution can be acted upon and facilitated by timely and careful human intervention. As farmers help corn to grow and physicians help wounds to heal (and the patient to recover), so designers can help (or hinder) the growth of assemblages by exploiting the evolutionary forces already at work and by playing with the multiple constraints and opportunities hidden in the existing technological and institutional infrastructure. While the complex, quasi-autonomous dynamics of the installed base tends to discourage architectural or engineering approaches, it allows careful 'growing' and 'nurturing' activities that help the installed base evolve and expand.

For sure, the agricultural metaphor helps us grasp the essence of what we are about when dealing with large-scale ICT systems, sensitising us to the influence of endogenous forces and processes. Yet, when used to develop a design strategy, it may lead to a simplified view of the complexity of change and of the practice of design *as it really happens*, underestimating critical features of real life design situations.[24] This is most apparent in the 'design kernel theory' recently proposed by Hanseth and Lyytinen (2004), which is to my knowledge the most systematic and complete treatment of the point. The theory focuses on the architectural and technical features of information infrastructures, outlining a strategy of how to deal with standard setting and the technical features of the installed base. But the normative and institutional components of the installed base and their influence on design are kept out of the picture or put in the background, as is the legal process underlying standard setting. Moreover, the theory discounts the political complexity of ICT and implementation generated by the presence and interaction of multiple agents, none of which can guide and monitor the design process individually. What the theory misses, it seems to me, is the fact that the development or 'cultivation' of information infrastructures is more an institution building endeavour rather than an engineering exercise. It critically depends both on the interplay between the technology and the existing institutional frameworks and on the social interactions among the actors involved.

A more articulated picture seems to emerge from our research work. To begin with, the design of an infrastructure does not take place in the technical domain only, but critically entails the transformation of normative regulations, the (re)design of organisational routines, and the learning of new skills. Many of the problems and bottlenecks arising in the development of information infrastructures seem to stem from institutional constraints and limited learning capabilities rather than from the intrinsic features of the technology. Rather than dealing with socio-technical systems we are dealing with a complex assemblage of rules, practices, values and imageries embedded in institutional and normative frameworks that need to be 'cultivated' as well, and eventually redesigned, otherwise no technical system will be able to operate. Standard setting is thus not only a technical activity, but an institutional process in its own right, entailing *town plannng + ICT design* (handwritten)

formal agreements among actors and the design of legal frameworks, that is, a great deal of institutional design. Moreover, in the formulation of Hanseth and Lyytinen (2004) it is implied that there is some pre-ordained agent (individual designer, chief engineer, organisation or public agency) who has the authority to enforce instructions about what should be done, when and by whom regarding the ICT. Unless the bureaucratic and project authority structure is monolithic and unchallengeable, this is not an easy condition to obtain. But even when this is the case, it is the ICT itself that makes the exercise of (established) authority problematic. As our studies show, most of the time in complex ICT-based innovation there are several 'farmers' attending to their own business in the same 'growing' field, and often they want to grow different crops on the same field at the same time, in some cases even advancing exclusive proprietary claims on the field or parts of it. We must then acknowledge that the activity of design, however one may wish to define it, is distributed across a variety of actors who have specialised skills, mixed interests and different expectations in time, and who play on a field over which property and control rights are often overlapping, ambiguous and controversial. The actual configurations of assemblages result from the interactions of multiple agents following multiple logics and having different priorities and timescales. Actors are seldom synchronised. The real challenge for design then becomes how to bring the agents together and make them cooperate to cultivate and grow the ICT.

Patterns of design

Our studies open multiple windows on the processes by which assemblages come about in different institutional settings. They tell different stories – each showing a specific mix of technical and institutional dynamics, evolutionary phenomena and deliberate design, structure and contingency. Each story discloses something that the other stories hide or don't talk about. In the following, by looking at the similarities and differences in the stories, I will sketch the features that seems to me to stand out in the different development experiences.

Multiple actors and authority structures. The design setting is characterised by multiple actors – government, corporate, technical or other – none of them exercising full control over the entire project, but each in charge of only one segment of the system. Although the design process is sensitive to the authority structure in the domain, even in heavily hierarchical settings and top-down implementation processes, such as Austria and Finland, central authorities with global reach cannot actually 'reach' and track all the local threads of the project in a comprehensive way. Monocentric structures can better facilitate a more 'compact' design than distributed, policentric ones, but they can also hinder grassroots initiatives and local innovation.

Institutional sponsors and project champions. In the various settings studied different actors may assume a critical leading or integrative role in promoting innovation and taking responsibility for coordination: for example, the Department of Constitutional Affairs for England and Wales' MCOL, which relied on a mix of hierarchy and subcontracting; the Ministry of Justice in Italy's TOL and Finland's *Tuomas* and *Santra*, which used hierarchical authority; the Federal Computing Centre in Austria, a mixed public-private body; the Research Institute on Judicial Studies (IRSIG) in Italy's JOP, which acted as a project champion and facilitator, becoming a critical enabler of network communication and project coordination. There is always an initiating point or platform for (re)design: for example, in the JOP case it is the home made website initially developed by the director of the JOP local office; in MCOL it is the County Court Bulk Centre (CCBC), the agency that manages the bulk money claim system (on top of which MCOL is built); in TOL the starting point for design is the code of civil procedure.

Episodes, discontinuous activities and situated interventions. Because of multiple engagements and commitments, actors attend to one thing at a time. Their activity can be described as a sequence of situated interventions, bounded in space-time, striving to make something happen and keep the process going; actors engage in commitments and transactions with one another and then make decisions leading to some kind of autonomous or joint activity that is continued for a while. However, actors' attention and activities are often diverted or deflected by the occurrence of incoming events. As a consequence, implementation tends to be intermittent and discontinuous in character: there are episodes of intense activity and close cooperative work followed by long periods in which little or nothing happens and actors seem to leave the project and go back to dealing with their own affairs. Usually the timing and speed of the process are dictated by the time-frames of bureaucracy and the political process rather than by the technology, and the speed of development varies considerably from project to project.

Adapting, repairing and redesigning available components. Design activity tends to be 'local' and fragmented, focusing on single components or aspects of the system; it can never be comprehensive of the entire system or assemblage, and, perhaps with the notable exception of Trial OnLine, it is never configured as the implementation of a blueprint plan or concept, fixed *ex ante*. Most of the design activity focuses on components that are already in place and need to be adapted and redesigned. Many of the design questions that pop up during the process are of the kind: How can we use what we have here and make it do something different from what it does? What functionalities should be added to the existing systems so that we can get what we want? How do we streamline and simplify existing procedures so that they can be seamlessly run online by the software?

Converting, linking, and plumbing. Most of the design consists in converting and linking functionally related components into a more complex assemblage by making different kinds of links, interfaces and channels; for example, MCOL is an assemblage produced out of 'ready-mades' of other systems, which were already in place. Subsequent configurations are built in layers, one on top of the other. In all cases the critical design challenge and the bulk of the activity of construction concern the complex underlying 'plumbing' that supports relatively simple applications and services; they only marginally concern the software applications as such, or the functionally specialised information systems, the development of which is relatively straightforward.

Redesigning administrative routines, interfaces and jurisdictions. Functional systems that once were being run in separate domains are connected by being 'hooked' to the technical infrastructure, and begin to have an effect on one another; consequently they have to be properly interfaced and made compatible by designing and implementing new intra- and inter-organisational routines. ICT components migrate or are moved across existing administrative boundaries, and this tends to generate ambiguity in authority and jurisdictions, which are sometimes contested: Where should such and such a facility be located? Who should be in charge of its operations? Who should or should not have access to it? To what extent, for instance, can database management be outsourced to private companies? (see Chapter 4 by Cordella and Willcocks, in this volume).

Characteristics of the installed base. The technical installed base can be more or less obtrusive or enabling, depending on the degree of modularity and re-combinability of its components and on the gateways that can be adopted. Standards for data exchange, user interface and connectivity are developed at different degrees of structuredness and completeness: for example, while UK's MCOL can rely on a well established e-government Interoperability Framework, such a condition does not yet hold in Italy. In addition, the institutionally installed base makes a difference: norms and regulations, bureaucratic procedures, organisational tools and practices, the administrative culture itself (formalistic versus pragmatic, legalistic and procedural versus outcome oriented, top-down versus bottom-up, trust-based versus control-based) may influence design frameworks, paths and choices, and even system architectures.

These features of the design process suggest that, in spite of the complex structural dynamics characterising techno-institutional change, innovation can be facilitated or induced by concerted design efforts based on 'local' intervention.[25] Indeed, the peculiar features of ICT systems and their installed base provides a ground and a starting point for developing a design approach compatible with the evolution and the complexity of assemblages. Firstly, because systems are open, heterogeneous and loosely integrated, they always have some 'slots' in their fabric which human agency can fill. Systems exhibit global inertia and locally sensitive points at the same time, and by touching these points remarkable effects can be produced. As a whole, systems tend to show high resilience, but locally they are always up for grabs. Secondly, the evolution of systems is punctuated by contingencies that may have generative effects and can be exploited by human actors for influencing future configurations.[26] These elements create a space, both practical and conceptual, where opportunities emerge for human agency and intervention. In the end, as in the ongoing maintenance and renovation of an old edifice, it is precisely the gaps, the imperfections and the overall inefficiency of the system that call for intervention. Though perhaps modest and distant from the Faustian ideal, intervention is the only mode of design compatible with systems complexity and evolution.

Administrative action across the assemblages: dislocations, concatenations, and interoperabilities

The emergence of the assemblages as distinctive composites of technical and institutional elements has a number of implications for the ways we understand organisations as empirical entities and define organisation as a phenomenon. The advent of ICT produces a re-ordering effect on the organisational landscape of the public sector: it simply makes new things available and new actions possible, while making some of the pre-existing options impossible.

First of all, administrative action is 'dislocated'. Some critical functionalities and operations, which are typically performed by and within organisations, are transposed and inscribed in the ICT infrastructure and in technical devices, often in a simplified form. Procedure is not contained within fixed boundaries but runs across the heterogeneous segments of the assemblage. Administrative, procedure-based action tends to become a set of 'concatenations' of technical devices and human actions crossing the assemblage. The outcomes of administrative action are not enforced by the authoritative implementation of pre-established rules, but rather stem out of the 'concatenations' of the administration with technological implements and components, some of which are privately designed, built and run by private ICT companies, which are now part of the governmental landscape. Consequently, new organising effects emerge from a combination of persons, devices and material rather than from authoritative enforcement and conformity to rules (Barry, 2001).

One of the major consequences of such 'dislocation' is that administrative capabilities are now increasingly enabled by the technical infrastructure. Technological devices form and support capabilities for thought and action, and new web- and Internet-based capabilities are added to a core of traditional paper-based operations. Coordination and control are increasingly supported by technical standards, which are set by external regulatory authorities, and routine operations are delegated to the machine. As Dunleavy, Margetts, Bastow and Tinkler (2006) have noticed governments and public authorities no longer run their own functions, at least not entirely, nor are they fully in control of their own information resources. 'The Weberian concept of a government organization as a self-contained, socio-technical system, where agencies are defined by their in-house operations and technology, no longer seems adequate' (Dunleavy, Margetts, Bastow and Tinkler, 2006, 15). 'Many agencies become their websites – where the electronic form of the organization increasingly defines the fundamentals of what it is and does' (Dunleavy, Margetts, Bastow and Tinkler, 2006, 3).[27] It seems that agencies, as we know them in the public domain, undergo a double transformation: from in-house to open assemblage operations and from material to digital.[28]

For example, the web portal of the JOP Office (see Chapter 8 in this volume) enacts a new way of delivering and using judicial services within a digital medium. When relevant components of the agencies migrate to the digital space, a new organisational topography emerges where places, spaces, times, relations, circuits, formal procedures and practical routines are redefined. This networked configuration results from re-assembling materials and functional elements that already existed but are now embedded in/ supported by a different kind of ICT infrastructure. The JOP Office with its front desk services is extended into its virtual image on the web, reaching out to its customers (solicitors, law firms, public and private agencies, citizens) with messages, memos and file documents every time it is needed. For their part, the lawyers or the generic users can enact the JOP front desk on the screens of their desk top computers asynchronously and at their will. Basically, what in 'real-space' looks like two distinct organisational entities, the judiciary office and the law firm – well defined by their respective boundaries, tend to merge into one another in the digital space, creating a virtual system of online activities where new things and actions and new forms of integration are made possible by the underlying infrastructure.[29] The JOP portal works as a 'boundary object', that is, an object situated at the boundary of two or more interacting communities of agents (Star and Griesemer, 1989). The portal connects, but at the same time it is an ambiguous and controversial object, because it is perceived in different ways by the interacting groups: while the JOP office staff perceive it as an outer extension of the office – an online *public service* that should be made openly available to all citizens, the lawyers tend to regard it first as a *commodity* that should be bought and sold on the market. Then, as they proceed in their testing experiments, they come to see it as an *office tool* producing value added effects for their firms and helping to reduce costs for the lawyers and, in the long run, for their customers. A further, and different image of the web portal is entertained by the developers themselves, who perceive it as an *experimental object*, which allows design experiments and the building up of new knowledge on ICT and institutional dynamics. Around the JOP portal – a digital artefact – and by means of it, a still uncharted and contested territory takes shape, together with an emerging network of organisational and institutional relationships. The agents' perception of the portal as an ambiguous object reveals a sense of displacement: whoever the agent is that interacts with it, the object must be 'positioned' within a new organisational and semantic topography, so that it can help organisations to make sense of their new environment and their position within it.

Dislocations and transformations of the kind just described are not usually painless for organisations. They entail a fair bit of friction, learning and re-positioning. For one thing, organisations must learn to share resources with other agencies and make their own resources more widely available. To this end, they must make decisions about ownership of data, access to data bases containing sensitive data, authority, boundaries, and so on. Second, they must learn to design and implement new routines by which they can link to a broad variety of agencies, so that they can do joint work with them. At the same time they must also be able to destroy or update the old routines. Third, they must develop new skills to operate the new technical devices or simply to communicate in a network, and that requires expensive staff training programmes. All this generates pressures to new forms of coordination and organising, but in a typically ambivalent manner: organisations must conform to shared standards and protocols if they want to enjoy the 'commons' of the ICT infrastructure and coordinate with other bodies; at the same time they must delegate large components of their agency to technology if they want to operate at all. The emergence of assemblages calls for both higher flexibility and higher compatibility and acceptance of each other's administrative processes between public agencies or between private and public. Both are critical conditions for the proper functioning of a complex administrative system.

These remarks on organisational implications lead to a more comprehensive understanding of the dynamics of ICT-based innovation. Innovation cannot be framed exclusively as a socio-technical endeavour. Rather, it involves a process of institutional design where system compatibility must be broken down into three major components and interoperability must be obtained in at least three critical domains.[30]

Technical compatibility. Compatibility between the technical components of the information infrastructure (standards, protocols, modules, interfaces, linkages, gateways, coding conventions, and so on); technical compatibility is a necessary condition for the interoperability of different ICT systems and software applications, which, so far, has been the major concern of research on information infrastructures;

Functional compatibility. Compatibility between the technical and the normative/institutional components of the assemblage. This is the problem of *functional equivalence* between two regulative regimes – law and technology. Functional equivalence can be obtained by *functional simplification* of administrative procedures so that they can be handled by the technology, essentially by software programs; basically, it entails the switch and the communication between two distinct regimes of regulation and between two different sets of work practices – law-driven and ICT-driven. When administrative procedures cannot be fully aligned to ICT because they are too complex, interoperability is jeopardised and can only be re-established by decoupling and offline handling.

Institutional compatibility. Compatibility between the multiple organisational and institutional agencies involved in the design and innovation process, which entails, for example, compatible administrative languages and routines in order to allow for communication, mutual understanding, accountability and coordination among different administrative bodies, in the absence of which it becomes very difficult to freely share and circulate information resources or run services and administrative functions which run across multiple domains of competence and responsibility. Institutional compatibility supports joint interpretation of data and overall assessment of problematic situations.

In our studies we found that the most serious problems for the effective development of ICT derive not from rigid or sloppy technology, nor from inefficient standard setting, but largely from misunderstandings and ambiguities among administrative agencies within and across government levels, from normative gaps and incoherence, and more generally from pre-existing, engrained institutional practices. Even the relatively simple administrative actions contemplated by MCOL, ELC, or the JOP e-services are not exclusively 'owned' by a single actor, but require the coordinated and synchronised contributions of multiple actors, which must acknowledge each other's procedures. A legal or administrative procedure must be able to travel across the assemblage without raising exceptions of sorts or problems of recognition, legitimacy, accountability or validity. In other words, technical interoperability must be supported by functional and institutional interoperability built into the assemblages. When large information resources are collectively shared and managed by multiple administrative agencies and when they are made more widely accessible and available across different organizations and communities of users, governmental authorities are burdened with a new set of critical requirements and responsibilities. Legal rules and organisational and inter-organisational routines need to be redesigned to ensure dissemination of information resources or to protect rights when resources are compiled from different sources. ICT infrastructures, if they are to work properly, must be embedded in complex institutional settings, where some institutional interoperability must be granted among multiple agencies. If the institutional component of interoperability is not properly taken care of, expansion of ICT capabilities among large communities of users will be limited, or not spread widely enough so as to generate increasing returns for innovation.

Government and governance in the digital: emerging questions

The structure of government and the modalities by which governance is exercised are critically affected by the rise of assemblages. The emerging electronic environment combines features of the existing institutional order with features that come with the new technology. Again, in mapping out the processes, we must make an effort to go beyond the overly simplistic, linear logic of 'impacts' of ICT on institutions (or, symmetrically, of ICT as a 'social construction') and further develop the dual reasoning that we have been pursuing in the course of the present analysis: as ICT is deployed and 'hosted' within an institutional environment, so institutional components and governmental functions are inscribed in (and delegated to) the technology; as ICT yields regulatory effects, so it demands to be regulated (Koops, Lips, Prins and Schellekens, 2006); as the existing legal and institutional order 'embeds the digital' (Sassen, 2006), so the digital 'turns institutional'.[31] As Sassen (2006) has pointed out, processes of de-territorialisation, re-scaling of traditional hierarchies, re-positioning of authority, disassembling and re-assembling of institutional structures and re-distribution of powers can be observed. Out of this complex encounter new 'imbrications' and new domains of activities are formed. What then are the main implications for government of this emerging ICT-mediated institutional environment, as it can be perceived in its current unfolding? How do government and ICT respond to one another? And what problems emerge for governance? Only sketchy indications will be offered here.

To begin with, it seems appropriate to say that government and institutional frameworks at large suffer some kind of displacement and drift as a result of the ICT. The studies in this volume suggest that the major implications concern authority structures and their re-positioning in a new institutional landscape that we have tried to capture in its unfolding, but is still largely uncharted. Problems of territoriality emerge when government agencies must be mapped onto the architectures of the ICT infrastructure (and the other way around), and domains of competence and responsibility must be redefined. Legal jurisdictions do not match the morphology and scale of information infrastructures. Electronic networks are not isomorphic to bureaucracy. ICT naturally enacts a cross-border electronic territory and a non-territorial electronic membership (or citizenship). Indeed, one of the design problems encountered in the development of ICT for the judiciary is how to match the strictly territorial jurisdictions typical of the law and the state with electronic networks, which are largely non-territorial (see on this Lessig, 1999, chapter 14). Experience shows that patterns of institutional response to this problem can vary. One possible response is, as is the case of Italy, trying to make ICT-based services compatible with existing territorial and legal jurisdictions by designing and scaling their functionalities in the shape of government agencies and levels. Another option is to create a separate jurisdiction for the ICT domain and assign it to a dedicated non-territorial agency or authority, which may be strictly governmental (MCOL, England and Wales) or made up of an association of public bodies and private companies (ELC, Austria). In either case problems of coherence, conversion and compatibility of multiple jurisdictions emerge, which can be solved by designing appropriate interfaces and integrative normative devices to ensure institutional compatibility and interoperability.

Next, ICT opens up new communication channels and circuits through which authority and agency can circulate, while at the same time it makes others obsolete or ineffective. New institutional capabilities enacted by the ICT compensate for the loss of existing ones. Traditional hierarchies do not disappear but are variously de-scaled and re-scaled with the disassembling and the re-assembling of institutional structures. In the de-scaling/re-scaling process the relationship between local and global is re-shaped: local agents emerge whose action, because of the technology, can have a global reach, scope and impact (Sassen, 2006). In the networked electronic environment peripheral nodes can act like centres and micro-worlds can have a global span.[32] Also, spatial-temporal framings of action are re-shaped, as a result of ubiquity, simultaneity, generalised access to information resources, and asynchronous communication. In principle, public access to digital and informational resources does not need the scaled and selective mediation of government agencies who claim ownership rights or special jurisdiction on the resources. This phenomenon is often perceived as a centrifugal trend by government authorities, leading to a loss of bureaucratic control and to the spreading of administrative disorder. In its efforts at counteracting the perceived disorder government produces tighter controls and normative regulations whose effects are always controversial and difficult to assess.

In our case studies the displacement in government functions surfaced in a set of recurring questions. Some have to do with control rights: Who has the right of control? Who should be responsible for what? Who should authorise whom and for what? Who is entitled to have access, and under what conditions? Others instead concern property rights: Who owns the data and the procedure? Who is the master of the portal and the e-services? Who owns the infrastructure or specific components of it? And where are the boundaries between the 'territories' of different agencies? These questions naturally stem from the difficulty of locating action in the digital, and consequently from the difficulty of holding agencies and other public bodies accountable. The answers to the questions differed in the different cases, but also shifted in the process of development. The range or type of answers that were provided or admitted depended in turn on the features of the existing institutions – structural and cultural. Most typically, the answers to questions of ownership and control could not be given at the outset, but had to be searched for through inquiry and learning. In some cases inquiry led to the discovery that the questions themselves were misleading and had to be reformulated. In other cases questions were left unanswered.

As a consequence of the advent of the ICT, new objects, which have both a technical and a juridical dimension, appear in the new institutional landscape. They may support or hinder basic governance functions depending on a number of circumstances. Networks, standards, codes, protocols for access, firewalls, linkages, converters, portals, applications and other technical paraphernalia are such objects. They are intrinsically ambiguous: on the one hand they provide new possibilities for administrative action; on the other hand, in order to use them appropriately, one has first to discover and learn what can and cannot be done with them. Design and use depend not only on considerations of technical feasibility and usability, but also on normative interpretations, legal arguments, authoritative jurisdictions, power relationships, or administrative procedures. A technical link allowing for network-wide communication is also interpreted by government as an institutional and normative link. When an 'agency-to-server' or a 'server-to-user' connection is designed, it must then be enclosed within a normative shell, or it must be normatively 'assisted'; otherwise it will not be legitimately established or enacted within the existing framework. Unfortunately the normative shell can itself turn into a hindrance by preventing the diffusion of innovation. One such case, for example, is the enforcement of measures restricting access to data bases and web-based e-services for security, privacy or other bureaucratic reasons. The requirements of strict ID certification and validation for obtaining access to services may reduce attractiveness and drastically curb the critical mass of users needed to yield the increasing returns on adoption that will make the innovation take off.

To make a final comment, at many points in this essay we have underlined that ICT cannot be regarded only as a set of efficiency-enhancing instruments and resources that are made available to the administration for management purposes, often subsumed under the category of Rationalization or the heading of New Public Management.[33] Most crucially, and it is worth recalling it again, ICT is a *Gestell*, that is a way of enframing reality that entails a re-ordering of the state's administrative structures and of government itself. With the advent of ICT many government functions and mechanisms are inscribed in and delegated to the technology, which then 'acts' as a regulatory regime with enforcement capabilities. This may have both positive and negative consequences for government performance: the emergence of assemblages in the traditional fabric of government can be disruptive, but may also contain new possibilities for coordination and social enhancement. As Ulrich Beck has pointed out, in complex postmodern societies technology never comes without risk (Beck, 1992). Digital technologies always show a dual, ambivalent face, empowering and hindering at the same time (Ciborra, 2005). They greatly extend the scope of government by making governance-at-a-distance a real possibility, but may have risky and as yet unclear implications for democratic governance, political transparency and public accountability. This predicament was always present in the research work that led to this book and, albeit in different forms, runs through all the contributions that follow.

Notes

1. According to Barry (2001) technology becomes a 'political object' as it becomes an object of public debate and controversy, an issue at stake, gaining relevance in the arena of political interests and public decision-making.
2. The argument and discussion developed here are largely based on the findings of the research project on ICT and Justice, which are reported in the second part of this book and to which I make frequent references (see Chapters 5, 6, 7, 8 and 9).
3. I take the concept of *assemblage* from a growing body of literature in social and organisational research. My effort here is to give it more analytical depth so that it can be more effectively employed in the study of innovation and institutional change. The concept has been used by Robert Cooper to capture the peculiar features of postmodern organisations, such as multiplicity, becoming, fragility, otherness, and so on (Cooper, 1998). It has been referred to in organisational analysis by Lanzara and Patriotta (2001, 2007), and by Ciborra (2005) in the field of ICT development. The concept has been very recently transposed to the field of sociology and institutional analysis by Saskia Sassen, who used it to describe the imbrications of digital networks and political/institutional authorities (Sassen, 2006). Both Cooper and Sassen questionably trace its genealogy to Deleuze and Guattari's use of the concept (Deleuze and Guattari, 1980). Our notion of assemblage is here closer to Ong and Collier's definition: 'An assemblage is the product of multiple determinations that are not reducible to a single logic. The temporality of an assemblage is emergent. It does not always involve new forms, but forms that are shifting, in formation, or at stake' (Ong and Collier, 2005, 12). See also how Bruno Latour refers to the activity of 're-assembling the social' in the context of Science and Technology Studies and Actor Network Theory (ANT) (Latour, 2005). We have further

extended the idea of assemblage to account for the phenomena observed in our empirical studies.

4. In this connection, see also Kallinikos (2006): 'The involvement of technology in organisations is so thorough that the pattern of inter-actions it gives rise to defies interpretation in terms of a straightfor-ward instrumental logic that considers technology as just a means to pre-established ends' (154). A purely instrumental view of technology 'tends to conceal the distinctive forms and processes by which tech-nology is involved in the making and regulation of human affairs' (Kallinikos, 2005, 189).

5. That of course does not amount to saying that technology *is* a political or legal institution *tout court*: the two concepts and domains must be kept analytically distinct.

6. See Czarniawska's remarks in Chapter 2, this volume. Also: Czarniawska and Hernes (2005).

7. Technology produces 'effects' on human behaviour, so that agents spontaneously comply with the instructions embedded in the artefact or tool. In this connection the image of traffic lights or speed bumps acting as 'silent policemen' is often evoked (see Latour, 1991). For an illustration of the inscription-delegation strategy, on a larger scale, see also Lanzara and Patriotta's (2007) study on the construction of a green field automotive factory.

8. It should be noticed here that 'functional simplification' does not always lead to simplified procedures and outcomes. Luhmann's term is ambiguous: he really means 'functional reduction', that is, complex-ity reduction according to functional requirements.

9. In other words, administrative objects and procedures must become 'machine-representable', that is, programmable in Turing's terms, hence executable by a computer.

10. Chapter 7 by Jannis Kallinikos, this volume, provides vivid illustra-tions of this.

11. In this volume the two perspectives are variously represented and modu-lated in the different chapters. In the development experiences reported, the institutional dynamics and the rise of assemblages of different kinds are instantiated in multiple ways with specific reference to the adoption and use of ICT in the administration of justice. Although the develop-ment stories originate from situated contexts or 'micro-worlds', made up of specific work practices, technical devices and institutional framings, they enrich our understanding of a range of complex technical and insti-tutional processes, pointing at a more general phenomenon: the recon-figuration of the space of government (Barry, 2001).

12. For example e-mail messages popping up on our computer screens carrying electronic reminders of book return deadlines: definitely a useful and cost-saving feature for the library user, but at the same time subtly suggesting that the user's behaviour is being 'surveyed' by the system.

13. In this sense, as economic historians have remarked by drawing an analogy with the electric dynamo, ICTs are 'enabling technologies' or General Purpose Technologies, whose effects can propagate in time throughout a wide range of sectors in the economy, government and organisations. While their short term effect on productivity might not be dramatic, as historical data seem to show, their long-term, partly indirect impact on the reframing of economic activities (markets, firms, institutions) can be remarkable (see Bresnahan and Traitenberg, 1995; David and Wright, 1999).

14. Changes of this kind cannot be easily conceptualised as 'transitions', a term which evokes a cinematic movement from a definite spot in space and time to another definite, presumably terminal, spot. A transition implies a beginning and an end, which are conceived as relatively stable states, while what falls in-between is transient, elusive and ontologically less relevant. Unfortunately the widespread and largely unreflective use of transition theories in mainstream political science and institutional analysis has prevented a deeper understanding of phenomena such as frictions, strains, asymmetries and, in general, historical hysteresis that make much of the complexity of political and institutional change (not to mention the empirical difficulties of defining when a transition begins or ends and when a system is *not* in transition ...). In my opinion, it would be more theoretically rewarding to use the concept of 'transformation', which, if properly applied, would allow a deeper analytical treatment of the complex topology of institutional change.

15. The notion of 'installed base' has been used in a purely technical sense in industrial economics and in economic history. See for example, Hughes (1983) and David and Bunn (1988). With the same expression, but in a broader sense, Ciborra and Hanseth (1998) have translated the Heideggerian notion of *Gestell*, which can be variously rendered as Ordering, Enframing, Standing Reserve, or even Infrastructure (see Martin Heidegger, 1977).

16. Sometimes the presence of non-technological components, such as power and authority structures, organisational features or legal frameworks, in the installed base is acknowledged in these studies, but their influence on the design process and outcomes is hardly analysed (see Hanseth and Lyytinen, 2004).

17. Outcomes of such dynamics depend on the morphological features of the installed base, which may embed different and conflicting elements. A more detailed analysis of the characteristics and the dynamics of the installed base in the judiciary is developed by Francesco Contini in Chapter 9 of this volume.

18. Marco Fabri in Chapter 5 of this volume compares Finland's and Italy's experience, illustrating the enabling and hindering processes that characterise the emergence of assemblages.

19. See for the latter perspective the ANT mainly developed by Callon (1991), Latour (1991, 2005) and Law and Hassard (1999). For the specific application to the analysis of Information Infrastructures, see Monteiro (2000) and Hanseth and Monteiro (1997). In this volume the conceptually closer contribution to the ANT framework is Barbara Czarniawska's (Chapter 2).

20. We speak here of a 'dilemma' and not of a 'trade-off', because each choice or action taken may expose or lead to a conflict of values, that is, values which are held to be important but cannot be met at the same time. In a dilemma situation no matter what choice is made it always leads to consequences which violate at least some of the actor's critical values.

21. To define the phenomenon Donald Schon coined the term 'dynamic conservatism' (Schon, 1971). It is appropriate here to recall the well-known Lampedusa syndrome: '*Se vogliamo che tutto rimanga com'è bisogna che tutto cambi*' (If we want everything to stay the same, everything must change). Giuseppe Tomasi di Lampedusa, *Il gattopardo* (Milan, 1958).

22. We know from systems dynamic theory that complex systems tend to respond to externally applied forces with internal processes that absorb, neutralise, displace or counteract the external forces. Non-linearity may make change and innovation efforts self-defeating (Forrester, 1971).

23. This can be taken as a complex illustration of the classic figure/background problem: in order to be able to 'see' the object and trace its contours, one has to be able to first 'see' the medium in which the object is hosted. And here the medium itself is undetermined and shifting.

24. As all metaphors, the cultivation metaphor throws light only on certain aspects of the phenomenon and obscures others. See on metaphor-making Ortony (1979) and Schon (1979).

25. The term 'local' refers here to the system, not to the territory or jurisdiction, therefore retaining a functional, not spatial meaning. It is opposed to 'global' or 'comprehensive' design intervention. Even in the most hierarchical, centrally managed and top-down ICT implementation frameworks, like most of the cases studied, central authorities

and agencies have to put together component resources from different sources, in a segmented and discontinuous process, over which they do not have full jurisdiction. In other words, they are not sitting at their workshop desks with all the pieces laid out on the desk ready to be assembled, like Herbert Simon's watch-maker (Simon, 1969). They intervene in the process of assembling by letting other assemblers assemble what is locally available, or preventing them from so doing.

26. 'Contingency is the affirmation of control by immediate events over destiny [...] Contingency is the licence to participate in history [...]' (Gould, 1989, 282–283).

27. In a different perspective, when organisations go digital, much of what organisations are in the real-space (structures, identities) is transplanted and inscribed into the electronic medium (see Oberg, Schollhorn and Woywode, 2003).

28. Reflecting on the fragility and on the management problems posed by such 'dislocation to the digital' of administrative action, a public prosecutor evoked a compelling metaphorical image: 'it's like handling a giant soap bubble with golden handles' (Bologna, 13 April 2007).

29. Barbara Czarniawska calls this new type of link 'action net' (Czarniawska, 2004).

30. *Interoperability* is usually defined as the ability of a software application or system to work with other systems or products without special redesign or customisation effort on the part of the user. A broader definition, and more appropriate to the present context, is provided by Miller (2000): 'to be interoperable, one should actively be engaged in the ongoing process of ensuring that the systems, procedures and culture of an organization are managed in such a way as to maximise opportunities for exchange and re-use of information, whether internally or externally'.

31. For each phenomenon or process that we may observe, it is as if we also observe the 'duality' of it. In the dual version constraints turn into opportunities, variables turn into constraints, dependent variables turn into independent variables or effecting forces. The challenge for the analyst is to be able to entertain both versions at the same time and switch from the one to the other when necessary.

32. It is the so-called Small World phenomenon, which can arise in dense networks, as described by Duncan Watts (1999).

33. Particularly, in the Fourth Chapter of this volume Cordella and Willcocks make it clear that the introduction of ICT in government should not be conceived as a way of dismantling public bureaucracy and a move towards a market logic in the delivery of public services to citizens, but

as a way of making bureaucracy more responsive to its original and true mission in modern democracies, that is, public service delivery according to principles of impersonality, equality and fairness.

References

Avgerou, C. (2002), *Information Systems and Global Diversity*. Oxford, UK: Oxford University Press.

Barley, S. (1986), 'Technology as an Occasion for Structuring: Observations on CT Scanners and the Social Order of Radiology Departments'. *Administrative Science Quarterly*, 31, 78–108.

Barry, A. (2001), *Political Machines. Governing a Technological Society*. London: The Athlone Press.

Beck, U. (1992), *Risk Society. Toward a New Modernity*. Thousands Oaks: Sage Publications.

Benkler, Y. (2006), *The Wealth of Nations, How Social Production Transforms Markets and Freedom*. New Haven: Yale University Press.

Bijker, W.E., Hughes T.P. and T. Pinch (1987) (eds), *The Social Construction of Technology*. Cambridge, MA: MIT Press.

Bresnahan, T. and M. Traitenberg (1995), 'General Purpose Technologies: Engines of Growth'. *Journal of Econometrics*, 65, 83–108.

Broadbent, M. and P. Weill (1999), 'The Implications of Information Technology Infrastructure for Business Process Redesign'. *MIS Quarterly*, 23(2), 159–182.

Callon, M. (1980), 'Struggles to Define What Is Problematic and What Is Not: the Sociology of Translation'. In Knorr, K.D., Krohn, R. and R.D. Whitley (eds), *The Social Process of Scientific Investigation: Sociology of the Sciences Yearbook*, 4. Dordrecht: Reidel.

Callon, M. (1986), 'Some Elements of Sociology of Translation: Domestication of the Scallops and the Fishermen'. In Law, J. (ed.), *Power, Action and Belief: A New Sociology of Knowledge*. London: Routledge and Kegan Paul (196–233).

Callon, M. (1991), 'Techno-Economic Networks and Irreversibility'. In Law, J. (ed.), *A Sociology of Monsters. Essays on Power, Technology and Domination*. London: Routledge (103–131).

Chae, B. and G.F. Lanzara (2006), 'Self-Destructive Dynamics in Large-Scale Techno-Change and Some Modest Countervailing Mechanisms'. *Information Technology and People*, 19 (1), 74–97.

Ciborra, C. (2000) (ed.), *From Control to Drift. the Dynamics of Corporate Information Infrastructures*. London: Oxford University Press.

Ciborra, C. (2002), *The Labyrinths of Information*. Oxford: Oxford University Press.

Ciborra, C. (2005), 'Interpreting e-Government and Development. Efficiency, Transparency or Governance at a Distance?' *Information Technology and People*, 18 (3), 260–279.

Ciborra, C. and G.F. Lanzara (1994), 'Formative Contexts and Information Technology. Understanding the Dynamics of Innovation in Organizations'. *Accounting, Management and Information Technology*, 4 (2), 61–86.

Ciborra, C. and G.F. Lanzara (1999), *Labirinti dell'innovazione. Tecnologia, organizzazione, apprendimento*. Milano: Etaslibri.

Ciborra, C. and O. Hanseth (1998), 'From Tool to *Gestell*: Agendas for Managing the Information Infrastructure'. *Information Technology and People*, 11 (4), 305–327.

Cooper, R. (1998), 'Assemblage Notes'. In Chia, R.C.H. (ed.), *Organized Worlds. Explorations In Technology and Organization with Robert Cooper*. London: Routledge (108–129).

Czarniawska, B. (2004), 'On Time, Space, and Action Nets'. *Organization*, 11 (6), 777–795.

Czarniawska, B. and T. Hernes (2005) (eds), *Actor Network Theory and Organizing*. Copenhagen: Liber Abstract.

Dahlbom, B. and L.E. Janlert (1996), Computer Future. Unpublished manuscript.

David, P.A. and G. Wright (1999), 'General Purpose Technologies and Surges in Productivity: Historical Reflections on the Future of the ICT Revolution'. Paper presented at the Symposium on Economic Challenges of the 21st Century in historical perspective. Oxford, UK, 2–4 July, 1–20.

David, P.A. and J.A. Bunn (1988), 'The Economics of Gateway Technologies and Network Evolution: Lessons from Electricity Supply History'. *Information Economics and Policy*, 3 (winter), 165–202.

Deleuze, G. and F. Guattari (1980), *Mille Plateaux*. Paris: Editions de Minuit.

Duffield, M. (2001), *Global Governance and the New War*. London: Zed Books.

Dunleavy, P., Margetts H., Bastow S., and J. Tinkler (2006), *Digital Era Governance. It Corporations, the State, and E-Government*. Oxford: Oxford University Press.

Forrester, J. (1971), 'Counterintuitive Behavior of Social Systems'. *Technology Review*, 73 (3), 52–68.

Genschel, P. (1997), 'The Dynamics of Inertia: Institutional Persistence and Change in Telecommunications and Health Care'. *Governance*, 10 (1), 43–66.

Gould, S.J. (1989), *Wonderful Life: the Burgess Shale and the Nature of History*. New York: W.W. Norton and Company.

Hanseth, O. (1996), Information Technology as Infrastructure. Unpublished PhD Thesis, Goteborg University.

Hanseth, O. (2000), 'The Economy of Standards'. In Ciborra, C. (ed.), *From Control to Drift. The Dynamics of Corporate Information Infrastructures*. Oxford: Oxford University Press (56–70).

Hanseth, O. (2002), 'From Systems and Tools to Networks and Infrastructures – from Design to Cultivation. Towards a Theory of ICT Solutions and Its Design Methodology Implications'. Retrieved from http://heim.ifi.uio.no/-oleha/Publications/ib_ISR_3rd_resubm2.html. Visited 30 October 2006, 1–30.

Hanseth, O. and E. Monteiro (1997), 'Inscribing Behaviour in Information Infrastructure Standards'. *Accounting, Management and Information Technologies* 7 (4), 183–211.

Hanseth, O. and K. Lyytinen (2004), 'Theorizing about the Design of Information Infrastructures: Design Kernel Theories and Principles'. *Sprouts. Working Papers on Information Environments, Systems, and Organizations* (207–241). Retrieved from http://sprouts.case.edu/2004/040412.pdf. Visited 10 October 2006.

Hanseth, O. and N. Lundberg (2001), 'Designing Work Oriented Infrastructures'. *Computer Supported Cooperative Work*, 10, 347–372.

Heidegger, M. (1977), 'The Question Concerning Technology'. *The Question Concerning Technology and Other Essays*. Transl. by W. Lovitt. New York: Harper and Row.

Hughes, T.P. (1983), *Networks of Power. Electrification in Western Society, 1880–1930*. Baltimore: Johns Hopkins University Press.

Hughes, T.P. (1987), 'The Evolution of Large Technical Systems'. In Bijker, W.E., Hughes, T.P. and T. Pinch (eds), *The Social Construction of Technology*. Cambridge, MA: MIT Press.

Joerges, B. (1998), 'Do Artefacts Have Politics?' *Social Studies of Science*, 29 (3), 411–431.

Joerges, B. and B. Czarniawska (1998), 'The Question of Technology, or How Organizations Inscribe the World'. *Organization Studies*, 19, 363–385.

Kallinikos, J. (2005), 'The Order of Technology: Complexity and Control in a Connected World'. *Information and Organization*, 15 (3), 185–202.

Kallinikos, J. (2006), *The Consequences of Information*. Cheltenham: Edward Elgar Publishing Company.

Koops, B., Lips M., Prins C. and M. Schellekens (2006) (eds), *Starting Points for ICT Regulation*. The Hague: Asser Press.

Kuran, T. (1988), 'The Tenacious Past: Theories of Personal and Collective Conservatism'. *Journal of Economic Behavior and Organization*, 10, 143–171.

Lanzara, G.F. (1999), 'Between Transient Constructs and Permanent Structures. Designing Systems in Action'. *Journal of Strategic Information Systems*, 8, 331–349.

Lanzara, G.F. and G. Patriotta (2001), 'Technology and the Courtroom. An Inquiry into Knowledge Making in Organizations'. *Journal of Management Studies*, 38 (7), 943–971.

Lanzara, G.F. and G. Patriotta (2007), 'The Institutionalization of Knowledge in an Automotive Factory. Templates, Inscriptions, and the Problem of Durability'. *Organization Studies*, 28, 1–26.

Latour, B. (1991), 'Technology Is Society Made Durable'. Law, J. (ed.), *A Sociology of Monsters. Essays on Power, Technology and Domination*. London: Routledge (103–131).

Latour, B. (2005), *Reassembling the Social. An Introduction to ANT*. Oxford: Oxford University Press.

Law, J. and J. Hassard (1999) (eds), *Actor Network Theory and After*. Oxford: Basil Blackwell.

Lessig, L. (1999), *Code and Other Laws of Cyberspace*. New York: Basic Books.

Lessig, L. (2007*), Code and Other Laws of Cyberspace. Version 2.0*. New York: Basic Books.

Luhmann, N. (1990), *Essays on Self-Reference*. New York: Columbia University Press.

Luhmann, N. (1996), *Social Systems*. Stanford, CA: Stanford University Press.

March, J.G. (1991), 'Exploration and Exploitation in Organizational Learning'. *Organization Science*, 2 (1), 171–187.

Miller, P. (2000), 'Interoperability. What Is It and Why Should I Want It?' Retrieved from http://www.ariadne.ac.uk/issue24/interoperability/; visited 5 March 2007.

Monteiro, E. (2000), 'Actor-Network Theory and Information Infrastructure'. In Ciborra C. and others (eds), *From Control to Drift. The Dynamics of Corporate Information Infrastructures*. London: Oxford University Press.

Monteiro, E. and O. Hanseth (1999), 'Developing Corporate Infrastructure: Implications for International Standardization'. In Jacobs, K. and R. Williams (eds), *Proceedings of SIIT 1999, Standardization and Innovation in Information Technology*, IEEE, 75–79.

Oberg, A., Schollhorn, T. and M. Woywode (2003), 'Isomorphism in Organizational Self-Representation in the World Wide Web? Institutionalization Processes Regarding Internet Presentation of Organizations'. Paper presented at the 19th EGOS Colloquium, Copenhagen, July 2003.

Ong, A. and S.J. Collier (2005) (eds), *Global Assemblages. Technology, Politics and Ethics as Anthropological Problems*. Oxford: Blackwell Publishing Company.

Ortony, A. (1979) (ed.), *Metaphors and Thought*. Cambridge: Cambridge University Press.

Powell, W.W. and J. DiMaggio (1991), *Neo-Institutionalism in Organizational Analysis*. Chicago: University of Chicago Press.

Rhodes, M. (1997), *Understanding Governance. Policy Networks, Governance, Reflexivity and Accountability*. Open University Press, Buckingham: Philadelphia.

Sassen, S. (2006), *Territory, Authority, Rights. From Medieval to Global Assemblages*. Princeton, NJ: Princeton University Press.

Schon, D.A. (1982), 'The Fear of Innovation'. In Barnes, B. and D. Edge (eds), *Science in Context: Readings in the Sociology of Science*. Cambridge, MA: MIT Press (290–302).

Schon, D.A. (1971), *Beyond the Stable State*. Harmondsworth: Penguin Books.

Schon, D.A. (1979), 'Generative Metaphor: A Perspective on Problem Setting in Social Policy'. In Ortony, A. (ed.), *Metaphors and Thought*. Cambridge: Cambridge University Press (254–283).

Simon, H.A. (1969), *the Sciences of the Artificial*. Cambridge, MA: MIT Press.

Star, S.L. and J.R. Griesemer (1989), 'Institutional Ecology, "Translations" and Boundary Objects: Amateurs and Professionals in Berkeley's Museum of Vertebrate Zoology, 1907–39'. *Social Studies of Science*, 19, 387–420.

Star, S.L. and K. Ruhleder (1996), 'Steps Toward an Ecology of Infrastructure: Design and Access for Large Information Spaces'. *Information Systems Research*, 7 (1), 111–134.

Tomasi di Lampedusa, G. (1958), *Il gattopardo*. Milano: Mondadori.

Wagner, A. (2005), *Robustness and Evolvability in Living Systems*. Princeton, NJ: Princeton University Press.

Walsham, G. (2001), *Making a World of Difference: IT in a Global Context.* Chichester: Wiley Publ. Co.

Watts, D. (1999), *Small Worlds.* Princeton, NJ: Princeton University Press.

Weber, M. (1978), *Economy and Society: an Outline of Interpretive Sociology.* In Roth, G. and C. Wittich (eds) (translators E. Fischoff and others), Berkeley: University of California Press.

Weill, P. and M. Broadbent (1998), *Leveraging the New Infrastructure.* Cambridge, MA: Harvard Business School Press.

CHAPTER 2

How institutions are inscribed in technical objects and what it may mean in the case of the Internet

Barbara Czarniawska

> The Internet really could create a global village, but I think the politicians will prevent it from doing so.
>
> (Richard Rorty, 2006, p. 65)

Introduction

In this chapter I review the idea that institutions are inscribed in machines and technical norms, in order to see what consequences it may have for such projects as e-justice and e-government. I therefore turn to recent writings commenting on the developments of and the on Internet, noting that they focus mostly on the issues of control *of* the Internet, rather than control *by* the Internet. This issue remains open to speculation, and I end the chapter by considering gains to be accrued from an increased consideration of the ways the Internet and its norms can join the mechanisms of societal control.

Technology as a writing pad

In a 1998 article, Bernward Joerges and I pointed out that technical objects that surround contemporary people in their everyday lives are thoroughly inscribed, and that the majority of these inscriptions originate with legal persons, that is formal organisations. This observation was connected to but also diverged from the then popular metaphor of *technology-as-text*.

No matter whether one judges this metaphor as successful or not, it certainly succeeded in returning the attention of social scientists, including organisation theorists, to the matters of machine technology, mostly of information and communication machines. Responding to this surge of interest, and borrowing the notion of inscription from studies of science and technology (Latour and Woolgar, 1979/1986), we attempted to reconcile a concern for institutional order with an understanding of technology in organising processes. We suggested that technical norms are one of the ways in which the institutionalised patterns of action are inscribed in technology.

We hoped that our contribution would enrich previous technology studies from the social science perspective, especially from an organisation theory perspective. Like other social science disciplines, organisation studies have had difficulties in grasping 'the inner structure of the artefact', to use Elaine Scarry's expression (Scarry, 1985). While technology studies have proliferated at times, the processes inside machines were mostly described and explained in either engineering or ideological terms.

Thus studies in the Tavistock tradition, where the notion of socio-technical systems was first introduced (see for example Rice, 1958), began to acknowledge the importance of the 'technical', but focused mostly on the 'social' and steadfastly assumed that there exist two different worlds that interact. Some authors revived the concept in the late 1980s (see for example Burns and Dietz, 1991). These studies, however, remained in the same dichotomising spirit, even if new notions of technological design, choice, and regulation enriched the 'social' part of the term.

Indeed, contingency theory, until recently the dominant approach to technology in organisation theory, originated from a strong interest in relations between technology and control systems (Burns and Stalker, 1961/1996; Woodward, 1965), but ended up actually obscuring tangible artefacts, focusing on quasi-objects such as task structures (see for example Scott, 1990). Even in new institutionalism there were attempts to separate 'institutional' from 'technical' environments (e.g., Meyer and Scott, 1983), as if there existed somewhere in the contemporary world machines free of institutions and institutions independent of machines.

It took several serious catastrophes to re-introduce material technology as a central concern in organisation studies. Indeed, catastrophe studies (such as Turner, 1978; Perrow, 1984; Rochlin, LaPorte, and Roberts, 1987; Weick, 1988; Vaughan, 1990; Shrivastava, 1993) prepared the ground for a re-evaluation of the issue of technology in organisation studies. More recently, Weick and Sutcliffe (2001) dedicated a whole volume to the theme of reliable organisations. But even this refreshing and interesting work focuses on sensemaking and other cognitive processes; machines remain dumb. Yet, most people would agree that any kind of organising – expected and unexpected – takes place simultaneously in three dimensions: symbolic, political, and material – or practical (Czarniawska-Joerges, 1993/2006). While many studies are dedicated to the first two aspects of organising, the practical dimension is often missing. For instance, this was the conclusion reached by Goodman and Sproull (1990, p. 260–261) in their overview of technology studies within organisation theory:

> While there appears to be a movement to focus primarily on technology as socially constructed, we feel that some balance is necessary. There are issues that concern technology as a physical reality. These have not been well addressed and have implications for doing work on technology and organizations. [...] We feel that a fruitful approach would be to increase our understanding of both the social and the physical aspects of technology. [...] The real contribution, however, will be understanding the intersection between both forms of reality.

The problem is partly connected to the persistent misuse of the term 'socially constructed' as synonymous with 'unreal', or 'immaterial', or 'to be changed at will'. Russian *konstruktivists*, such as Tatlin, Pevsner and Gabo are probably turning in their graves on seeing this use of the term they coined to oppose the idea of *creation* (from nothing) by the robust term borrowed from the building industry, to emphasise the fact that art always consists of assembling a new work from existing materials. Another point worth making is that, as Latour pointed out, the better they are constructed, the more real things become (e.g., Latour, 1996). Thus, for example, opposing 'symbolic' to 'material' is nonsensical, as there can be no immaterial symbols,[1] while any artefact (or organism for that matter) can be used in the work of symbolisation.

In contrast, a lively Foucauldian school, using all kinds of technical metaphors for organisational discipline, power and control, made differentiation impossible. As Anne Loft (1995, p. 132) observed: '[...] *Foucault's use of machine metaphors to describe techniques of discipline led him to conflate techniques and technologies and to ignore the role of machinery in discipline.*' Technology was forgotten again. The neo-contingency organisation studies promised to fill this gap by way of defining workflow:

> Workflow is the process whereby inputs, including raw materials, manufactured components and parts, machine capacity and human effort are organised in order to transform them into output. It presupposes

differentiated arrays of machines, jobs, organizational sub-units, people with specific skills and knowledge, and it consists of the technical and social arrangements that allow human effort, machine capacity and material inputs to be brought together to achieve output goals [...] 'Work' may be done by machines or by humans or by a combination of the two. In the course of technical change, boundaries between human and machine work are changed, and combinations of the two also change. Variables should therefore be able to reflect such shifts rather than be biased by them. (Sorge, 1989, p. 27)

The remaining problem was that the variables favoured by the neo-contingency theorists were so abstract ('workflow continuity', 'product variability'), that although they might be useful as evaluation variables, they did not do their work as explanatory variables. This is perhaps unavoidable, in that they rely upon ostensive rather than performative definitions (variables are treated like physical attributes; for a critique of this stance, see Czarniawska, 2007), and aim at structural correlations even when focusing on processes. As a result, the affinities between technologies and institutional orders have been observed but, as Sorge admitted himself, the nature of these affinities was 'not precise enough' (1991, p. 168).

Within a symbolist perspective in organisation studies, researchers demonstrated that artefacts are symbols that can be real, above and beyond their practical use (see for example Gagliardi's collection, 1990). While authors of such studies would undoubtedly agree that tools and machines not only symbolise, but also do work, they still seem to assume that it is necessary to separate, or even contrast the two uses.

Joerges and I suggested that technologies could be conceived of as carriers of institutionalised patterns of action. This is possible, among other reasons, because contemporary societies trust machines more than persons (machine trust is 'system trust'; Giddens, 1990). Thus technical artefacts can be seen as exteriorised institutions, engraved in matter and therefore constituting material bases of societal processes. Over time, we claimed, societies have transferred various institutional responsibilities to machine technologies and so removed these responsibilities from everyday awareness. As organised actions are externalised in machines, and as these machineries grow more complicated on ever-larger scales, norms and practices are entrusted to things. Inscribed in machines, institutions become literally black-boxed (Whitley, 1972).

It was high time, we postulated, to ask a question about what is hidden behind the neutral term 'technical norms'. There exist numerous studies concerned with the political and economic functioning of units and agencies responsible for technical normalisation and standardisation (see for example Brunsson and Jacobsson, 2000). In this literature, the notion of technical norms is rarely explicated, however. Rare exceptions suggest that technical norms are dictated by the economy of cognition and are meant to make technical knowledge available in the form of a public good. Thus Charpentier (1977, p. 632; quoted after Joerges and Czarniawska, 1998):

> Simplification according to the spirit of normalization means searching for the essential; recording the fundamental rhythms of nature to which man [sic] is attuned. Likewise, simplification includes the search for the guiding threads that make it possible to clarify the inextricable and contribute to a state where everyone can afford common knowledge.

Yet, we stressed, such simplification and affordability of common knowledge is more complex that that. We use computers as the most obvious example. At that time, we had just acquired a new PowerBook, and watched its user's guide with fascination. A smiling face welcomed us and softly informed us that we were about to learn, and be instructed in, the norms (mostly technical-procedural) of the Mac community, to be imbibed into us via a step-by-step action programme. The instructor in the programme was a man and the learner was a woman.

This changed very quickly: most users are by now sensitive to gender-related issues. Still, it is assumed that it was the software, the social part of the machine that could have been discriminatory. It is also assumed, in this case as in many other cases of critical analysis, that machine control is a case of an intentional managerial control. In contrast, Joerges and I wanted to bring to light the instances where the controlling power stems from the fact that a given practice has been institutionalised, and therefore is taken for granted. Obviously, individuals and groups often seek to exploit institutions for their political purposes, but we wished to draw attention to one of the ways in which society controls itself: it socialises its members by unobtrusive measures, and thereby constantly re-constructs itself.

Our claim was therefore that technical norms are the institutional structure of machinery. We distinguished technical from non-technical norms by two criteria: technical norms are inscribed by organisations, and they contain an explicit or implicit reference to a quantitative measure. Technical norms thus were organisationally imposed action prescriptions that referred to measures and/or formal procedures (algorithms) justified by natural or engineering science discourses. Further, we distinguished three sub-genres of technical norms:

1. Norms for human action, defining human rights and duties (e.g., 'turn the bottle cap clockwise' or 'so many units per hour' in piece work).

2. Norms for machine behaviour, which prescribe not only how specific technical artefacts are to be constructed, but also how they are to function (e.g., DIN A4, a standard page in Europe or 220 V, the regulation voltage in Europe).

3. Norms for the natural environment, prescribing the extent to which incursions of ecological or bodily environments by machinery and other technical undertakings are to be tolerated (e.g., emission and immission limits for CO_2, or the nitrate content of ground water).

We also pointed out that such technical norms are strongly intertextual, and linked to various technical supertexts consisting of a multitude of interrelated general procedural norms and maxims. Partly because we wanted to make our argument – that technical norms function as social norms – stronger, we had various prescriptions for building and using hardware mostly in mind.

We realised that, like every classification, ours, too, can be only pragmatically evaluated, with criteria appropriate in a given time and space. Even if our classification was found useful at the time of its conception, it was obvious that the three realms of application of technical norms were not safely fixed within the three sub-genres. Blurring genres and redefining their boundaries was only to be expected. Indeed, one of the most important corrections of our classification happened shortly afterwards and targeted precisely the space between the first and the second of our genres: the code. Before I move to this missing point, however, let me summarise the main conclusions of the article written by Joerges and myself.

We emphasised the fact that technical norms tend to operate out of awareness of their habitual 'readers'. Smoothly and reliably prescribed machine-technical operations and assemblies become more or less sealed-off from ongoing representations and questioning. Take the legal order inscribed in day-to-day urban traffic-action nets: once through the driving test, drivers never activate the knowledge of transportation acts, and even deviant behaviour prompts only a partial activation. Nevertheless, drivers, cars, roadside trees, pedestrians, bicycles, red lights, timetables and all the other actants associated with urban transport effortlessly follow this order through the trail of inscriptions it has left. And so do computer users.

Code is law but is law everything?

The main message and focus of interest of the work of Joerges and myself was the phenomenon of legitimate collective agents inscribing an institutional order into machines, partly unnoticed by the machine users, and partly controlled by other legitimate instances. These inscriptions arrived one by one, or at the most in sets, and blended with one another and with older inscriptions in ways that brought to mind the metaphor of palimpsest.

Lessig's *Code and Other Laws of Cyberspace* (1999) considered a much more shocking possibility: that a whole new institutional order – better or worse than the one already existing – may be inscribed into a new technological creation, the Internet. Rightly, he reminded those who saw the Internet as a harbinger of an unlimited freedom that the word 'cyberspace' denotes a space where control at a distance is being exercised. The questions were, whose control, and what control.

Lessig drew the attention of his readers to the fact that he is a US citizen and that he is a lawyer. Both are indeed significant in assessing his proposals. His is an attitude of a US liberal, so well expressed by Richard Rorty: *Take Care of Freedom and Truth Will Take Care of Itself* (a collection of interviews with Rorty edited by Mendieta, 2006). In Lessig's rendition, 'Guarantee the structural (a space in cyberspace for open code), and (much of) the substance will take care of itself' (1999, p. 8), the substance stands for freedom of speech and fair trade, and privacy. European history teaches us, in contrast, that since ancient Greece and Rome, freedom of one man has meant the slavery of another (and especially of women). Further, being a lawyer means that Lessig tends to assume that laws are all that there is to an institutional order (although he does – innovatively – assume that laws are understood through stories, not through rules). Again, the same history taught us in Europe that laws can be horrible and that they can be disobeyed, and that an institutional order can partly exist against the law. Before I explore alternative views, however, I will briefly summarise Lessig's argument.

Lessig pointed out that the idea that the Internet offers unlimited freedom and anarchy is an illusion – all architectures (codes) permit control, although of different kinds. His claim, well corroborated since his book was written, was that the Internet was being remade to fit the demands of commerce, and that an increased 'regulability' will be a by-product of this remake. What is needed is an additional, or meta, regulation – of the code. Much as there are agencies controlling the technical norms that are allowed to be inscribed in the machines, there need to be similar or the same (government) agencies that will regulate the architecture of the cyber-space, that is, the code. Thus while Joerges and I pleaded for an increased awareness on the part of the agencies regulating technical norms that, in fact, they also regulate social norms, Lessig pleaded for agencies that are well aware of the social effects of their regulations to realise that these can be extended to technical norms. The difference lies mostly in that what Lessig saw as a new institution (governmental regulation of the code), we would see as an extension of a well-established practice.

Lessig welcomed the governmental regulation of the Internet. Does that mean that he parted company with his fellow liberal[2] Rorty, whose utterance quoted at the outset was obviously critical? No; he is well aware that regulation can go awry. He envisions the open code (open source software) as an effective check against possible governmental excesses, because of its transparency and because of some of its possibilities to oppose other regulations.

Also, by his open Americanism, Lessig makes the readers realise that the United States has much to say in terms of regulation of cyberspace by code, and that it is not necessarily the case that the values dear to US citizens have to be equally cherished by all the rest of us. Nevertheless, the solution suggested by Lessig applies to all countries outside the United States as well: a public debate about what values should be reflected in code. It is somewhat unclear (and therefore creating an opening for another interesting debate) if Lessig's ideas concerning the role of the state in regulating the regulative code are closer to the interventionist role of the law in the Swedish welfare state (reducing inequalities by creating positive rights) or to the classic liberal idea of the state as a protector of negative rights (Bertilsson, 1995).

Seven years later, Yochai Benkler (2006) took Lessig's argument and carried it on with great enthusiasm. His main idea, however, concerned the productive side of the Internet: the fact that the excess of capacity of personal computers can be linked into a distributive computing source which, coupled with the excess of energy on the part of young people, can boost the 'networked information economy' beyond any expectations based on performance of markets and states. He also hoped that such an economy would liberate the public sphere from the mediation of commercial mass media, in favour of opinion exchange on the Internet. He was concerned with the regulative aspects only insofar as they related to the regulation of the Internet, not the regulation by the Internet, the main topic in the present volume. Still, his notions of *relevance filtration* and *accreditation* are pertinent not only to the networked economy but also to justice-online and e-government:

> A communication must be relevant for a given sender to send to a given recipient and relevant for the recipient to receive. Accreditation further

filters relevant information for credibility. Decisions of filtration for purposes of relevance and accreditation are made with reference to the values of the person filtering the information, not the values of the person receiving the information. (2006, p. 167)

The latter can be a problem, if the values of the person receiving the information do not coincide with those of the person doing the filtering. 'Values' is perhaps too strong a word here, as the recipients of administrative and legal information usually complain of lack of relevance, not of value disparities (although filtering can be used as a value education; see the study of Norén and Ranerup (2005), described in greater detail below). Benkler's solution was that even relevance and accreditation must be produced in a distributed fashion: users can compare notes as to what they think relevant. (Observe that this assumes a different mechanism from the now common 'users' feedback', which can be manipulated by the designers or owners of the portal). This idea of a distributed decision on relevance and credibility is close to certain industrial solutions that I describe in the next section.

Code in the service of law

Lessig's insights are very important in understanding the legal aspects of cyberspace, but the focus of the present volume is actually the reverse. The question is, how can Information and Communication Technologies (ICT) be used in the service of law, that is, in facilitating legal services? The more appropriate analogy could then be the so-called Enterprise Systems, or ES, which use computers to standardise and to monitor tasks performed by a company's employees. While the ES can be seen as an update of a Fordist assembly line (Head, 2007), the truly interesting and presently relevant aspect is the use of ES in service companies.

> At call center companies such as AmTech and TeleTech, call centers companies to whom many corporations outsource their 'customer relations management', agents must follow a script displayed on their computer screens, spelling out the exact conversation, word by word, they must follow in their dealings with the customers. (Head, 2007, p. 43)

While Simon Head was mostly interested in ES as systems controlling the workforce, I wish to build an analogy to the situation of the customer. (This does not exclude the possibility of using something like ES to control the work of legal advisors and administrative workers, but this is not yet the primary objective of introducing ICT to legal services). It is easy to imagine the situation of a customer whose problems deviate – in any way – from those included in the ES scenarios (a situation known to all of us when we are pushed around through 'The most frequently asked questions' dialogue in any Help program). Afraid of sanctions, the call centre employee would do anything to fit the customer's request into an already existing template. In the case of legal services, the template will be the only fit.

In the same review by Head, which was mainly dedicated to the issues of micromanagement made possible by ICT use, there was an opposite example, still related to the producer's side of services, but possibly translatable into the situation of legal services. John Seely Brown and Paul Duguid (2000) reported a successful project at Xerox, where they were able to convince Xerox to abandon the plan of monitoring copy machine technicians by an ES in favour of collecting the technicians' experience into a generally accessible database called Eureka. Brown and Duguid took inspiration from Julian Orr's (1996) famous study of such technicians, where he was able to demonstrate that they shared and developed their expertise by telling each other stories about specific cases of repair. Now it was Eureka that collected such stories. This was what Brown and Duguid had to say about the difference between Eureka and other databases ('reps' are 'technical representatives' who service and repair Xerox machines at clients' sites):

> [...] a database for technical information is not in itself original. But most such databases are [...] top-down creations. People who are not themselves reps usually fill these databases with what they think reps ought to know. [...] Eureka was designed differently, however. It drew directly on the reps own insight and their own sense of what they needed.
>
> Of course, such a database would be of no use to anyone if it filled up with everybody's favourite idea [...] Such a database must be selective. But again it would be a mistake to filter these from a top-down, process perspective. Instead, as with scientific articles, the reps' tips are subject to peer review, drawing on those same lateral ties that make the reps resources for one another. (Brown and Duguid, 2000, p. 112)

A faulty analogy needs to be pointed out: especially in social sciences, peer reviews actually tend to eliminate original and deviant articles in favour of generally accepted truths. But in the case of reps, it need not be a disadvantage. A deviant idea can be tried out, and rejected only later. Also, a common practice in fact needs generally accepted truths.

The researchers at Sintef Group, collaborating with the Norwegian University of Science and Technology, introduced storytelling as a stable trait of an Intranet at Computas, a computer consultancy. 'Scheherazade's divan' presents all the stories sent in by the staff, revealing – the managers claim the different points of view of different storytellers – and thus helping to deal with conflicts (Gisvold, 2005/2006).

Similarly, reported Head (2007), the Regenstrief Institute in Indianapolis, a centre for medical research, created a database that is shaped by all the people who use it – patients, general physicians, specialists, hospital managers and local health officials. While this database provides almost all kinds of relevant information, it does not make automated decisions, which are left to the physicians. These databases inscribe in machines a very important social norm which says that narrative knowledge is the primary knowledge used by professionals.

While many of these positive presentations can be seen as the reflection of the new managerial fashion, storytelling as a management tool, the idea behind it is certainly worth considering. One observation that needs emphasising is the importance of the context of use (which the stories report) as contrasted to the context of design.

The arc of reciprocation is always wider than the arc of projection

Lessig, Benkler and Head all focused on the designers – in order to praise, criticise or advise. Their reasoning may be summarised as follows: properly designed laws (including labour legislation) will guarantee a proper structure; if the structure (architecture) is right, the right processes will follow. I share their sympathy for open source, for freedom of speech, for dignity of labour and for fair trade. However, my knowledge gathered in many years of studies of organising prevents me from completely sharing their beliefs. No matter whether we focus on free market or open source, a structure might facilitate processes, but guarantees nothing. Only processes can control processes; that is, a regulation must be constant.

Further, even the best designed laws may not function in practice; this defect can be counteracted by flexibility (dropping one's tools, to use Karl Weick's, 1996, metaphor), but also by an unprejudiced observation of spontaneous practices, with a goal of stabilising and making permanent those that seem promising. In other words, design must be seen as a never-ending process, and code as permanently tentative.

To support my stance I shall rely on the theory offered by Elaine Scarry in her *The Body in Pain* (1985). Her basic claim was that an artefact's 'reciprocation' (the ways in which it can be used) always exceeds the designer's projection. How is this possible? Well, for one thing, the context of use is always richer than the context of design; or, to put it differently, the contexts of use are many, the context of design only one. Here, among other things, lies the strength of open source, as it combines the stances of the designer and the user – as does, at least in principle, participatory design. But one can also say that the uses tend to surprise the designers because designers project more than they intend. They project ideas inculcated in them by the institutional order of which they – and the users – are a part.

One striking example of this was the design of the virtual newscaster, Ananova (Gustavsson and Czarniawska, 2004). Carefully crafted as beyond-race-and-stereotype, she turned out, in the eyes of critical readers, to embody (virtually) all the stereotypical virtues of a (UK) woman, and those of an ideal employee as well. The designers confronted with such an interpretation by the users were shocked: the reading was the opposite of their intentions. A similar case that ended in a different way appeared in Sweden: newspaper journalists established far-reaching similarities between a virtual financial adviser, Hera Qraft, and the sexy virtual figure of the *Tomb Raiders* series, Lara Croft. The designers of Hera Qraft protested their innocence, but seemed not at all displeased by this interpretation (Gustavsson and Czarniawska, 2004).

Another example, closer to the focus of the present book, is Norén and Ranerup's (2005) description of creating educational portals in Sweden. The governmental agencies, with the best intention of helping citizens in need of education, designed Internet-based Web portals whose very use required an acceptance of the political objectives those agencies represented. Their conclusions were as follows: 'System designers take the idea of individualisation in the liberating and disciplining conceptions of the market as a point of departure for their construction of tools for qualification and calculation to be used by the citizen in Internet Web portals' (Norén and Ranerup, 2005, p. 204).

Norén and Ranerup seem to assume that the enrolment in political camps is intentional: I would like to point out that the point of intention, as in the analysis of literary texts, is moot. When the authors/designers are displeased with interpretations/uses, they deny that these were their intentions; when they are pleased, they will admit to non-existing intentions or accept the results gratefully.

It is therefore safe to conclude that designers cannot control the arc of projection because they say more than they realise (the institutional order speaks through their work); and that designers cannot control the arc of reciprocation because they cannot foresee the contexts of use. The situation seems to be paradoxical: if code is to regulate, how can it be designed if its use cannot be controlled? Perhaps there is an analogy between Lessig's idea of the regulating intervention of government to be harnessed by the open source: the designers will never be able control the uses, but they might find consideration of context – prior to design and well into use – rewarding. I will therefore dedicate the last part of this chapter to spelling out in greater detail what the general term 'context' can mean.

What can be fruitfully considered 'a context of use'?

I have the following suggestions to make considering the ways context can be understood:

1. Other texts relevant for (called for) the text/object that we hold in focus. This understanding of context derives both from the etymology of the term (con-text; the texts that are considered together with the text in question), and from the distinction between figure and ground introduced by *Gestaltpsychologie*. In order to deal with the irreducible complexity of the world, people's perceptions focus on one point, one part of an image, one text; all around recedes into background. This does not mean that the background ceases to exist. On the contrary, its noises, lights, and interferences are constantly interplaying with the way the figure is seen. The designers try to remember this, and imagine the settings where their products will be used. But the physical settings are only a minute part of the context. There will be a large number of other elements that will play a role. How could designers ever know what they are? Luckily for the designers, the contexts of use are at least in part common with the context of design. One step in widening the extent of the considered context is self-observation: the designers themselves would do well to observe and analyse their own contexts much more. This is especially pertinent for things that are not easily visible or tangible.

2. That which is beyond the frame (as in *framing* = composing a picture, not as in framing = setting a frame around). This insight comes from Goffman (1974), who used the cinematographic metaphor to explain how the actual differentiation between a figure and a ground takes place. Framing is only seemingly borderless and unlimited; in fact, the directors and the camera operators develop certain conventional ways of framing, which facilitate their work but also bring about a risk of stereotyping. A political

framing is usually different from an economic framing of the same event; a conscious effort is needed to see beyond the frame (all political events have economic consequences and all economic events have political meaning). Even more effort is required in order to become aware of one's own framing, which designers develop as automatically as camera operators.

3. An institutional context of actions. This is much more than a relevant legal framework, although it is often thus understood. Most routine collective actions are parts of some institution or other, and therefore are taken for granted: this goes for designing laws as much as for designing hardware and software. Each such action is connected to other actions within the same institution; the production of software for sale is intimately connected with the present state of the market institution. What is more, the actions seemingly belonging to one institution usually have aspects of or are related to actions connected to completely different institutions. The designers of Ananova did not think that by designing the avatar as they did, they supported gender discrimination, highly institutionalised in present societies.

In all cases, I speak of effort, of awareness, of directed reflection – all of these colliding with the institution of effective production, so strongly embedded in the present institutional order that, unlike gender discrimination, it is almost never contested or questioned. Why, then, to undertake such effort? What are the possible gains? My point is that artefacts are inscriptions of institutions in the matter, but they also offer a possibility of a revolt against an institution. I am not alone in suggesting this: Elaine Scarry (1985) said the same, as did Donna Haraway (1991), who used the cyborg as a metaphor for the discursive codes that program people's biological existence, and so said William Gibson in his cyberfiction. Open source is an example of an attempt to modify the existing institutional order; perhaps it will turn out that changing the code is quicker than relying on evolution, and less painful than any kind of revolution.

At this point it must be emphasised that institutions do not change rapidly – either by design or by acts of subversion. Among many predictions concerning the possible consequences of the entrance of the Internet into our public and private life, another quote from an interview with Richard Rorty may be worth citing. Asked if the Internet will cause an emergence of a new sub-discipline, such a cyber-philosophy, Rorty answered: *'Maybe, but I see no special reasons to think so. The telephone and the telegraph didn't create a tele-philosophy* [...]' (2006, p. 111).

Adapting this for the present purposes one could say that e-justice and e-government need not be much different from the current forms of justice and government. The old institutions are resistant and, even when vanishing, leave sediments. The institutions of the post-socialist countries resemble at present much more those of the socialist institutional order than they did in 1917 or 1945. But a new technology, coupled with a new awareness of its institution-inscribing powers, may open ways of gnawing at the bars of the iron cages of institutions, or for that matter of installing shiny new stainless steel ones. The consideration of the contexts of use may be of great value in such an endeavour.

Notes

1. *Symbolein*, as Umberto Eco (1985) reminded us, means 'half of the coin', standing for the missing half.
2. Lessig usefully reminds the readers of the difference between a liberal (a progressive in the United States of America) and a libertarian (an enemy of governmental intervention of any kind).

References

Benkler, Y. (2006), *The Wealth of Networks. How Social Production Transforms Markets and Freedom*. New Haven, NJ: Yale University Press.

Bertilsson, M. (1995), 'Inledning'. In Bertilsson, M. (ed.), *Rätten i förvandling. Jurister mellan stat och marknad*. Stockholm: Nerenius and Santérus Förlag, (7–38).

Brown, J.S. and P. Duguid (2000), *The Social Life of Information*. Cambridge, MA: Harvard Business School.

Brunsson, N. and B. Jacobsson (2000) (eds), *The World of Standards*. Oxford, UK: Oxford University Press.

Burns, T. and G.M. Stalker (1961/1996), *The Management of Innovation*. London: Tavistock.

Burns, T.E. and T. Dietz (1991), 'Technology, Sociotechnical Systems, Technological Development: an Evolutionary Perspective'. In Meinholf, D. and U. Hoffmann (eds), Technology at the Outset. Frankfurt/Boulder, CO: Campus/Westview, (206–238).

Czarniawska, B. (2007), *Shadowing, and Other Techniques for Doing Fieldwork in Modern Societies*. Copenhagen: Liber, Copenhagen Business School Press.

Czarniawska-Joerges, B. (1993/2006), *The Three-Dimensional Organisation: A Constructionist View*. Lund: Studentlitteratur.

Eco, U. (1985), 'The Modern Concept of Symbols'. *Social Research,* 52 (2), 383–402.

Gagliardi, P. (1990) (ed.), *Symbols and Artefacts: Views of the Corporate Landscape.* Berlin: de Gruyter.

Giddens, A. (1990), *The Consequences of Modernity.* Cambridge: Polity Press.

Gisvold, M. (2005/2006), 'From Scheherezade's Divan'. Gemini, SINTEF/ NTNU, Trodnheim, Norway. Retrieved from www.ntnu.no/gemini/ 2002–06e/18–21.htm; visited 10 October 2007.

Goffman, E. (1974), *Frame Analysis.* New York: Harper and Row.

Goodman, P.S. and L.S. Sproull (1990) (eds), *Technology and Organizations.* San Francisco: Jossey-Bass.

Gustavsson, E. and B. Czarniawska (2004), 'Web Woman: the Online Construction of Corporate and Gender Images'. *Organization,* 11 (5), 651–670.

Haraway, D. (1991), *Simians, Cyborgs and Women: the Reinvention of Nature.* London: Free Association Books.

Head, S. (2007), 'They're Micromanaging Your Every Move'. *New York Review of Books,* 16 August, 42–44. New York Review of Books, Vol. 54, n. 13.

Joerges, B. and B. Czarniawska (1998), 'The Question of Technology, or How Organizations Inscribe the World'. *Organization,* 19 (3), 363–385.

Latour, B. (1996), *Aramis or the Love of Technology.* Cambridge, MA: Harvard University Press.

Latour, B. and S. Woolgar (1979/1986), *Laboratory Life: the Construction of Scientific Facts.* Princeton, NJ: Princeton University Press.

Lessig, L. (1999), *Code and Other Laws of Cyberspace.* New York: Basic Books.

Loft, A. (1995), 'Time is Money'. *Studies in Cultures, Organizations and Societies,* 1 (1), 129–145.

Meyer, J. and W.R. Scott (1983), *Organizational Environments: Ritual and Rationality.* Beverly Hills, CA: Sage.

Norén, L. and A. Ranerup (2005), 'The Internet Web Portal as an Enrolment Device'. In Czarniawska, B. and T. Hernes (eds), *Actor Network Theory and Organizing.* Malmö/Copenhagen: Liber/ CBS Press, 188–207.

Orr, J.E. (1996), *Talking about Machines: an Ethnography of a Modern Job.* Ithaca: Cornell University Press.

Perrow, C. (1984), *Normal Accidents: Living with High-Risk Technologies.* New York: Basic Books.

Rice, A.K. (1958), *Productivity and Social Organisation: the Ahmedabad Experiment*. London: Tavistock.

Rochlin, G., LaPorte, I.T. and K. Roberts (1987), 'The Self-Designing High-Reliability Organization: Aircraft Carrier Flight Operations at Sea'. *Naval War College Review* 40, 76–90.

Rorty, R. (2006), *Take Care of Freedom and Truth Will Take Care of Itself: Interviews with Richard Rorty* (edited by E. Mendieta), Stanford, CA: Stanford University Press.

Scarry, E. (1985), *The Body in Pain: the Making and Unmaking of the World*. New York, NY: Oxford University Press.

Scott, W.R. (1990), 'Technology and Structure: an Organizational Level Perspective'. In Goodman, P.S. and L.S. Sproull (eds), *Technology and Organizations*. San Francisco: Jossey-Bass, (109–141).

Shrivastava, P. (1993), 'Crisis Theory/Practice: Towards a Sustainable Future'. *Industrial and Environmental Crisis Quarterly*, 7 (1), 23–42.

Sorge, A. (1989), 'An Essay on Technical Change: Its Dimensions and Social and Strategic Context'. *Organization Studies*, 10 (1), 23–44.

Sorge, A. (1991), 'Strategic Fit and the Societal Effect: Interpreting Cross-National Comparisons of Technology Organization and Human Resources'. *Organization Studies*, 12 (2), 161–190.

Turner, B.A. (1978/1996), *Manmade Disasters*. London: Wykeham Press.

Vaughan, D. (1990), 'Autonomy, Interdependence, and Social Control: NASA and the Space Shuttle Challenger'. *Administrative Science Quarterly*, 35, 225–257.

Weick, K.E. (1988), 'Enacted Sensemaking in Crisis Situations'. *Journal of Management Studies*, 25, 305–317.

Weick, K.E. (1996), 'Drop Your Tools: an Allegory for Organization Studies'. Administrative Science Quarterly, 41(2), 301–313.

Weick, K.E. and K.M. Sutcliffe (2001), *Managing the Unexpected*. San Francisco: Jossey-Bass.

Whitley, R. (1972), 'Black Boxism and the Sociology of Science'. *Sociological Review Monograph*, 18, 61–92.

Woodward, J. (1965), *Industrial Organization: Theory and Practice*. Oxford, UK: Oxford University Press.

CHAPTER 3

The regulative regime of technology

Jannis Kallinikos

Introduction

A widespread understanding across the social sciences construes the impact or influence which technology has on institutions and organisations as being heavily contingent on the local practices and the specific characteristics of the contexts in which the technology is applied. Such an understanding is, wittingly or unwittingly, premised on a strong contrast between, on the one hand, technologies (i.e., the functionalities they embody) and, on the other hand, the complex fabric of local practices and conditions in which technologies are thought to be embedded. It assumes accordingly that the forms through which technological artefacts become involved in local contexts do not depend, at least not predominantly, on the properties of these artefacts. They rather emerge during the process of local implementation, as the functionalities of technologies are negotiated, shaped, undone or undermined *in situ* (see, for example, Suchman, 1996; Orlikowski, 1992, 2000; Grint and Woolgar, 1997; Woolgar, 2002). In other words, the character and the design of a technological artefact do not dictate the way it is used. Only local practice seems able to do that.

Despite the fact that it has been unclear as to what is exactly the object of *in situ* negotiation (for what is negotiated must have an identity of a sort), the assumption of local negotiability of technology has over the last two decades increasingly acquired the character of a tacit and often unquestioned belief. The outcome has been the limited attention given to the strategies of technological objectification and the generic forms by which technologies become entangled with human affairs. Technologies may not impose unambiguous courses of action, as engineers may like to believe, but they matter nevertheless. They make some things easier to accomplish and render others difficult. I find it regrettable that social science lacks a vocabulary and a conceptual strategy for describing technologies and artefacts in systematic ways that permit comparisons across contexts. Contrary perhaps to what is often believed, conceiving of technologies in generic terms reflects a profound social concern for a fuller appreciation of what is gained or lost, as technologies become involved in human affairs. New habits and conventions are established, occupational skills become obsolete or change, goods and services become cheaper, more costly or easier to access, life chances and freedoms emerge or decline as technological artefacts and traditions dissolve into one another over time (see, for example Zuboff, 1988; Borgmann, 1999; Lessig, 2006). There is no way of appreciating these far-reaching consequences of technological shifts unless one conceives of technology in terms that transcend the limited horizons of local contexts (see Lanzara Chapter 1). This chapter deals with some of the challenges raised by the attempt to conceptualise technology in abstract, generic forms.

The chapter is structured as follows. The next section discusses some of the limitations consequent upon the disproportionate space given to local conditions in attempting to understand the impact of technology in organisations. I provide some reasons and examples as to why such an over-reliance cannot address the key question relating to the forms through which technologies participate in the construction of the local by virtue of being negotiated *in situ*. I subsequently state the case for the need to conceive technology as a generic form of regulation that cuts across contexts. In so doing, I outline the distinctive character of technological regulation, which I identify with the strategies of functional simplification and functional closure and the modality of automation. I then contrast technological regulation to the two principal regulative regimes in concentrated systems (e.g., bounded and hierarchical organisations), that is, social structure (formal role systems and hierarchy) and culture (normative regulation) and I identify the distinctive configuration of modalities by which all three operate. The chapter ends with a reflection on current technological developments (information growth, the Internet) and technological regulation.

Artefacts, systems and contexts

Considered from a longer time span, the need to move beyond an understanding of technology framed predominantly in technical, engineering terms has been closely associated with the distinctive nature of the Information and Communication Technology (ICT)-based systems and applications and their expanding involvement in social and economic life. On the one hand, ICT-based systems and artefacts convey an aura of plasticity and flexibility that older, materially based artefacts and technologies seem to lack. In contrast to hard-wired artefacts, software can always be reconfigured or even rewritten to fit particular purposes. On the other hand, the diffusion of ICT in social life has often implied the breaking away of technology from the heavily regulated circuits of institutions and organisations (Nardi and Kallinikos, 2007). The organisational use of technology has been considerably predicated upon the model of concentration, often justified on the basis of economies of scale and calculations of costs and benefits. ICT, by contrast, is seen as favouring scalability and dispersion (Castells, 2001; Zuboff and Maxmin, 2003; Benkler, 2006). Both these developments have reinforced the belief in the malleability of ICT-based artefacts and underscored the need of alternative ways of conceiving the relationships between humans and technologies.

But even the implementation of large-scale systems in organisations, often predicated on the logic of concentration, has been disclosed as a tenuous project, replete with problems of one kind or another. Indeed, the claim has regularly been made that despite the consumption of considerable resources, large-scale systems like Enterprise Resource Planning (ERP) have often failed to deliver their promises (see, for example, Ciborra, 2000; Markus, Axline, Petrie and Tanis, 2000). The reasons behind the complexity associated with the implementation of ICT-based systems in organisations are surely many and some of them could well be heavily contingent on unique factors. But two lessons seem to emerge rather straightforwardly. First, ICT-based systems and applications are themselves much more ambiguous and open than has commonly been assumed. Design may influence but does not determine the use of technology. Second, organisations are quite complex technical and social entities that exhibit considerable recalcitrance and resistance to technologically induced change (e.g., Zuboff, 1988; Orlikowski, 2000, 2007). Closely associated to this is the fact that the local appropriation of technologies is as a rule contingent on a wide range of professional skills and practices, which being the outcome of longstanding learning processes may be easy to overlook.

The awareness of the complex technical and social issues surrounding the implementation of particular technologies and the decline of technological determinism among students of technology have, however, brought to the fore novel questions. Design may not unambiguously determine use but it may not be devoid of implications either. Indeed it would be reasonable to assume that design and use, possibility and actuality are interrelated in many and complex ways that have to be disentangled conceptually and studied empirically. A key question thus pivots around the degree to which core properties of a technological system may condition its very negotiability and local appropriation (Hughes, 1987; Kallinikos, 2002, 2004b,c).

Interpretivist, situationist accounts of technology may, in this respect, suffer from an over-reliance on the local 'remaking' of technologies (Pollock, Williams and Procter, 2003; Pollock and Williams, 2008). Such an exclusive focus on local processes is often in danger of bypassing the formation over time of nucleii of technological and also institutional constraints. Some of these constraints may be negotiable in the short or medium term; others are the outcome of path dependent processes in which successive strategies of objectification (innovations) have been laid upon one another (Hanseth, 2000, 20004).

Technological objectification and the design of artefacts are as a rule the outcome of considerable periods of development, whereby technologies emerge as a series of technical and social innovations that gradually coalesce into complex and recalcitrant textures (Hughes, 1987; Kallinikos, 2004c). Its creative nature notwithstanding, the design of artefacts is a complex social activity, a practice conducted within an established web of significations that are conditioned by a variety of methods, techniques and discourses (see, for example Norman, 1999). Considered over a longer time span, technological development is partly shaped by cumulative collective learning, itself occasioned, at least to some degree, by the use of technical artefacts. Indeed, patterns of use, solidified over long periods of practice and engagement with particular artefacts, become taken for granted, drop out of awareness and may thus be more difficult to change than hard-wired properties of artefacts. Few technologies develop *ex nihilo* and many of them may indeed be claimed to have path dependent histories of development, partly driven by the lessons the use of technology delivers over time (Hughes, 1987; Hanseth, 2000). It is thus crucial to observe that use, in this wider sense, is not just a situated accomplishment as has often been assumed but is a complex social and time-evolving pattern that would be better described as a *Praxis*. Rather than being the outcome of a deliberate choice that celebrates the operations of a detached subjectivity, use emerges as a historical force that constructs the user (Kallinikos, 2006). Thus understood, the user is not a transcendental being whose predilections dictate how an artefact is used but a historical construction, in the sense of embodying the longstanding lessons of experience that may often transcend the life span of individuals.

The growing awareness of some of the conditions underlying the situated reshaping of technology as briefly described above may thus form the basis for transcending some of the limitations of interpretivism and a-historical constructivism while accommodating, at the same time, the lessons they have taught us. Indeed, it would seem highly relevant and timely to question the understanding of technology as primarily a situated exercise, without needing to resort to the old simplifications, typical of a naïve technological determinism. The elusive yet crucial issue of *what* becomes locally negotiable and transformable needs to be readdressed (Hacking, 1999). Are there any core properties that define the identity of particular artefacts or are technologies just a random bundle of characteristics? To what extent are ICT-based systems and applications malleable and interpretable? What limits or renders an artefact or technology malleable? The answer to these questions makes necessary the investigation of the character of particular technologies and the appreciation of the constraints and limits to their malleability and situated remaking (Kallinikos, 2002). Which of these constraints derive from the local or organisational context to whose activities the ICT-based artefact is applied, and which could ultimately be attributed to the artefact itself and the institutional history that its development and use embody (Arthur, 1994; Hanseth, 2000) constitute issues that need to be studied in considerable detail.

The controversies surrounding the issue of the local negotiability-interpretive flexibility versus the causal status of technology may well seem to be part in many respects of an old and tired debate (e.g., Grint and Woolgar, 1992, 1997; Kling, 1992; Winner, 1993, 2001; Orlikowski, 2000; Bijker, 2001; Woolgar, 2002). But they are not. They emerge forcefully again in the debate concerning information appliances versus generative artefacts (Norman, 1999; Benkler, 2006; Zittrain, 2007), automation and search engines versus the semantic web or in the more infected (economically and politically) debate over the regulative power of code, copyright law and the fate of commons (Lessig, 2002, 2006; Grimmelmann, 2005; Benkler, 2006). Indeed, there is no way to avoid taking a stance on the key issue of the ontology of technical artefacts and how they shape life. I find it therefore crucial to situate the argument of this chapter as clearly as possible within the rather complex conceptual and empirical landscape which the research on the social and organisational impact of information and communication technologies currently represents.

The central idea I develop in this chapter is that technology could be seen as a distinctive constituent of organisational and institutional life and a major *regulative regime*. By regulative regime I mean a technical, social and institutional system of forces that shape human agency both in the direct way of embodying functionalities that engrave particular courses of action and in the rather unobtrusive fashion of shaping perceptions and preferences, forming skills and professional rules. In this respect regulation should not be understood in negative terms, as something posterior and exterior brought in to constrain the space of action of a community already alienated by technology. In the broad way I use the term here, regulation is constitutive of its regulative domain as well. Technological regulation in particular instruments processes, frames possibilities and perceptions, and brings forth skill profiles and modes of conduct. As I hope to be able to demonstrate in this chapter, the regulative significance I attribute to technology is closely associated with the distinctive forms by which technology is implicated in human affairs and the shaping of social practices accomplished by technological means. This is to some degree demonstrated by the case of *Money Claim Online* I present and analyse in this volume (see Chapter 7). In concentrated systems like organisations, the distinctive character of technological regulation emerges against other regulative regimes such as *formal role systems* (bureaucratic regulation) and *normative/cultural rules* and the different ways these latter are implicated in the governance of organisational action. In the wider context of society, technology also differs from the ways the *state*, the *law* and the *market* are involved in the governance of human affairs (Benkler, 2006; Kallinikos, 2006; Lessig, 2006). It is extremely important to understand how such distinctions arise and most crucially to appreciate what implications it may have. In this chapter, however, I will primarily deal with formal organisations and the way technology is involved in the governance of bounded and hierarchical organisations.

Technological regulation

Technology can be said to be involved in the shaping of social relations in two basic and in principle inseparable ways. The first of these seems rather obvious and is closely associated with the *specific functionalities and procedures* embodied in the technological medium. Each technology is a technology of some sort, for example electronic patient record systems, accounting and finance systems, profiling techniques. It is reasonable to expect that once introduced in a local setting, a technology, by virtue of being a technology of some sort, cannot but come to influence, in one way or another, the *tasks* which it has been called upon to monitor and the *social relations* clustering around the accomplishment of these tasks. Such influence may well be subject to varying degrees of local reinterpretation and remaking. Yet, it is reasonable to assume that local responses are themselves conditioned by the core functionalities of the technological medium (Ciborra and Lanzara, 1994). Granted that particular technologies have life spans, it comes as no surprise that their involvement in organisations is also associated with the formation and diffusion of skill profiles necessary to operate or interact with them.[1]

However, technology is involved in the shaping of human affairs in another less obtrusive and easily overlooked way, that is as a *generic form for regulating* social and organisational relations. Indeed, particular technologies could be seen as specific instantiations (tokens) of the generic form that defines technological involvement in social affairs. If technologies were just assemblages of specific functionalities then it would probably have been superfluous to speak of technology in the singular. If the label 'technology' is not just a linguistic convention or even an illusion (and some may claim so) then there ought to be at least a minimal set of conditions which the overwhelming majority of technological artefacts must satisfy. I suggest that it is on the basis of such a minimal yet vital set of requirements (which I will make an effort to defend below) that technological artefacts are recognised as different from, say, cultural or social artefacts (Kallinikos, 2006; Simon, 1969). The generic form through which technology is involved in the making of human affairs might accordingly be said to coincide with that minimal set of requirements on the basis of which certain human devices come to be recognised as technological rather than as social or cultural artefacts. Routines and standard operating procedures are, in this respect, social or cultural artefacts. By contrast, computer software is a technological object. Routines and standard operating procedures may demand technological objects for their execution and technological objects may necessitate routines or standard operating procedures in order to be successfully operated. However the mutual implication and interpenetration of technologies with cultural or social artefacts does not make them similar. That all human artefacts are ultimately social does not spare one the task of showing the distinctive facets that make up the mosaic of contemporary social life (Luhmann, 1995, 1998; Gellner, 1996). The alternative is indeed to assume an undifferentiated hodge-podge in which everything is deemed social.

Generic forms then, I claim, cut across specific instantiations and disclose an overall orientation vis-à-vis the world. For instance, in his widely acclaimed essay *The Question Concerning Technology*, Heidegger (1977) suggests that modern, science-based technology (as opposed to older premodern techniques) regulates human life through *Enframing* (Gestell), which he describes as a distinctive ordering (standing reserve) of the world that technological regulation imposes upon (sets upon) man and nature. No matter whether one agrees with Heidegger's highly suggestive yet speculative description of technology, his way of accounting for the distinctive character of modern technology is indicative of what I would call generic forms of technological regulation. I would like to explore in this paper this perhaps 'essentialist'[2] idea and seek to find ways to capture and describe the generic modes of technological regulation. In so doing, I will juxtapose the way technology is involved in the making of social relations to what I consider to be two other major regimes of regulation in organisations, that is hierarchies (formal role systems) and normative-cultural forms of governance.

The detailed study of particular technologies and their specific implications has tended to monopolise the attention of IS and organisational research and to a certain degree research undertaken from a broader social theory-based perspective (Bijker, Hughes and Pinch, 1987; Bijker, 2001). Indeed, one could make a case for stating that the study of particular technologies (as opposed to technology as generic form) is just the right avenue for understanding their human and organisational implications (Kling, 1996). Could there then be any rationale for dealing with technology in the singular? I suggest so, although the usefulness of such an approach has to be demonstrated rather than assumed *a priori*. Particular technologies never exhaust what I call the distinctiveness of the technological, in perhaps the same way that a token cannot exhaust the type of which it is an occurrence. The understanding of technology as a major regulative regime would seem therefore to necessitate the appreciation of the distinctive generic forms it takes in contemporary life (see for example Borgmann, 1984, 1999; Castells, 1996, 2000, 2001). After all, an important part of the scientific endeavour aims at disclosing how generic forms are implicated in particular instantiations and vice versa (Cassirer, 1955).

Taking these observations as a point of departure, I would like to consider technology as a generic form of regulating human affairs. In this form, technology embodies a distinctive mode of involvement in social and organisational relations that emerges as distinct precisely in the juxtaposition of technological regulation with the two other major regulative regimes in organisations, that is formal role systems (i.e., bureaucracies/hierarchies) and rationalised action schemes predominantly deriving from the prevailing cultural models of thinking and doing (Kallinikos, 2004a, 2006). In more general terms, the regulative mode of technology could be juxtaposed to the ordering achieved through social structure and culture. Generic forms of regulation are analytic or abstract categories and their regulative valence has to be extracted from a bewildering array of cues and situations that make up the concrete and messy world of everyday life. It is for this reason, perhaps, that the distinctiveness of technology as a generic form has been overlooked and bypassed in the Information Systems (IS) research and, with few exceptions (e.g., Perrow, 1967, 1984), in organisational and social research as well.

Following one of the great social theorists of our time, namely Luhmann (1993), I would like to suggest that the distinctive and generic form by which technology is involved in organisations or other social settings is captured in the instrumentation of the very tasks and operations to which a technological system or application is applied along the lines of *functional simplification* and *functional closure* (see also Kallinikos, 2005, 2006). This should imply that despite their differences, each technological system must satisfy this minimal set of requirements that functional simplification and closure epitomise. Wireless technologies (a family of technologies in their own right) differ, for instance, from search engines and both differ rather spectacularly from enterprise systems. However, all three embody the twin strategy of functional simplification and closure by means of which they seek to regulate or monitor their respective domains. There are also differences in the ways technologies embody these strategies, and there is undeniably much to be learned by reflecting on the power and limitations of these strategies, and the ways different technologies embody them. This is a task, however, which will not be pursued in this chapter.

As a rule, functional simplification and closure in complex social systems take the form of a set of operations which are lifted out of the surrounding institutional and organisational complexity to which they belong, with the purpose of reconstructing them as simplified causal and, in the case of ICT, procedural sequences, sealed off from their environment. Three major objectives are accomplished that way. *First*, the causal or procedural sequences that make up the circuit of technology represent a considerable reduction of complexity; for such sequences furnish a carefully designed series of steps that have been selected and instrumented either as cause-effects or as procedural transactions out of a much broader range of choices. *Second*, by sealing off the operations thus instrumented from their environment, it becomes possible to diminish (but perhaps never eliminate) unwanted and uncontrolled interferences from the outside. *Third*, a significant part of the technological operations that are thus simplified and sealed off from surrounding conditions can be detached from the social actors in terms of immediate execution and embody that execution in a variety of material devices and objects.

The essence of functional simplification and closure then coincides with the fact that a series of operations is thus organised so as to be considerably cleansed from the ambiguities that may surround their planning and, most crucially, their execution. Thus instrumented, operations become possible to manage in, comparatively speaking, smooth and often efficient ways, by having a considerable part of the carrying out of the operations entrusted into material and mechanical devices or tools that embody pre-arranged causal or procedural sequences (in the case of software) in closed circuits. Sealing off and functional closure often implicate the automatic or considerably automated firing of the steps that make up the technological sequence.

In the technological realm, functional simplification and closure are thus unavoidably tied to the particular 'animation' of the material, or object universe, by having a significant part of the operations carried out as closed sequences of pre-arranged and automated or considerably automated steps (Mumford, 1952, 1970). Automation, closure and functional simplification implicate one another.[3]

As already indicated, an essential prerequisite for clearing ambiguities from targeted operations and transforming them into closed processes coincides with the decoupling or sufficient separation of the technological operations from the institutional and social complexity of the wider system into which these operations are embedded. Ideally the two systems should be completely separated and their interactions take place only periodically, under a highly strict regime of rules that decree who, when and under which conditions it is permissible to interfere with technological operations. This applies equally well to the operations of nuclear factories, aircraft flight operations, or database use. When the interaction of the two systems cannot be avoided altogether, then it must be so designed as to take place along controlled pathways (i.e., a strictly regulated interface between the two systems) that do not disturb the pre-arranged and automated unfolding of technological sequences.

Under the conditions technological regulation epitomises, it should be possible to offload and externalise accruing and unforeseeable complexity that may occur, for one reason or another, within the confines of the technological system, through controlled pathways back to the institutional/organisational system, which should be able to handle it in traditional ways (Kallinikos, 2005, 2006). Obviously, the states described here represent ideal conditions that are only variably met by different technological systems. At the same time, they disclose the entire philosophy of technological regulation and provide a yardstick against which technological sophistication can be measured.

These observations suggest that functional simplification as a description of the regulative geist of technology does not refer to the technological medium *per se*. This latter could indeed be very complex in technical or instrumental terms, that is, in its ability to efficiently perform particular functions, as is often the case with many software packages. It rather describes the *relationship* which the technological medium has with the overall context within which technological operations unfold and to those activities, operations or tasks to which it is applied. The functional simplification which *Money Claim Online* embodies does not entail the description of the software applications (at the front and back-end) through which the service is sustained but the *straightforward character of the very operations that define the service.* As explained in the corresponding chapter, these operations represent a substantial simplification of the judicial processes associated with money claims, even though the technical execution of these operations may be carried out in technically complex and eventually efficient ways. One could go so far as to claim that the efficiency of technical operations is partly due to the functional simplification of the environment within which they are carried out. Indeed, efficiency often provides the rationale (or the legitimation) for decoupling a series of operations from the surrounding organisational and institutional complexity and entrusting their execution to technologies.

The description of the relationship which the technological medium has with its wider functional context in terms of functional simplification is somehow elusive and abstract and needs to be illustrated by reference to other examples as well. The appreciation of the functional abilities of, say, vehicles as technical artefacts make it necessary to place their understanding within the wider system of technological conditions and relationships within which they are used. Smooth vehicle driving demands reasonably simplified terrain conditions and clearly stipulated traffic rules. The relationship of the technical artefact (the vehicle) to its environment is functionally simplified in this sense, that is terrain conditions have been flattened and constructed in standardised forms that allow smooth vehicle traffic under a clear-cut and rigid regime of traffic rules. These latter have themselves been selected out of a much wider option of possible moves to make vehicle traffic an unambiguous and predictable operation. Similarly, Automatic Teller Machine (ATM) transactions necessitate a simple interface, procedural standardisation (sequence of steps to be executed) and standardised information items and inputs for identifying the user and his/her bank details.

The same holds true for much more complex applications and techniques such as those of profiling. Profiles of people are constructed through the identification and relation of standardised data items in large databases. In such a framework, data items are understood as tokens of behaviour. The algorithms of the application are indeed complex and sophisticated but the relationship with the activities (the behaviour of people) they bear upon is thin and functionally simplified; that is certain behavioural characteristics are selected out of a large variety of characteristics and reconstructed on the basis of interrelating data tokens, understood as the traces of particular actions or behaviours. Reflecting on these examples, it would indeed be possible to claim that the more technically complex an artefact is (e.g., aircraft) the more functionally simplified the environment (landing and take-off conditions) within which it operates tends to be.

A crucial implication of functional simplification and closure is the possibility these strategies provide for magnifying the scale (an aspect of technical efficiency) in which the execution or unfolding of the tasks and operations that define the technological circuit takes place, for example information search through search engines or profiling applications, motorway or railway traffic, nuclear power production, mass production technologies. Indeed, the gains in efficiency, often associated with design and implementation of technologies, are the outcome not simply of better opportunities for controlling and monitoring technological operations (Beniger, 1986) but crucially of the possibilities which technological design offers for magnifying the scale in which operations take place (Kallinikos, 2005). The widely used engineering technique of black-boxing (that is functionally closing) operations into a technological medium could in this respect be seen as just one expression of a much wider strategy, geared to magnifying the scale or intensifying the technological operations through functional simplification, closure and automation.

Regimes of regulation

Functional simplification and closure must be understood as providing the generic premises through which technology is involved in social systems and organisations. Those activities, tasks or operations that define the object domain of technological regulation must be cleared of ambiguities, standardised and streamlined to a reasonable degree to make technological intervention possible and smooth. As Perrow's (1967) pioneering work on technology shows, ambiguity and recurrent exceptions from the standard ways which a set of tasks is handled defeat the goal of bringing technology to regulate organisational operations though pre-specified and standardised responses. Complex and ambiguous tasks can partly be handled with the help of technology but this necessarily implies *ad hoc* and contingent responses. These latter transcend significantly the functional jurisdictions of technology and what can be regulated through the automation of functionally simplified and closed off operations.

The streamlining of operations brought about by functional simplification and the protective cocoon of functional closure are to a certain degree used by other strategies of instrumenting predictable worlds. Indeed, classical texts in organisation theory construe the construction of organisations as largely coinciding with the conception and instrumentation of functionally simplified action patterns, routines and standard operating procedures (March and Simon, 1958/1993; Thompson, 1967; Simon, 1977;

Mintzberg, 1979). Bounded within a rationalised and technically simplified space, organisational agents are given the chance to pursue the accomplishment of the organisations' objectives, relatively undisturbed from environmental contingencies. Organisational boundaries (closure) are key to such a project.

It is therefore important to distinguish how technological regulation differs from such significant modes of governing action in organisations. As already indicated, a way of understanding the particular profile of technological regulation is by juxtaposing it to two other key forms of regulation in bounded systems, that is *hierarchy/formal role systems* and *cultural rationalisation/normative regulation*. By the latter, I mean predominantly the individual or collective interiorisation of norms, the shaping of expectations and the adoption of standard, publicly available, action schemes. Norms, expectations and modes of conduct may be specific to organisations or derive from the wider institutional system in which the organisation is embedded.[4] Indeed, this claim must further be extended to portray technology as a major means of social regulation alternative to *social structure* and *culture*. In this respect, technology could be considered as either a functional complement or even an alternative mechanism to regulation accomplished though social structure building (that is social stratification, hierarchy and role patterning), or other rationalised action schemes involving culturally embedded action scripts, routines, rules, conventions or policies (Perrow, 1967, 1986; Beniger, 1986; Scott, 2001; Thornton, 2004). Little wonder there is a close and historically substantiated relationship between technology, social structure and culture, whereby the one implicates or is driven by the others (Mumford, 1934, 1952, 1970; Noble, 1984, 1985; Winner, 1986; Introna and Nissenbaum, 2000). Also the development and deployment of technological applications necessitate access to rules and operational regimes and a host of other regulations but these should be distinguished from the very task and procedures embodied in (and thus regulated by) the technological system or artefact itself.

Their mutual implication notwithstanding, there are, I suggest, important insights to be gained by analytically distinguishing between these generic forms (i.e., technology, social structure and culture) of making and regulating social relationships. In so doing, it is important to clarify some key similarities and differences. To begin with, social structure and formal role systems as an instance of it also presuppose ordering through a variety of strategies that bear a strong resemblance to functional simplification and closure. They too represent a considerable reduction of complexity through careful specification of duties, the standardisation of their execution and the stratification of their monitoring and evaluation (see Table 3.1). As already

Table 3.1 Regulative regimes in concentrated systems (organisations)

	Technology	Social structure	Culture
Strategies	Functional simplification, closure	Stratification, functional simplification	World framing
Modalities	Automation	Routines, standard operating procedures	Norms, perceptions, expectations
Agency forms	Skill profiles	Formal role systems	Models of action, modes of conduct
	Objectification versus **subjectification**		

indicated, routine and standard operating procedures are in many respects defining characteristics of organisations (March and Simon, 1958/1993). However, these similarities notwithstanding, formal role systems and procedure instrumentation through rule stipulation can never be sealed off from the institutional and social complexity surrounding them, at least not in the way technological systems are. Nor can their execution be entrusted, other than in a trivial fashion, to material and technical means, as is the case with automation. Automation, it should be pointed out, is crucial to technological regulation. Functional simplification is crucially undertaken for the purpose of black-boxing and automating the processes or sequences that become thus simplified. In this respect formal role systems and technology stand as functional alternatives, as Beniger's (1986) study of the economic origins of information technology suggests.

This latter observation indicates that comprehensive *material objectification* and *automation* are essential to technology. The steps by which technological operations unfold in self-firing, chained sequences distinguish technological regulation from the management of complexity by means of formal role systems. But self-firing or automation is but a consequence of the distinctive forms through which technological objectification works. Formal roles systems are generally mapped onto the task segmentation and standardisation they are applied to (Mintzberg, 1979; Sinha and Van de Ven, 2005) but the two systems remain separate. By contrast, technological objectification is both exclusive and expansive. It seeks to translate or replace altogether formal role systems with technological sequences. This may and often does imply the regulation of technology through higher-order technologies, in a cascade or even a hierarchy of technological systems (Luhmann, 1993; Hanseth and Braa, 2000; Kallinikos, 2005). In this last case, technological regulation involves the trade-offs of low impact/high frequency risks to high impact/low frequency ones, as previously unrelated or loosely coupled processes are tied together. The irruption of unforeseen contingencies into the closed circuit of technological operations that unfold in a magnified scale may have devastating effects, as Perrow (1984) demonstrates in his theory of 'Normal Accidents'.

The distinction between technology and norms, rules, conventions and other culturally embedded action scripts may seem easier to make and more straightforward than perhaps the description between social structure and technology. In a sense, technology and culture seem at a remove from one another. Yet in a different and more general sense, technology is itself a major cultural artefact in the sense of being the product of the particular technical-scientific orientation of the West. In *Technics and Civilization*, Lewis Mumford dedicates the first 60 pages of this monumental work to what he calls the cultural preparation for the technological take-off of Europe (Mumford, 1934). In this respect, technology does embody key cultural orientations that have been, for some time, the object of substantial debate and controversy (e.g., Ellul, 1964; Heidegger, 1977; Borgman, 1984, 1999; Winner, 1986).

However, having branched out of a particular cultural orientation, technology has gradually become an independent and, as I claim in this paper, distinctive realm of contemporary life. Cultural schemes, norms and rules may well rely on simplification, standardisation and often substantial ritualisation of behaviour but these means of regulating social relations differ substantially from functional simplification, closure and automation, as described in this chapter. Perhaps, a key difference between cultural and technological regimes of regulation pivots around the emphasis put upon material objectification as a key strategy of control and coordination. No matter what values and predispositions particular technologies may express and what rules they make necessary, they cannot exist as technologies unless the functions they embody are externalised, materialised and carried out by elaborate and interrelated systems of devices and materially supported processes, including lines of code, as in software technology.

Culture, on the other hand, makes extensive use of material artefacts but predominantly as a means of expressing cultural predispositions rather than as a means of instrumenting cause-effects or procedural sequences. By contrast, technology has an unmistakable outcome orientation (Castoriadis, 1987). It may be used in symbolic ways (gaining legitimacy, signalling modernity) but only by virtue of its pronounced instrumental orientation and the connotations that may be involved in such an orientation. In this respect, perhaps the major difference between technology and culture as regulative regimes lies in the varying and, to some degree, reverse emphasis given to the objectification versus subjectification processes. Culture constructs subjects in an immediate way. Technology may accomplish such a task only indirectly by means of constructing an object universe that turns upon subjects, aspiring to direct and channel their behaviour by engraving the paths along which subjects can explore their agency (Kallinikos, 2004b).

The differences between the key regimes of regulation identified here are of course subtle and shifting. Most crucially, they presuppose one another and would seem to work successfully under conditions in which each one provides adequate support for the others. For instance, skill profiles and patterns of use that are associated with particular technologies are essential to technological regulation and are to some degree modes of interiorising (through learning) established patterns of action (culture). They also furnish a significant set of criteria (expertise) for designing formal role systems, which are key governance mechanisms for social structure. But the interpenetration of technological, structural and cultural modes of regulation provides no excuse for failing to differentiate between them and expose the distinctive logic they exhibit. The differences between the three key regimes of regulation discussed in this chapter can, in a somewhat simplified form, be summarised as found in Table 3.1.

Postscript

I have in this chapter presented a few key ideas concerning the distinctive mode by which technology is involved in the instrumentation of tasks and the governance of social relationships centring on the execution of these tasks. I have referred to this distinctive mode of task instrumentation and social governance as the regulative regime of technology and juxtaposed it to the modes by which social structure and culture are involved in the making and regulation of organisations. The reference has always been to the dense and concentrated instrumental and social space of organisations as distinct from society. How the alternative regulative regimes of the law, the market and the state may operate within the open space of society has not been considered here. Obviously, not all of these ambitious tasks can be accomplished in a text like this. My main purpose has been predominantly directed towards charting new directions, by opening up a space for theorising about technology.

Little wonder that the ideas presented in this chapter need further elaboration. Most crucially, they make necessary the substantial clarification of those nested territories whereupon technology, social structure and culture encounter one another in ways that make it difficult to disentangle one from another and to assess them separately (see Lanzara in this volume). There is also a need to more clearly spell out the implications for both practice and theory as regards what can be learned by such an abstract and generic treatment of the subject. Two sets of implications seem to be straightforward but there may be others as well. The first is related to the hypertrophic trends of technological growth, which, if we are right, inevitably replace judgements and actions derived from other regulative regimes, for example norms, formal role systems based on expertise. In vital sectors of the society like health care and justice (but in many others as well) key decisions will increasingly seek to accommodate the heavy involvement of technology in these domains. I think such a performatisation of professional domains like the law expressed in a variety of actions pursued on the basis of instrumental/technological rather than professional criteria can be read in many case studies in this volume. Technology accomplishes what other domains cannot or are not willing to do (see also Schmidt, 2007).

Second, there is the issue of the processes of technological development that the theory here predicts as considerably autonomous from particular groups of actors and pursuits. The relatively independent logic of technological regulation suggests that significant technological developments in particular domains will reflect the allure of functional simplification rather than the intrinsic realities of these domains (Pollock and Williams, 2008). What will the consequences of these processes be in the long run? In the theoretical reflection on the case study of *Money Claim Online* in the justice system of England and Wales I have drawn attention to some of these issues.

Finally, the current developments manifested in the increasing significance of information, information infrastructures and the expansion of the Internet disturb the balance established over the last century between the operative independence of technology, social structure and culture and the regulative regimes thus constructed (see for example Kallinikos, 2006). The way information, goods, services and processes diffuse across populations challenges the model of concentration and the primacy it has achieved in the production of goods and services. In particular, Benkler's (2006) notion of *social (non-market) production* in which highly valuable goods (e.g., open source software, Wikipedia) are produced in ways that challenge the model of concentration, and the indissoluble ties to property such a model has maintained, may suggest that the key distinctions I make in this chapter need be rethought, modified or expanded. It is my firm belief, nevertheless, that the appreciation of the far-reaching character of these developments makes necessary the deep understanding of the generic forms through which technology, social structure and culture have been involved in the making and coordination of contemporary life (see, for example Lessig, 2006). As suggested in the introduction to this chapter, the fuller appreciation of what is currently at stake, what may be lost and gained, necessitates the adequate understanding of technology as a regulative regime and the way it both differs and is entangled with other regulative regimes in constituting and governing organisational and social life.

Notes

1. The debates on deskilling, reskilling and e-literacy are indicative in this respect.
2. Indeed, technological regulation obtains its distinctive character only against the background of differences it obtains vis-à-vis other regulative regimes. No hidden essentialism is therefore involved. See for example Kallinikos (2006, chapter 2).
3. I obviously distinguish here between tools and more complex artefacts like machines in which a series of chained operative sequences are black-boxed. Tools are appended to humans, machines and complex artefacts may not be. For more details see Kallinikos (1992) and Mumford (1934, 1952).
4. For instance, the justice system in all of the case studies of this volume.

References

Arthur, B.W. (1994), *Increasing Returns and Path Dependence in the Economy.* Ann Arbor: The University of Michigan Press.

Beniger, J. (1986), *The Control Revolution: Technological and Economic Origins of the Information Society.* Cambridge, MA: Harvard University Press.

Benkler, Y. (2006), *The Wealth of Networks: How Social Production Transforms Market and Freedom.* New Haven: Yale University Press and www.benkler.org; visited 15 June 2008.

Bijker, B. (2001), 'Understanding Technological Culture through a Constructivist View of Science, Technology and Culture'. In Cutcliffe, S. and C. Mitcham (eds), *Visions of STS: Counterpoints in Science, Technology and Society Studies.* New York: State University of New York (19–34).

Bijker, W.E., Hughes, T.P. and T. Pinch (1987) (eds), *The Social Construction of Technological Systems.* Cambridge, MA: The MIT Press.

Borgman, A. (1984), *Technology and the Character of Contemporary Life.* Chicago: The University of Chicago Press.

Borgman, A. (1999), *Holding on to Reality: The Nature of Information at the Turn of the Millennium*. Chicago: The University of Chicago Press.

Cassirer, E. (1955), *The Philosophy of Symbolic Forms: Vol. 1: Language*. New Haven: Yale University Press.

Castells, M. (1996), *The Rise of Network Society*. Oxford: Blackwell.

Castells, M. (2000), 'Materials for an Explanatory Theory of the Network Society'. *British Journal of Sociology*, 51 (1), 5–24.

Castells, M. (2001), *The Internet Galaxy*. Oxford: Oxford University Press.

Castoriadis, C. (1987), *The Imaginary Institution of Society*. Stanford, CA: Stanford University Press.

Ciborra, C. (2000) (ed.), *From Control to Drift: The Dynamics of Corporate Information Infrastructures*. Oxford: Oxford University Press.

Ciborra, C. and G.F. Lanzara (1994), 'Formative Contexts and Information Technology'. *Accounting, Management and Information Technologies*, 4 (2), 611–626.

Ellul, J. (1964), *The Technological Society*. New York: Vintage Books.

Gellner, E. (1996), *Conditions of Liberty: Civil Society and its Rivals*. London: Penguin.

Grimmelmann, J. (2005), 'Regulation by Software'. *The Yale Law Journal*, 114, 1719–1758.

Grint, K. and S. Woolgar (1992), 'Computers, Guns and Roses: What's Social about Being Shot?' *Science, Technology and Human Values*, 17 (3), 366–380.

Grint, K. and S. Woolgar (1997), *The Machine at Work: Technology, Work and Organization*. Cambridge: Polity Press.

Hacking, I. (1999), *The Social Construction of What?* Cambridge, MA: The Harvard University Press.

Hanseth, O. (2000), 'The Economics of Standards'. In Ciborra, C. (ed.), *From Control to Drift: The Dynamics of Corporate Information Infrastructures*. Oxford: Oxford University Press (56–70).

Hanseth, O. (2004), 'Knowledge as Infrastructure'. In Avgerou, C., Ciborra, C. and F. Land (eds), *The Social Study of Information and Communication Technology*. Oxford: Oxford University Press (103–118).

Heidegger, M. (1977), *The Question Concerning Technology and Other Essays*. New York: Harper and Row.

Hughes, T.P. (1987), 'The Evolution of Large Technological Systems'. In Bijker, W.E., Hughes, T.P. and T. Pinch (eds), *The Social Construction of Technological Systems*, Cambridge, MA: The MIT Press (51–82).

Introna, L. and H. Nissenbaum (2000), 'The Politics of Search Engines'. *Information Society*, 16 (3), 169–185.

Kallinikos, J. (1992), 'The Significations of Machines'. *Scandinavian Journal of Management*, 8 (1), 113–132.

Kallinikos, J. (2002), 'Re-Opening the Black Box of Technology: Artefacts and Human Agency'. In *23rd International Conference in Information Systems*, 287–294. Barcelona 14–16 December.

Kallinikos, J. (2004a), 'The Social Foundations of the Bureaucratic Order'. *Organization*, 11 (1), 13–36.

Kallinikos, J. (2004b), 'Deconstructing ERP Packages: Organizational and Behavioural Implications of ERP Systems'. *Information Technology and People*, 17 (1), 8–30.

Kallinikos, J. (2004c), 'Farewell to Constructivism: Technology and Context-Embedded Action'. In Avgerou, C., Ciborra, C. and F. Land (eds), *The Social Study of Information and Communication Technology*. Oxford: Oxford University Press.

Kallinikos, J. (2005), 'The Order of Technology: Complexity and Control in a Connected World'. *Information and Organization*, 15, 185–202.

Kallinikos, J. (2006), *The Consequences of Information: Institutional Implications of Technological Change*. Cheltenham: Edward Elgar.

Kling, R. (1992), 'When Gunfire Shatters Bone: Reducing Sociotechnical Systems to Social Relations'. *Science, Technology and Human Values*, 17 (3), 381–385.

Kling, R. (1996), *Computerization and Controversy*. San Diego, CA: Academic Press.

Lessig, L. (2002), *The Future of Ideas: The Fate of Commons in a Connected World*. New York: Vintage.

Lessig, L. (2006), *Code: Version 2.0*. New York: Basic Books and pdf. codev2.cc/ Lessig-Codev2.pdf; visited 1 July 2008.

Luhmann, N. (1993), *The Sociology of Risk*. Berlin: de Gruyter.

Luhmann, N. (1995), *Sociol Systems*. Stanford, CA: Stanford University Press.

Luhmann, N. (1998), *Observations on Modernity*. Stanford, CA: Stanford University Press.

March, J. and H. Simon (1958/1993), *Organizations*. New York: Free Press, Second Edition.

Markus, L.M., Axline S., Petrie D. and S.C. Tanis (2000), 'Learning from Adopters' Experiences with ERP: Problems Encountered and Success Achieved'. *Journal of Information Technology*, 15 (4), 245–265.

Mintzberg, H. (1979), *The Structuring of Organizations*. Englewood Cliffs, NJ: Prentice Hall.

Mumford, L. (1934), *Technics and Civilization*. San Diego, CA: HBJ.

Mumford, L. (1952), *Arts and Technics*. New York: Columbia University Press.

Mumford, L. (1970), *The Myth of the Machine: The Pentagon of Power.* New York: Columbia University Press.

Nardi, B. and J. Kallinikos (2007), 'Opening the Black Box of Digital Technologies: Mods in World of Warcraft'. *23rd EGOS Colloquium*, 5–7 July 2007, Vienna.

Noble, D. (1984), *Forces of Production: A Social History of Industrial Automation.* New York: Alfred, A. Knopf.

Noble, D. (1985), 'Social Choice in Machine Design: The Case of Automatically Controlled Machine Tools'. In MacKenzie, D. and J. Wajcman (eds), *The Social Shaping of Technology.* Milton Keynes: Open University Press.

Norman, D.A. (1999), *The Invisible Computer.* London: The MIT Press.

Orlikowski, W.J. (1992), 'The Duality of Technology: Rethinking the Concept of Technology in Organizations'. *Organization Science*, 3 (3), 398–427.

Orlikowski, W.J. (2000), 'Using Technology and Constituting Structures: A Practice Lens for Studying Technology in Organizations'. *Organization Science*, 11 (4), 404–428.

Perrow, C. (1967), 'A Framework for the Comparative Analysis of Organizations'. *American Sociological Review*, 32 (2), 194–208.

Perrow, C. (1984), *Normal Accidents: Living with High Risk Technologies.* New York: Basic Books.

Perrow, C. (1986), *Complex Organizations.* New York: Random House, third edition.

Pollock, N. and R. Williams (2008), *Software and Organizations: the Biography of the Enterprise-Wide System or How SAP Conquered the World.* London: Routledge.

Pollock, N., R. Williams, and R. Procter (2003), 'Fitting Standard Software Packages to Non-Standard Organizations: The Biography of an Enterprise-Wide System'. *Technology Analysis and Strategic Management*, 15 (3), 317–332.

Schmidt, A. (2007), 'ICT and the Judiciary in the Netherlands – A State of Affairs'. *Computer Law and Security*, Rep. (2007), doi:10.1016/j.clsr.2007.03.006.

Scott, R.W. (2001), *Institutions and Organizations.* London: Sage, second edition.

Simon, H.A. (1969), *The Sciences of the Artificial.* Cambridge, MA: The MIT Press.

Simon, H.A. (1977), *The New Science of Management Decisions.* Englewood Cliffs: Prentice Hall.

Sinha, K.K. and A. Van de Ven (2005), 'Designing Work Within and Between Organizations'. *Organization Science*, 16 (4), 389–408.

Suchman, L. (1996), 'Supporting Articulation Work'. In Kling, R. (ed.), *Computerization and Controversy*. San Diego, CA: Academic Press (407–424).

Thompson, J.D. (1967), *Organizations in Action*. New York: McGraw Hill.

Thornton, P. (2004), *Markets from Culture: Institutional Logics and Organizational Decisions*. Stanford, CA: Stanford University Press.

Winner, L. (1986), *The Whale and the Reactor. A Search of Limits in the Age of High Technology*. Chicago: The University of Chicago Press.

Winner, L. (1993), 'Upon Opening the Black Box and Finding It Empty: Social Constructivism and the Philosophy of Technology'. *Science, Technology and Social Values*, 18, 362–378.

Winner, L. (2001), 'Where Technological Determinism Went'. In Cutcliffe, S. and C. Mitcham (eds), Visions of STS: Counterpoints in Science, Technology and Society Studies. New York: State University of New York.

Woolgar, S. (2002) (ed.), *Virtual Society? Technology, Hyperbole, Reality*. Oxford: Oxford University Press.

Zittrain, J.L. (2007), 'The Generative Internet'. *Harvard Law Review*, 119, 1974–2040.

Zuboff, S. (1988), *In the Age of the Smart Machine*. New York: Basic Books.

Zuboff, S. and Maxmin, J. (2003), *The Support Economy*. London: Allen Lane.

CHAPTER 4

ICT, marketisation and bureaucracy in the UK public sector: critique and reappraisal

Antonio Cordella and Leslie P. Willcocks

Introduction

In the private sector the major trend towards Information and Communication Technology (ICT) outsourcing from the early 1990s through to 2008 has been driven by a range of financial, business, technical and micro-political factors (Lacity and Hirschheim, 1993, 1995; McLellan, Marcolin and Beamish, 1995; Clark, Zmud and McCray, 1997; Kern and Willcocks, 2001; Willcocks and Lacity, 2006). The research of the 1990s and more recent research suggests that four main drivers seem to be operating (Willcocks, Lacity and Fitzgerald, 1995; Lacity and Willcocks, 2008). First, ICT outsourcing is often a response to the hype and publicity surrounding the subject – a bandwagon effect leads to senior managers asking: 'why don't we outsource ICT?' Second, outsourcing may be a response to tough economic and competitive climates and the need to cut, or at least control costs. Third, it may be conceived as part of a larger and longer term change in how organisations are structured and managed – part of what we would call a move towards the 'contractual organisation'. Following on from the seminal work of Pralahad and Hamel (1990) and Quinn (1992), there has developed a strong literature arguing the case that organisations need to focus on their core competences and activities, while contracting out to the market that work which can be done more cost-effectively or acts as a distraction from core activity. Finally, outsourcing may reflect the desire of senior managers to get rid of a troublesome function that finds it difficult to demonstrate its business value (Willcocks and Lacity, 2006; Lacity and Willcocks, 2008).

Most of these drivers translate across into the market testing, compulsory competitive tendering, Private Finance Initiative (PFI) and privatisation initiatives encouraged in the UK public services by the British government from the early 1990s, through successive Conservative and Labour governments to the present day. Market testing proposals made in November 1992, for example, saw ICT activities in 13 government departments cited as an essential part of the increased 'businessisation' and competition desired by government (Willcocks, 1994a). Contracting out could range from selective outsourcing as occurred in many parts of the National Health Service (NHS) and local government in the 1990s through to large 'total' outsourcing deals as subsequently progressed through to 2008 in the earlier named HM Inland Revenue (IR) and Department of Social Security. Alternatively these proposals meant the privatisation of in-house ICT departments, or the hiving-off of ICT departments to agency status within the public sector. Subsequent governments continued the emphasis on outsourcing ICT, as can be seen in major central government projects initiated in the last five years in the NHS, the renewal of the IR arrangement (though with switched suppliers) and the letting of contracts for the National Identity Card scheme in 2007/8.

In retrospect these initiatives would seem to have been driven by two features inherent in government policy throughout the 1992–2008 period: a concern to lower costs dramatically in the public sector (or at least reduce the Public Sector Borrowing Requirement [PSBR]), and the political belief that private sector companies tend to be more efficient, and that competition will increase efficiency and effectiveness of management and operations in public services. These both support a more fundamental reappraisal of the core role of government that occurred in particular in both the United Kingdom and the United States from the mid-1990s (Margetts and Willcocks, 1994; Margetts, 1999; West, 2005; Dunleavy, Margetts, Bastow and Tinkler, 2006). These governmental predilections, however, tend to ignore a largely private sector debate about the ways in which information-based assets embodied in assemblies of technologies and skills can themselves form core competences differentiating companies in terms of organisational efficiencies and offerings to customers (Quinn, 1992; Willcocks, Petheridge and Olson, 2002). Moreover there is little recognition of the very mixed record that long-term large-scale ICT outsourcing deals have had in the *private* sector, let alone the public sector. Thus using objective criteria based on cost savings, delivery against objectives, and stakeholder satisfaction levels, in one research study covering 63 ICT sourcing decisions in the private sector, only two such deals were successful and five a failure, with marked deterioration in the satisfaction levels for contract terms and service levels after the initial five years (Lacity and Willcocks, 1996a; see also Lacity and Willcocks, 2001). By comparison, selective ICT outsourcing recorded 22 successes and four unsuccessful deals (Lacity and Willcocks, 1996a). Finally, there is a very mixed record where significant contracting out of ICT took place in the public services in the 1990s, with Wessex Regional Health Authority, the Child Support Agency and several local authorities being only high profile examples of the kind of difficulties that were experienced (Willcocks, 1994a; Collins, 1996). Unfortunately, such results seems to have continued into the 2000–2008 period as recorded by a succession of National Audit Office and House of Commons Committee of Public Accounts reports and academic research studies alike covering NHS, IR, National Identity Card and many other marketised initiatives (see as example only Dunleavy, Margetts, Bastow and Tinkler, 2006, HCCA, 2007a,b,c,d; NAO, 2006; Willcocks and Lacity, 2006; Davies and Hosein, 2007).

In this chapter we offer a critique of the concept of 'the contract state', and suggest how more disciplined uses of outsourcing can assist the performance of government agencies. This discussion will first focus on the managerial level but then moves to the level of central government strategic intentions, in terms of democracy, citizenship, and public service, focusing here primarily on the United Kingdom context. We suggest that erosion of the bureaucratic form inherent in outsourcing and marketisation initiatives needs to be rethought, and propose a re-evaluation of how a distinctive public services management ethos can be developed to harness ICTs in support of democratic values and effective public services. In this paper 'outsourcing' is defined as the contracting out of ICT services/activities to third party management for the required result. This can also be done on short or long-term contracts. A further option is 'insourcing', that is buying in resources from an external supplier to work under in-house management. This can be on a short term and one-off, long-term 'preferred supplier' basis (Lacity and Willcocks, 2001).

The UK public sector: towards the contract state?

There has been considerable interest in recent years in notions of 'the contract state' (Osborne and Gaebler, 1993; Hambleton, 1994; Sorabji, 1994; Mintzberg, 1996; Dunleavy, Margetts, Bastow and Tinkler, 2006; Le Grand, 2007). In the public sector, the contract state can refer to contracting between public service organisations and their users/members of the public; contracting with external providers; or contracting between different parts of the public service. While these are important distinctions, in recent years UK government policy has often seemed to collapse them into the notion that public service organisations are best managed as if they were 'businesses' (Hambleton, 1994). In particular, underlying a number of key government policy shifts has been the move, begun in the 1990s, to replace monolithic state services with numerous competing providers, with the role of the public service often portrayed as being 'enabling, not providing', and the dominant focus being on extending markets and contracting with external providers (Stewart, 1995; Walsh, 1995). Critics of this approach have pointed to other ways of radically reforming the public services whereby service efficiencies can be improved, and public bodies can still deliver many services, some as businesses, others operating in a more 'business-like' manner, while all remain publicly accountable (Osborne and Gaebler, 1993; Hambleton, 1994; Mintzberg, 1996; West, 2005). Mintzberg (1996) put forward several models for managing government. He attacked the traditional, dominant Government-as-Machine model, where government is viewed as a machine dominated by rules, regulations and standards. But he also attacks its replacement by the managerialism of the Performance-Control model where the principles of 'Isolate, Assign and Measure' are applied within a conglomerate-like divisional structure. He further attacks the taking of this model to its natural limit, and the development of a Virtual-Government model – the assumption here being that the best government is, in fact no or very little government. The latter two are cited as particularly underlying the UK government's framework for the contract state in the 1990s (Sorabji, 1994; Mintzberg, 1996). In the 2000–2008 period, one can discern strong elements of both the Performance-Control and Virtual-Government models in Labour government policy, enabled, in their view, it would seem by the virtuality made by possible by ICTs – expressed in the e-government initiative of this period, and also in the continuing outsourcing to private companies of major ICT operations and innovations.

As major resources in the public service, information and communication technologies are inevitably bound up in these debates and developments. Indeed, by 1996 ICT privatisations and market tests had led to contracts worth more than £2 billion. By 2008 this figure regularly exceeded £15 billion annually. Such outsourcing represents operationalisation of the Performance-Control model as applied to public services, with some contracts (e.g., in the case of the IR Customs and Excise) demonstrating the ICT component of a further move towards a 'Virtual-Government' model being applied to the centre of government.

Emerging issues and critique

One of the ironies observable in the adopting of private sector practices by the public sector has been the application of practices actually considered outmoded or indifferent by leading privates sector corporations (Willcocks and Harrow, 1992). A major example occurs in outsourcing. Lacity and Willcocks' (2001) research on a range of ICT sourcing practices in Europe, Asia Pacific and the United States in both private and public sector organisations endorses fairly strongly the prescriptions implied in the following analytical framework

1. **Differentiator or commodity.** An ICT activity/service is a differentiator where it provides a basis for competitive advantage or, in the public sector, represents a leading competence advantage (Cronk and Sharp, 1997). A commodity activity does not distinguish the organisation, and has to be done competently, but no more. A typical example would be payroll.
2. **Strategic or useful.** 'Strategic' activities are integral to the organisation's achievement of goals and critical to its existing and future business direction. 'Useful' activities make incremental contributions but do not affect strategic direction or competitive positioning.
3. **Degree of uncertainty** – about future business environment and business needs and, hence, longer term ICT needs.
4. **Degree of technology maturity associated with the ICT activity/ service.** Maturity is low when the technology is new and unstable; or where an existing technology is being used in a radically new application; and/or where the organisation has little in-house experience in implementing the technology in the current application.
5. **Level of ICT integration.** Highly integrated systems have complex and extensive interactions with other technical systems and interface in complex ways with multiple business users.
6. **In-house capability relative to that of the market.** This factor relates both to relative capability and the in-house cost relative to what external suppliers will charge. This can be complicated in the public sector where pay constraints, and lower pay generally, can produce an inexpensive in-house service, one where it is difficult to attract and retain experienced and skilled ICT professionals.

We invariably find that the lowest risk route to using the market is to outsource useful commodities in conditions of low uncertainty (Willcocks, Fitzgerald and Feeny, 1995; Willcocks and Lacity, 2006). On the technical front, additionally it was important to reduce risk by outsourcing discrete, as opposed to integrated systems, in situations of high technology maturity where the market could provide comparable service at a more efficient price. In practice there will be trade-offs between these factors. Additionally, for public and private sector organisations alike, the following questions need to be answered positively if the outsourcing is to be effective:

- is there an economic rationale? This may not be straightforward. In the public sector, for example, outsourcing can be a way of avoiding capital expenditure and large outlays on ICT updating that can hit annual budgets hard.
- is there a low rate of technological change relevant to the content and length of the contract?
- can we manage ownership issues around asset and people transfers?
- is a suitable vendor available?
- is there sufficient in-house management capability to make and deliver on the decision? One aspect of this may be the need to separate out ICT planners/strategists from providers of ICT services to ensure objective advice.
- can we handle any significant human resource issues that will arise?

Clearly, much also depends on a tailored detailed contract and adequate evaluation systems in place to monitor vendor performance (Willcocks, Lacity and Fitzgerald, 1995; Willcocks, Cullen and Lacity, 2006). Finally, we would point out that use of the ICT services market need not be restricted to long-term large-scale or 'total' outsourcing – sometimes also called strategic alliances/partnerships (Henderson, 1990).

If these principles can be put forward as 'best practice' for outsourcing whether in the private and public sector, then it has to be pointed out that the levels of disappointment in the UK public sector on the outsourcing record would suggest that private sector 'best practice' is not being adhered to, despite what the research studies on outsourcing effectiveness indicate needs to be done. This research also points to the most neglected area of effective outsourcing practice, namely the building of retained in-house core capability to define, negotiate, and manage outsourcing arrangements. Willcocks and Craig (2007) summarise the requirement as evolving nine core capabilities to elicit and deliver on business requirements, manage external supply, retain control over the technical blueprint and strategy and lead govern and coordinate the ICT activity, thus keeping control of ICT destiny. However, a more typical scenario in many public sector organisations has been a residual ICT organisation developing, staffed by those not transferring over to the vendor for various reasons, whose tasks are reduced mainly to contract management. In such situations the organisations can quite quickly lose control of their ICT destinies, and their business requirements can become dictated by the technology available from the contracted supplier. Moreover, despite twenty-first century e-government initiatives, in practical terms 'joined-up' government can become very difficult when outsourcing is by department, thus cutting off opportunity for integrating systems across departments. Outsourcing ICTs in the public sector can also fragment ICT operations, losing the opportunities for synergistic use of integrated systems across organisations.

If our research work establishes the public services management benchmark, then in case after case one has to report that public sector outsourcing is indifferently managed, mainly through a failure to prioritise and invest in the need to build a distinctive public services management capability able to high perform in leveraging outsourcing for public service distinctive multiple purposes.

Moreover, where this is the case, there are inherent advantages in pursuing a focused selective sourcing rather than a total outsourcing approach to ICT even within the Performance-Control model. In the private sector, where organisations have applied a core competence model to their business, ICT has tended to be effectively totally outsourced mainly where the client company had considerable experience and maturity on managing ICT outsourcing and external suppliers. Relatedly, in the light of the disappointments with long-term single supplier contracts, and against, for example, the 1990s IR model of a contractual organisation, the emerging approach has been to contract with multiple vendors on staged, risk-reward contracts in order to mitigate risk (Cross, 1995; Lacity, Willcocks and Feeny, 1995; Willcocks and Lacity, 2006). Therefore, in looking across Lacity and Willcocks case work (collected in Lacity and Willcocks, 2008, Willcocks and Lacity, 2009) we must raise the issue as to whether, generically (with pockets of exceptions), the UK public sector environment today is actually appropriate for anything other than relatively short term contracts on a selective basis.

The attractiveness to government of large-scale ICT outsourcing must also be questioned, not least because of the private sector evidence of a mixed record on such arrangements (Willcocks, 1994b; Lacity and Willcocks, 1996a, 2001, 2008). The dangers of asymmetries of dependence developing over time, and working in the suppliers' favour are considerable. However, the size of such deals, as can be seen in the NHS and National Identity schemes between 2003–2008 and on-going, means that very few suppliers actually have the capability to deliver on the contract.

And sometimes they drop out either during contract performance – as was the case of Accenture and its NHS contract in 2006 – or withdraw from bidding because they cannot see how they would make money and/or perform well, as has been the case in both those major sets of contracts. Large contracts fall to very much the same few companies, Electronic Data System (EDS) being just one of them. This situation can be perpetuated when further similar contracts arise with only those companies having the size, experience and contacts to make a realistic bid. This can create a semi-monopoly situation. Not only would this be a long way from any government's original intention of creating increased competition in the public services; it would also increase public sector organisations' dependence on those few suppliers, make switching costs even more prohibitive, and possibly through less competition result in indifferent rather than superior performance by the suppliers. Again the multiple reports and research studies produced between 2003 and 2008 suggest that these are more than just possibilities, and too often realities.

Moves towards the contractual organisation can also lead to a much more formal, contractual, less flexible, and potentially more litigious set of arrangements. There are instances of such litigation. For example, in 1995–1996 the Department of Social Security and two suppliers were involved in writs and counter claims over acceptance tests for a £25 million system. Similar legal disputes were apparent between several police services and their suppliers in 1995 (Smith, 1997). New risks are also added, with the possibility of the vendor firm perhaps being taken over, going bankrupt, or making the organisation a low priority client once the contract is signed and the vendor needs to pursue more, perhaps larger contracts. This happened in the NHS contracts in 2005/6 with the failure of a software firm to deliver to Accenture, causing that firm to withdraw with losses of hundreds of millions of pounds, and consequent delays to the delivery of vital software to the project. This builds to the point that the public sector ethos of mitigating risk for the taxpayer and citizen can become seriously compromised where private sector practices and exposures are brought increasingly into play.

That said, if public services really do need to learn from better private sector practice, what can be learned from private sector experience of how the developing ICT services market can be leveraged in order to best achieve public service advantage? Given the on-going state of flux in the public services, carefully thought through selective sourcing would be the lower risk approach. This would lead to a mixed economy and a contractual organisation emerging, but one where the in-house capability on core ICT functions was high, where a capability to manage external suppliers was maintained, together with in-house capabilities to elicit and deliver on business/organisational requirements for ICT and maintain control of the organisation's ICT destiny. From recent research the latter would be delivered through retaining in-house capability to design technical architecture and arrive at ICT strategy, together with the ability to 'trouble-shoot' ICT problems that do not have standardised solutions (Willcocks and Craig, 2007). Thus a fundamental building block of a public service contractual organisation must be a high performing rather than a 'residual' ICT function.

While such an approach to ICT sourcing fits within the Performance-Control model of government posited several years ago by Mintzberg (1996), its usage is not excluded from those wishing to pursue reformist public service contractual models of organisation addressing more fully all three aspects of the 'contract state' as delineated above. Such proponents preserve the notion of public service provision but seek a radical reform of the manner in which this provision is undertaken. Unlike in the Performance-Control model, however, public service managers would have an important, indeed central role to play in delivering and managing reforms based more on strengthened democracy, citizenship participation and community values. But, according to such advocates, more cost-effective and responsive approaches can only be developed through exposure to countervailing pressures from outside the organisation (Hambleton, 1994). As far as ICTs are concerned, the need then would be to retain within the public service organisation the ability to address concerns and make decisions in the wider public interest on such issues as the maintenance of interagency data and its compatibility, the availability of data in the light of potential ICT supplier competition and commercial confidentiality, data security issues affecting the citizen, and the possibility of developing interagency ICT usage in synergistic ways. These additional concerns inherent in a broader understanding of the meaning of a 'contractual' public service organisation imply, on the ICT front, that the market needs to be carefully managed and controlled. In particular, the wider public service repercussions of inflexibilities and limitations in external contracting, and of possible asymmetries of dependence developing in favour of the vendor would always need to be addressed seriously in any ICT sourcing decision-making process.

Private vs public sector: the evaluation question

Let us now extend the argument further beyond the 'contractual organisation' notion and what makes for effective management practice in public sector contexts. As we indicated above, writing in the mid-1990s, Mintzberg expressed reservations about the Performance-Control model, and we have already suggested ways forward on that issue. But he also attacked the Government-as-Machine model along the lines by which bureaucracies are invariably attacked, by academic research, citizens, and politicians alike. Is there any rescue for bureaucracy, and if so what role would ICTs play in this development?

Let us reinforce the point that the dominant approaches to estimating the impact of outsourcing policies are mainly based on evaluation frameworks developed to assess outsourcing impacts in the private sector. These approaches mainly look at efficiency-driven performance measures, such as cost reduction and return on investment, and New Public Management (NPM) goal achievements, such as transparency and accountability, once again closely related to private sector economic standards. These approaches, however, neglect the fact that public sector strategies differ from private sector strategies because the former are driven by the overriding goal of creating public value while the latter should aim at creating private value (Moore, 1995). Private value can be estimated through financial measurements of profits, while public value is much more difficult to define, despite the all too many government-inspired documents already issued on Value For Money. Public value is related to the achievements of objectives set by government programmes and the delivery of public service to the citizenry. Public value is thus not related to efficiency of the action of the Public Administration (PA), but rather to the effectiveness in the achievements of government programmes. Moore (1995) points out that political power determines the action of the PA to so represent collective aspiration: 'The collective aspiration, in turn, establishes a presumption of public value as strong as the presumption of private value created by market mechanisms – at least if they can be achieved within the term of the mandate' (p. 30). In democratic States, above all, the fundamental values of collective aspiration are the values of fairness, equity and equality that cannot be evaluated in terms of: 'the economic market place of individual consumers, but (only) in the political market place of citizens and the collective decisions of representative democratic institutions' (p. 31).

Moore (1995) argues for techniques of programme evaluation and cost-effectiveness, distinguishing these from cost-benefit analysis on the basis that they presuppose the 'compelling collective purpose' of the outcome rather than optimising individual benefit across a range of competing alternative outcomes. Kelly, Mulgan and Muers (2002) observe that the 'NPM' of the 1980s and 1990s was 'premised on the applicability of management techniques across both public and private sectors' and that government value would be created 'by mimicking organizational and financial systems used by business' (p. 9). The result, they assert, was an emphasis on narrow concepts of cost-efficiency and a downplaying of non-functional objectives that were difficult to measure. We would suggest that this tendency has become ingrained into how public sector performance evaluation has continued during the 2000–2008 period.

New public management and the efficiency paradigm have been the main drivers for the development of the PA reform policies and their evaluation, including its e-government initiatives. This transformation in the logic underpinning the design and evaluation of public sector organisations has considerable implications for the nature of the services delivered by the PA, and also, we would suggest, serious consequences for the public value associated with the services delivered.

In practice, as discussed above, the attempted transformation of the PA along the lines of NPM, and private sector evaluation techniques based on efficiency, has led to a reconsideration of the role of bureaucratic organisation as natural organisational structure for the public sector. Outsourcing of public service delivery, and in general of PA activity, has often been envisaged as a solution to PA's continuous failure in delivering the expected services to citizens and businesses. This is still a live and on-going debate. Thus Le Grand (2007) suggests that market competition can provide a better solution for public service delivery. Choosing amongst a larger number of suppliers, as offered by competitive markets, he argues, the public sector is better positioned not only to become more efficient, but also more effective. Using quasi-market forces to deliver public services, he suggests, it is possible to differentiate the services provided, increasing the competition among the providers of these service. Increasing offers for services provides a richer set of alternatives to be chosen, allowing citizens to get served with the best alternative they are looking for. Two observations are merited. The first is that we have already commented on the risks inherent in marketisation and outsourcing, and these seem to be filtered out of Le Grand's account. Secondly, his model mainly looks from the users' perspective and very little attention is given to the role of traditional bureaucratic organisation as a value provider in public services delivery. Let us restore the balance, and not automatically assume that public sector bureaucracies serve outmoded purposes and tend to be dysfunctional in their net effects. We argue thus in line with Weber (1978) who pointed out that that the mere fact of bureaucratisation tells us little about the concrete directions in which it operates in any given context. Du Gay (2005) endorses the point for us commenting that a senior public administrator in British central government has needed to be something of an expert in the constitution, a bit of a politician, a stickler for procedure, and a stoic able to accept disappointments with equanimity. One needs to be quite precise about which bureaucratic ethics, comportments and capacities one is seeking to defend or criticise, and there are limits to the extent to which bureaucratic ordering can be pushed towards a single vision, for example managerialism, modernisation, audit, without significant costs attached to the endeavour (Du Gay, 2000).

Re-appraising bureaucracy

Government ICT policies are often informed by the assumption that the digitalisation of the public sector will allow reform of PA along the lines of private sector business management techniques and indeed will provide a support to the outsourcing of PA activities. E-government and outsourcing projects are intrinsically embedded in combination of political reforms and organisational change to enact, support, and push a profound transformation in the organisation of the public sector. ICTs have in fact become one of the most common solutions implemented to standardise work procedures and smooth information flows to make more efficient and transparent the overall organisational procedures, thus reducing the need for normative, rule-based mechanisms of coordination. Increased transparency and accountability are among the factors needed to introduce market-like coordination mechanisms (Malone, Thomas, Yates and Benjamin, 1987; Ciborra, 1993) such as outsourcing. Following this rationale, contemporary public sector reforms are often described as the right move to implement the changes that are needed to leverage the efficiency of public organisations' performances and to promote outsourcing of public sector services.

Such ideas of public sector reform are informed by the rationale that less bureaucracy in PA will improve the quality of the government's actions. But why has the bureaucratic setting been for so long the foundation upon which the public sector has been organised? Shedding light on the values that are enforced by bureaucratic structures, we are probably better positioned to assess if and how outsourcing can help public sector reform. Outsourcing is in fact not only a strategy to promote NPM reorganisation, but also possible solutions for reorganising and leveraging the effectiveness of bureaucratic organisations (Ciborra, 1993).

Before we analyse the possible effects of outsourcing on the internal organisation of bureaucratic institutions, it is necessary to consider why bureaucratic organisations are important for the operation of democratic States.

Government, democracy and bureaucracy

The relationship between citizenry and government is mediated by a complex set of institutional, normative and cultural settings. In order to understand the nature of this relationship it helps to study the institutional and bureaucratic mechanisms that define the procedures and the practices that govern the PA. In democratic regimes, the central role of PA is to mediate the relationship between citizens and the State, delivering services to every single citizen in precisely the same way, so that the basic principle of equality in front of the law and the State is enforced. Fulfilling this goal, the PA is the instrument throughout which democratic States enact their political choices. In order to guarantee the homogenous implementation of public policies and therefore guarantee impartiality in administrative action, the PA is organised and regulated following a legal-rational logic. The procedural nature of the PA is thus the outcome of the need to enforce the impartial enactment of public policies.

The enforcement of these prescriptive values is, according to Weberian bureaucratic thought (Weber, 1947), strengthened by three key features of bureaucratic organisations (Kallinikos, 2006). In the first place, bureaucracies have a formal and explicit hierarchical structure of authority. Secondly, bureaucracies have a detailed, rationalised division of labour. Thirdly, bureaucracies are governed by a set of formal, explicit, comprehensive and stable set of rules that are impersonally enforced in decision-making. Moreover, a fundamental stance of bureaucratic systems is the separation of the functions in the organisation from the person entitled to exercise that organisational function. According to Weber, the goal of bureaucracies and subsequently of the bureaucratic organisation was the need to maximise efficiency. He clearly stated that bureaucracies are instruments of administration that are technically efficient because institutionalised rules and regulations enable all employees to perform their duties optimally.

Democratic States have created bureaucratic institutions because bureaucratic organisational values enforce principles of impartiality and equality for the citizenry before the State and its apparatus (Peters, 2001). It follows that the normative propositions regarding the role of bureaucracy cannot be neglected in the formulation of policies that aim at reforming the nature of the relationships mediated by PA. The relationship between citizens and the PA is mediated by the offices of PA and therefore by the civil servants who work to provide the services. The administrative rationality and impartiality of the administrative action are therefore only enforced if internalised in the action of public servants while providing the services to citizens (Merton, 1968).

Is this just an argument rooted in history? Recently, because of complex economic and political changes, it has been argued that the mechanisms of control and regulation of the private economic system can more efficiently regulate PA action (Du Gay, 1994). Following this assumption, NPM suggests reforming the action of the PA and therefore its regulatory mechanisms along the line of the competitive market, envisaging the invisible hand of the market as the instrument that certificates impartiality in the action of the PA and therefore in the relationship that the citizens have with it. And outsourcing has been presented as a potentially effective instrument for strengthening some characteristics of the administrative system – in particular transparency, measurability and the efficiency of PA action – and therefore a means to facilitate the change of the mechanisms that regulate its action, moving from rule-based mechanisms of control to quantitative measurements typical of competitive markets. However, this change underestimates the consequences for the enforcement of the principle of equality and impartiality that govern the action of democratic states (Chapman, 1991; Du Gay, 1994).

Outsourcing as enablement

Outsourcing is not only a strategy for transforming bureaucracies into market-oriented organisations, but can also be conceived as a practice for supporting bureaucratic administrative functions. The choice to outsource existing administrative procedures can possibly improve the administrative system's efficiency and effectiveness without changing its underpinning logic (Nohria and Berkley, 1994). Since the 1980s outsourcing has been undertaken to provide the proper and adequate tools and solutions for the effective support of bureaucratic organisations both in the private and public sector. Outsourcing of repair and maintenance activities, and the outsourcing of the ICT function in particular, are some examples of market-mediated solutions designed to make PAs more effective and efficient. This has been achieved by incorporating in outsourcing contractual agreements multiple levels of controls. The increased layers of control and the more transparent and less expensive monitoring systems provided by market-based mechanisms can offer a superior and more efficient decision-making process, and help the design and production of more functional governmental bureaucratic systems.

As discussed in transaction cost theory, different organisation structures can be conceived to coordinate organisation activities. Market-like systems are very effective mechanisms of coordination when the complexity of the task and the specificity of the resources under exchange are low. This means that externalisation of service provision and organisational tasks are increasing the efficiency and the effectiveness of PA activities only when the outsourced tasks or services are very simple and not highly specific. Outsourcing can externalise part of the administrative complexity, delegating to market-based mechanisms of control the monitoring of execution of the tasks. Transaction cost theory elaborates a powerful framework to analyse the impact of outsourcing on organisation structures that comprises a clear argument about the potential effects of outsourcing on bureaucratic organisations. This argument is based on the assumption that failures in the bureaucratic organisational mechanisms can occur because of information-processing and handling-related problems. The transaction costs framework assesses different organisation structures on the basis of their ability to handle and process information and information-based relations.

As a response to the disappointments found in public sector reforms and outsourcing projects deployed along NPM lines (Dunleavy, Margetts, Bastow and Tinkler, 2005, 2006), we here propose an alternative set of ideas to inform outsourcing strategies in the public sector. This conceptual model for outsourcing policies, while considering the opportunities opened by externalisation of public service's activities and services delivery, does not neglect the role of bureaucratic organisation in enforcing fundamental democratic values, such as impartiality and equality for citizens before the State. In fact it relies upon the assumption that bureaucratic organisation has to be preserved as long as it is able to provide coordination better than alternative organisational structures, such as market-like organisations. This assumption does not pretend, unlike other forms of evaluation, to compare the costs of running a bureaucratic organisation vis a vis the cost of running a market-like organisation. Rather it compares the costs of running the two structures to provide the same set of organisational outputs. This means that it is not possible to compare market-like organisations and bureaucracies where they provide *different* organisational outputs. It follows that when outsourcing policies are implemented to reform PA organisation, and at the same time to change the nature of services provided by the same offices, we cannot compare these two different forms of organisation. This means that the values enforced by bureaucratic organisation such as impartiality and equality of the citizens in front of the State, are here considered valuable outputs to be preserved while still considering alternative forms to coordinate the action of public offices.

Accordingly, we suggest that it becomes very useful to study the role of bureaucratic systems in delivering public services using transaction costs economics. Following transaction costs theory, we would argue that bureaucracies have failed to deliver services effectively because they have not been able to handle the increasing amount of information and coordination activities nowadays needed to provide what have historically been considered traditional public services. As a consequence of the increased areas of intervention by the public sector, as part of the expansion of the welfare state, such as child care, education, retraining programmes, and a great many other services that promote social welfare in general, interdependences across sectors of the PA have increased dramatically, and the public sector has faced increasing difficulties in managing efficiently the administrative apparatus. The increased number of citizens, the larger size and number of public offices, the increased integration of public offices and facilities needed for producing and exchanging information between citizens, citizens and the PA, and amongst different branches of the PA have overloaded the bureaucratic organisation with information that now needs to be processed to provide the expected services. The increased complexity of administrative processes has dramatically reduced the efficiency of bureaucracy (Heeks, 2002) in delivering these services. So far the responses by public authorities and government advisors have not provided convincing solutions that keep at the centre of the focus the need to provide the given services, but instead has mainly concentrated on the design of solutions that change the nature of the services provided, and hence on the discussion of the best organisational solutions needed to efficiently supply these new services.

We would suggest that bureaucratic organisation is not necessarily the main reason for the crisis in public sector administration; rather a major cause can be found in the increased complexity of the administrative procedure needed to provide public services. The question arises: How can outsourcing be deployed to revitalise the capacity of public bureaucratic organisations to handle the increased complexity of the administrative procedures needed to successfully deliver public services? Cordella (2007) argues that e-government policies should be designed to make bureaucratic organisations able to cope with the increased administrative complexity rather than to eliminate them in favour of market-oriented service delivery. His suggestion is supported by the argument that, as we have previously discussed, bureaucratic organisations add value to public services.

The solution Cordella (2007) proposes is based on the notion of the e-bureaucratic form. This idea not only provides a possible strategic orientation for the design of e-government and ICT policies, but also a useful departure point for discussing when and where public services outsourcing will not adversely affect the public value guaranteed by the delivery of services via bureaucratic organisation. Following the transaction costs model (Malone, Thomas, Yates and Benjamin, 1987; Ciborra, 1993) bureaucracies are unambiguous organisational forms with very specific characteristics designed to achieve very specific goals. These are organisations that follow the logic of the bureaucratic coordinating mechanism, summarised in the norms and rules, to coordinate the execution of organisation activities and hence to deliver services (Kallinikos, 2006). This body of rules and routines represents the core information system that defines the bureaucratic coordination mechanism. Bureaucrats have in fact to fulfil the ordinary duties following these normative prescriptions that define how and when to deliver public services. This information system can fail to provide the efficient coordination mechanism needed where required to execute extremely complex and highly interdependent organisational tasks (Galbraith, 1977; Williamson, 1985). In this case, too many rules and norms have to be taken into consideration while executing the tasks. Coordinating and controlling in order to ensure that all the interdependent norms and rules are properly considered can jam the organisational processes, making impossible the final execution of tasks. In line with the transaction costs argument, bureaucracy is in fact efficient in coordinating organisation activities that do not deal with highly complex environments and highly interdependent organisational tasks. Typical examples of such failure are the delay in and waiting time needed to get proper answers from PA, and the failure of the PA in providing correct answers to a specific citizen's requests.

The solution to these failures has often been addressed proposing the outsourcing of part of the tasks and activities needed to pursue the PA duties with or without the implementation of e-government policies aiming at facilitating the externalisation of traditional PA functions. In these cases outsourcing is perceived as the proper solution to solve the administrative complexity faced by the PA in coordinating complex activities. It must be however recalled that the delegation to market-like mechanisms of control is only efficient if the outsourced activities are not complex and specific, without recognising that the complexity that is today faced by the PA is mostly related to the coordination of activities that are complex and specific. In these cases, outsourcing rather than simplifying the administrative complexity will increase it, making more difficult the coordination of the activities of the PA, and less efficient and effective the delivery and administration of such activities. The failures of the PA in delivering effective and efficient services are in fact due to the incapacity of the PA in managing the internal and external information flow and in processing this information flow along the line of the legal rational procedural mechanism.

Outsourcing, and public sector reforms policies in general, should first try to answer this problem. Following Cordella's (2007) argument, only when the use of ICT to support the bureaucratic function, or other reforms in the internal organisation of bureaucratic activities continue to fail to support the bureaucratic organisation is there space to re-think the nature of the services and the media channels through which they are delivered. In such cases, the use of market-oriented mechanisms such as outsourcing, are possible solutions. However, these decisions involve a balancing act for a complex set of factors that include cost, coordination efficiency, delivery of stated services, and maintenance of public values of equality, impartiality, and rights embodied in the public rule base. Outsourcing can support the distinctive bureaucratic forms found in the public services, and it is by no means clear that, in concrete cases, outsourcing will express the comprehensive intentions of such bureaucracies in terms of outputs and value. Therefore there is required a much richer analysis of the trade-offs and desired outputs than that implicit in much NPM thinking and in much government-initiated outsourcing policy.

In practical terms, transaction cost economics also raises doubts about the efficacy of public sector ICT outsourcing, as it has been conducted in the UK public sector at least, on a number of points. Firstly, one of the ironies in the UK public sector is that outsourcing has occurred in very large central ICT departments that often had quite good ICT functions relative to the market; but less so where the ICT functions were smaller and less strong. That is, their production costs were not noticeably different from that offered by suppliers. As one example, when the IR outsourced to EDS, its datacentres were very efficient, and indeed made no money from that part of the contract until it was able to achieve economies of scale by integrating the IR and Department of Social Security datacentres.

But, secondly, many such practices are quite capable of being achieved in-house without outsourcing – as Lacity and Hirschheim (1995) convincingly argue from their accumulated evidence. But thirdly, the key to efficacy is often NOT economies of scale, but applying superior ICT management practices (Lacity and Willcocks, 2001), something the UK public sector has all too reluctantly invested in, as discussed above, and which has not always been forthcoming from suppliers, despite the assumption imbedded in transaction cost economics theory. Fourthly, the founding assumption of transaction cost economics is that the market should be used if the production and transaction costs incurred using the supplier are still lower than the higher production costs and lower transaction costs incurred doing the work in-house. In many public sector outsourcing arrangements it is by no means clear that transaction costs are so low. For example, the IR believed in 1992 that its EDS deal would cost it £1 billion over ten years, but it eventually cost £2.4 billions. There are many reasons for such unheralded expenditure, including extra work not originally envisaged and contracted for, but transaction costs are also a key factor. For example, when EDS had to deliver on the new Self-Assessment Tax system by April 1997, it had to hire sub-contractors at premium price, because it did not have enough key staff. This pricing, plus a profit element was then charged to the IR. These are a mixture of production and transaction costs resulting from not having in-house capability. Lacity and Willcocks (2006) also point out that the costs of managing outsourcing deals (which are transaction costs) are often not weighed in the initial assessment of overall costs, but are regularly between 4–8 per cent of the total costs of any outsourcing arrangement.

One might also point out that, if administrative complexity needs to be managed down, as we have argued above, and it has not been, and it is subsequently outsourced, it is by no means clear that a private sector organisation can manage more cheaply the resulting processes than in-house public servants, who at least understand the complexity. Further transaction costs may then be incurred as supplier staff undergo a learning curve, though these costs might be sufficiently prohibitive for all parties, that only technical, rather than domain knowledge is delivered to the contract by the supplier, incurring other costs in the form of lower quality service, needing further in-house management attention.

Conclusion

Given the central role of government in protecting its electorate and citizens, a major question in public sector contexts is how can financial and other risks to taxpayers and citizens be kept to a minimum? The introduction of private sector ethos and practices in the form of ICT outsourcing can compromise this objective, but we show ways in which the risks can be mitigated. However, UK governments have perhaps moved too enthusiastically, and sometimes on too grand a scale down the road of contracting out ICT services. In doing so it has led to question marks being placed against its belief in the superior cost efficiency and effectiveness of increased competitiveness and of private sector companies as opposed to in-house teams. This, of course, need not be a necessary outcome. But the volatility of the political and legislative climate created by the governments of the 1990s and new century, and the lack of understanding of, and interest in, the ICT implications of their political mandates amongst government ministers and many senior civil servants hardly cr mate conducive to successful large-scale ICT outsourcing.

In retrospect, much of the ICT development necessitated by legislative and structural change would perhaps have been better handled on an insourcing basis. But this assumes a confidence in in-house public sector ICT departments not apparent amongst the governments of the day of whatever political hue. One major aim of market testing and privatisation of ICT services has been to achieve dramatic cost savings and reduce the PSBR. In the public sector the circumstances may be being created whereby, through widespread outsourcing to private sector ICT suppliers, ICT services will cost more, but still deliver not much greater tangible benefits than before.

Our chapter points to a less than thoughtful move to ICT marketisation and outsourcing throughout central government departments throughout the 1990–2008 period and calls for a more disciplined approach to outsourcing, which can in fact be learned from private and public sector experiences alike. A key part of this is rebuilding internal ICT skills in terms of ICT policy development and management capability, the latter translating into the ability to elicit and deliver on business requirements, manage external supply, achieve governance, and keep control of the ICT blueprint and of ICT destiny. Until PA can achieve high performance in these capabilities, it will be (and demonstrably has been) high risk to go down the route of large-scale ICT outsourcing. The NPM rhetoric has not only favoured outsourcing but also the denigration of bureaucratic structures and values, despite the fact that bureaucracies in specific concrete forms can be a rich repository for values, skills, efficiency and effectiveness, when supported by a distinctive public management ethos, and suitably supportive ICTs. We conclude, therefore, that a reconsideration of the value of bureaucracy, a rebalancing of outsourcing and in-house sourcing, and a reassessment of how flexible ICTs could be deployed, would seem to be a useful counterweight to the rhetoric of progress, modernisation, transformative ICTs and NPM that has shaped the public debate over the last 20 years.

References

Chapman, R.A. (1991), 'Concepts and Issues in Public Sector Reform: The Experience of the United Kingdom in the 1980s'. *Public Policy and Administration*, 6 (2), 1–19.

Ciborra, C.U. (1993), *Teams Markets and Systems*. Cambridge: Cambridge University Press.

Clark, T., Zmud, R. and G. McCray (1997), 'The Outsourcing of Information Services: Transforming the Nature of Business in the Information Industry'. In Willcocks, L. and M. Lacity (eds), *Strategic Sourcing of Information Systems*. Chichester: Wiley.

Collins, T. (1996), 'Whitehall Smothers Privatisation Report'. *Computer Weekly*, 29 February, 1–29.

Cordella, A. (2007), 'E-government: Towards the e-Bureaucratic Form?' *Journal of Information Technology*, 22, 265–274.

Cronk, J. and J. Sharp (1997), 'A Framework for Deciding what to Outsource'. In Willcocks, L. and M. Lacity (eds), *Strategic Sourcing of Information Systems*. Chichester: Wiley.

Cross, J. (1995), 'IT Outsourcing: British Petroleum's Competitive Approach'. *Harvard Busines Review*, May–June, 94–104.

Davies, S. and G. Hosein (2007), *Identity Policy: Risks and Rewards*, LSE, London, April.

Du Gay, P. (1994), 'Making up Managers: Bureaucracy, Enterprise and the Liberal Art of Separation'. *The British Journal of Sociology*, 45 (4), 655–674.

Du Gay, P. (2000), *In Praise of Bureaucracy*. London: Sage.

Du Gay, P. (2005) (ed.), *The Values of Bureaucracy*. Oxford: Oxford University Press.

Dunleavy, P., Margetts H., Bastow S. and J. Tinkler (2005), 'New Public Management is Dead – Long Live Digital-Era Governance'. *Journal of Public Administration Research and Theory*, 1–28.

Dunleavy, P., Margetts, H., Bastow, S. and J. Tinkler (2006), *Digital Era Governance*. Oxford: Oxford University Press.

Galbraith, J.R. (1977), *Organisation Design*. Reading, MA: Addison-Wesley.

Hambleton, R. (1994), 'The Contract State and the Future of Public Management'. Paper at the Employment Research Unit Conference: The Contract State: the Future of Public Management, Cardiff Business School, 27–28 September 1994.

Heeks, R. (2002), 'Reinventing Government in the Information Age'. In Heeks, R. (ed.), *Reinventing Government in the Information Age – International Practice in IT-Enabled Public Sector Reform*. London: Routledge (9–21).

Henderson, J. (1990), 'Plugging Into Strategic Partnerships: The Critical IS Connection'. *Sloan Management Review*, Spring, 7–18.

House of Commons Committee of Public Accounts (2007a), 'Central Government's Use of Consultants'. HMSO, London, HC309, June.

House of Commons Committee of Public Accounts (2007b), 'Delivering Successful IT-enabled Business Change'. HMSO, London, HC113, June.

House of Commons Committee of Public Accounts (2007c), 'HM Revenue and Customes: ASPIRE – the Re-competition of Outsourced IT Services'. HMSO, London, HC179, June.

House of Commons Committee of Public Accounts (2007d), 'Department of Health: the National Programme for IT in the NHS HMSO'. London, HC390, April.

Kallinikos, J. (2006), *The Consequences of Information: Institutional Implications Of Technological Change*. Cheltenham: Edward Elgar.

Kelly, G., Mulgan, G. and S. Muers (2002). 'Creating Public Value: an Analytical Framework for Public Service Reform'. Strategy Unit Discussion Paper, London: Cabinet Office.

Kern, T. and L. Willcocks (2001), *The Relationship Advantage*. Oxford: Oxford University Press.

Lacity, M. and R. Hirschheim (1993), *Information Systems Outsourcing*. Wiley: Chichester.

Lacity, M. and R. Hirschheim (1995), *Beyond the Information Systems Outsourcing Bandwagon*. Chichester: Wiley.

Lacity, M. and L. Willcocks (1996a), 'Best Practices In Information Technology Sourcing'. *Executive Report* No. 2, June. Oxford: Templeton College.

Lacity, M. and L. Willcocks (2001), *Global IT Outsourcing: Search for Business Advantage*. Chichester: Wiley.

Lacity, M. and L. Willcocks (2008), *Information Systems and Outsourcing: Theory and Practice*. London: Palgrave.

Lacity, M., Willcocks L. and L. Feeny (1995), 'IT Outsourcing: Maximize Flexibility and Control'. *Harvard Business Review,* May, 84–93.

Lacity, M., Willcocks L. and L. Feeny (1996), 'The Value of Selective IT Sourcing'. *Sloan Management Review,* Spring, 37 (3), 13–25.

Le Grand, J. (2007), *The Other Invisible Hand: Delivering Public Services Through Choice and Competition*. Princeton, NJ: Princeton University Press.

Malone, T.W., Thomas W., Yates J. and R.I. Benjamin (1987), 'Electronic Markets and Electronic Hierarchies: Effects of Information Technology on Market Structure and Corporate Strategies'. *Communications of the ACM*, 30 (6), 484–497.

Margetts, H. (1999), *Information Technology in Government: Britain and America*. London: Routledge.

Margetts, H. and L. Willcocks (1994), 'Informatization in Public Sector Organizations: Distinctive or Common Risks?'. *Informatization and the Public Sector*, 3 (1), 1–19.

Merton, R.K. (1968), *Social Theory and Social Structure*. New York: The Free Press.

McLellan, K., Marcolin B. and P. Beamish (1995), 'Financial and Strategic Motivations Behind IS Outsourcing'. *Journal of Information Technology*, 10 (4), 299–321.

Mintzberg, H. (1996), 'Managing Government, Governing Management'. *Harvard Business Review,* May–June, 75–85.

Moore M.H. (1995), *Creating Public Value Strategic Management in Government*. Harvard: Harvard University Press.

National Audit Office (2006), 'Department of Health – the National Programme for IT in the NHS'. HMSO, London, HC1173, July.

Nohria, N. and J.D. Berkley (1994). 'An Action Perspective: The Crux of the New Management'. *California Management Review,* 36 (4), 70–92.

Osborne, D. and T. Gaebler (1993), *Reinventing Government. How the Entrepreneurial Spirit is Transforming the Public Sector*. New York: Plume.

Peters, B.G. (2001), *The Politics of Bureaucracy*. London, New York: Routledge.

Pralahad, C. and G. Hamel (1990), 'The Core Competence of the Corporation'. *Harvard Business Review,* 63, 79–91.

Quinn, J. (1992), 'The Intelligent Enterprise: A New Paradigm'. *Academy of Management Executive*, 6 (4), 44–63.

Smith, S. (1997), 'The Truth Is Out There'. *Computer Weekly,* 10 April, 36–37.

Sorabji, D. (1994), '"Created Environments" and Public Management: A Preliminary Model of the Emerging Contract State'. Paper at the Employment Research Unit Conference: The Contract State: the Future of Public Management, Cardiff Business School, 27–28 September.

Stewart, J. (1995), 'The Limitations of Government by Contract'. *Public Money and Management,* July, 1–6.

Walsh, K. (1995), *Public Services and Market Mechanisms. Competition, Contracting and the New Public Management*. London: Macmillan.

Weber, M. (1947), *The Theory of Social and Economic Organization*. New York: The Free Press.

Weber, M. (1978), *Economy and Society* (2 volumes). Los Angeles: University of California Press.

West, D. (2005), *Digital Government*. Oxford: Princeton University Press.

Willcocks, L. (1994a), 'Managing Information Systems in UK Public Administration: Isssues and Prospects'. *Public Administration,* 72 (1), 13–32.

Willcocks, L. (1994b), 'Collaborating to Compete: Towards Strategic Partnerships in IT Outsourcing?' OXIIM Research and Discussion Paper 94/11, Templeton College: Oxford.

Willcocks, L. and A. Craig (2007), 'The Outsourcing Enterprise 4: Developing Retained Core Capabilities'. London: Logicacmg.

Willcocks, L., Cullen S. and M. Lacity (2006), 'The Outsourcing Enterprise 3: Selecting and Leveraging Vendor Capabilities'. London: Logicacmg.

Willcocks, L., Fitzgerald G. and D. Feeny (1995), 'Outsourcing IT – The Strategic Implications'. *Long Range Planning*, 28 (5), 59–70.

Willcocks, L. and J. Harrow (1992) (eds), *Rediscovering Public Services Management.* London: Routledge.

Willcocks, L. and M. Lacity (2006), *Global Sourcing of Business and IT Services.* London: Palgrave.

Willcocks, L. and M. Lacity (2009), *The Practice of Outsourcing: From Information Systems to BPO and Offshoring.* London: Palgrave.

Willcocks, L., Lacity, M. and G. Fitzgerald (1995), 'IT Outsourcing in Europe and the USA: Assessment Issues'. *International Journal of Information Technology*, 15 (5), 333–351.

Willcocks, L., Petheridge P. and N. Olson (2002), *Making IT Count.* Oxford. Blackwell.

Williamson, O.E. (1985), *The Economic Institutions of Capitalism: Firms, Markets, Relational Contracting.* New York, London: Free Press, Collier Macmillan.

PART II

Experiences: ICT, institutional complexity, and the development of e-services

CHAPTER 5

E-justice in Finland and in Italy: enabling *versus* constraining models

Marco Fabri

Introduction

All the countries in Europe have embarked on investments in Information and Communication Technologies (ICT).[1] The common motivation is that ICT should provide a means of increasing the speed and effectiveness of information exchange, while offering a formidable range of opportunities for institutional change and innovation. The variety of solutions adopted by individual countries, both technically and managerially, provide unique insights into the European justice sector (Fabri and Langbroek, 2000; Fabri and Contini, 2001; Fabri and Woolfson, 2001; Oskamp, Lodder and Apistola, 2004). However, the outcome of these investments varies widely from country to country. This chapter will deal with two very divergent examples in Europe: Finland and Italy, where indeed the outcome has been very different. The two cases will be described in terms of ICT governance[2] strategies, legal framework, and main applications developed.

In the Finnish case the road to e-justice is already paved and ICT has contributed to the development of a better service for the general public. In Italy, institutional complexity, and the lack of pragmatism and capacity to manage the actual situation in judicial offices by the ICT chief executive officers of the Ministry of Justice have so far stymied the effective development of e-services for the general public. This work shows how, on the one hand, in the Finnish case procedural law is seen as the enabler of technology while, on the contrary, in the Italian case technology is seen as an enabler of the law.

This work is based on extensive research carried out by the Research Institute on Judicial Systems of the Italian Research Council,[3] and some interviews specifically carried out for this contribution.[4]

Governance, basic ICT infrastructure, and legal framework in Finland[5]

Governance

The Judicial Administration Department of the Ministry of Justice of Finland is in charge of ICT infrastructures, networks, protocols, standards, applications development and management within the agencies of the administration of justice (i.e., prosecutor's offices, courts, prisons, and enforcement agencies). ICT governance is centralised in this department, with the twofold goal of firstly standardising the information provided by the courts and integrating the different ICT systems in the justice system, and secondly enabling the exchange of data within the public sector and between the judiciary and the general public.

The strategies of data administration are decided in the steering committee of the Judicial Administration Department, and then reported to the Minister for the final decision. When the matter is technical, the Department is assisted by the Data Administration Bureau of the Ministry, which is a semi-independent service unit. It is also worth mentioning that some technical activities are usually outsourced to private companies.

The information technology strategy follows a three-stage approach. The first stage is an assessment of the current situation, the second step is an extensive number of interviews carried out with users, interest groups (actors within the justice system, for example the police), and customers (actors outside the justice system, for example debt-collection agencies). The objective of these interviews is to identify the changes that are most urgent and to single out any problems that have come up with the existing technologies. Then, the final stage is an analysis of the state-of-the-art technology in order to adopt the ICT solution that best fits the reported needs, given the life-cycle of the technology to be adopted.

The courts themselves play an active role in the development of applications, and members of court personnel are included in the steering and project committee. Moreover, many projects have a *support group*, whose task is to evaluate the suitability of the application for the courts. The members of the support group will quite often continue as the *core group* for training in the use of the new application. However, some services are outsourced and the Ministry is in charge of dealing with suppliers in negotiating the services to be provided.

It is also worth noting that Finland enjoys one of the best technical infrastructures in Europe. Telecommunications are relatively inexpensive, the ICT literacy is very high, and the percentage of Internet users out of the total population is one of the highest in the world. The whole public administration has pretty much the same level of technology and, above all, it uses basic common standards and codes.

Basic ICT infrastructure

The Ministry of Justice has a justice network (data, voice, and video) which connects all the justice offices under its responsibility (i.e., prosecutor's offices, courts, prisons, and law enforcement agencies). The Justice network and the Police network are connected via intranet. These networks are also the platform for Voice over the Internet Protocol (VoIP), which is also used for video links between prosecutors, courts and the police.

The basic ICT infrastructure services of each justice office include a local area network, personal computers for all the personnel, office software (OpenOffice), intranet services (e.g., a legal information data base, rules of civil and criminal procedure), a Case Management System (CMS), e-mail, Internet access, and access to the so-called *basic registries*. These registers collect various data such as: information on natural persons (Population Register System), companies and associations (Business Register System), property (Real Estate Information System), buildings and houses (Building Register System), physical communication networks (roads and railways), and the natural environment.

These registers are the backbone of the public administration ICT system. The core of the basic registers is the *standardised code system*, that is the *personal identity number*, which is created for every Finnish citizen at birth, and the *real estate ID code*, which is used for all real estate transactions. On the one hand, this allows effective communication and exchange of data between the systems; on the other hand, it presents a challenge to the protection of privacy, as it is quite possible to make combinations of the data collected which are not necessarily desirable.

However, these registries are considered very useful, thanks to the fact that they are comprehensive, reliable and versatile. They are comprehensive because all units in a given category are recorded and provided with an official individual code (identifier). The reliability is due to the fact that the registers are kept by public authorities. The data is collected only once, and it can then be used by other branches of the public sector. This versatility is possible thanks to the standardised code system (personal identity number and the real estate identification code).

Finnish courts take full advantage of these registers and they, in turn, can provide data entries which benefit other registry users. For example, the district courts update the Real Estate Information System with titles or mortgages over property, so that people who apply for the registration of their title have only to return the deeds to the court, and the court can then obtain all the other information required from the Population Register and the Real Estate Information System. A bank can access information on real estate and mortgages, while negotiating a loan. Also, the courts update the Population Register with the information on divorces, custody, paternity and adoptions. Information on the addresses of people who are summonsed to appear in court can be retrieved from the Population Register.

Legal framework

ICT applications, and in particular applications that deal with electronic transactions, or Electronic Data Interchange (EDI), have benefited from two Acts: one on Electronic Communications in Court Proceedings which came into force in 1993 and was amended in 1998; and another Act issued in 2003 on Electronic Services and Communication in the Public Sector.

The first Act contains statements and principles that fostered the development of electronic transactions. Of particular importance among these are those that state that: (1) an application for a summons, a response and another comparable document may be delivered to a court by fax or e-mail or by direct computer transfer into the data system of the court (electronic message); (2) the Ministry of Justice may grant a party permission to deliver the information required for an application for a summons by direct computer transfer into the data system of a district court (i.e., *Sakari*); (3) the electronic message is considered to have arrived at the court at the moment when it can be printed by the receiving device or when it has arrived in the court's data system; (4) the responsibility that the electronic message has been delivered to the court lies with the sender (the same as when normal post is used); (5) the document does not need to be signed, as long as there is sufficient information in the message to enable the court to contact the sender if it doubts the authenticity of the message. In addition the law states that the court has to make a hard copy of the message if it is necessary according to the rules and regulations concerning court archives; and a court document other than a summons may be served on a party as an electronic message in the manner stipulated by that party.

It is interesting to note the fact that the Act on Electronic Communication in Court Proceedings inspired the subsequent Act on Electronic Services and Communication in the Public Sector, which includes several principles that had already been applied in the judicial field, so it would appear that the justice sector was ahead of the public sector as a whole.

Regarding the 2003 Act on Electronic Services and Communication in the Public Sector there are some provisions that should be emphasised such as: responsibility for the delivery of an electronic message lies with the sender (section 8). In the lodging and consideration of a matter, the written form required is also covered by an electronic document delivered to the authorities. An electronic document delivered to the authorities does not have to be signed, if the document includes sender information and there is no uncertainty about the authenticity or integrity of the document (section 9). An electronic message is considered delivered to the authority when it is available for the authority's use in a reception device or data system in such way that the message can be handled (section 10). The authority notifies the sender of an electronic message on receipt of the message without delay. The acknowledgement can be sent as an automatic reply through the data system or provided in some other way (section 12). In addition, the civil procedure (1993) and the criminal procedure (1996) were amended to allow the electronic lodging and exchange of legal documents. Based on this brief description, it is evident how the legal framework has been conceived to accommodate the use of ICT applications and, more generally, the development of e-services.

It is also worth mentioning that in Finnish law there is no clear definition regarding the nature of documents that can be used as evidence in legal proceedings. Generally all documents that contain significant information can be used as evidence since the evidentiary value of written evidence is defined by the free evaluation of the evidence. This means that electronic evidence such as video films, tapes, microfilms, and telegrams may also be integrated in the case documents. This helps to further develop the use of ICT in the judicial process.

A key to good results: in Finland ICT developed along with procedural reforms

Tuomas and *Santra*: the civil case management system with electronic transmission

In the 1990s, during the planning of the new civil procedure in Finland which then came into force in 1992, it was realised that the most numerous cases would be simple, undisputed money claim/debt-recovery cases. If the claim was contested, the procedure could continue in a preliminary hearing but most of them were undisputed or the evidence submitted was so clear that the decision could be taken summarily based on the available written evidence (it was estimated that this covered about 90 per cent of them). Therefore it was clear that this highly repetitive bulk of cases could easily be managed and would benefit from an automated CMS. During the planning stage it was noticed that information systems in banking and commerce contained basically the same information as the data required by the courts, so this information, which was already in electronic form, could be used in the CMS. In addition, in Finland debt-collection is concentrated within a few companies owned by banks or financial institutions. In order to use an automated tool, there were two obstacles in the legislation: the requirement of an original signature and the submission of paper documents, both of which were overcome with the introduction of the procedural rules mentioned earlier.

In the new civil procedure, it was decided to change the previous rules, so that the plaintiff in a money claim is not required to submit the written evidence (i.e., an invoice) to the court as long as it is specified in the written application.[6] This meant that the original document did not have to be sent to the courts, and the documents transmitted did not need to be signed in the traditional way. Therefore the application could be transmitted to the courts electronically by fax or e-mail, starting a multi-channel system to lodge cases in the courts.

Thanks to the new civil procedure rule the ICT application received a boost and two applications were implemented. The key point was that the new legislation made it possible to use electronic data extensively, and software was introduced immediately after the rules were changed: *Tuomas,* a robust new CMS, and *Santra,* the electronic file transfer system, took full advantage of this opportunity. The courts started receiving about 40,000 electronic applications a year directly via *Santra* from large case filers (i.e., debt-collection agencies) and some others by e-mail or fax (i.e., lawyers). It is noteworthy that these proceedings, which are usually quite repetitive and do not really need the expertise of a judge, can be delegated by the chief judge to a clerk of court, who will be responsible for the whole procedure. The plaintiff, if necessary, can be contacted by the court via e-mail or fax. Subsequently, e-mail addresses can be used in scheduling the hearing and summonsing the parties. However, it has to be emphasised that this option was not taken up by the lawyers very often at first, and it was, and it still is mainly used by the debt-collecting companies. Getting accustomed to the use of these tools took some time, but now the Finnish Lawyers Association[7] has its own secure e-mail service which allows lawyers to exchange information with the courts and vice-versa. The documents are produced by *Tuomas*, integrated with a word processor, and sent electronically via *Santra*. It should be remembered that this is possible without any original signature, since the summons does not need to be signed. In addition, in most cases, the original document relating to the application does not need to be sent to the courts. *Tuomas* and *Santra* are used during the entire proceeding, in setting the hearing and summonsing the parties to the hearing, as well as in managing the court calendar. The *Santra* system allows the sending of legal applications to the court mailboxes and then into the *Tuomas* CMS. Then, the summons are issued by post through an Electronic Posting Service (EPS) managed by the Finnish Post. Both *Tuomas* and *Santra* systems can send the summons automatically (see Figure 5.1).

Another advantage of *Santra* is that the plaintiffs, in debt-collection cases, will receive the decision back in their data system, which can then be used to enforce the decision, since the enforcement authorities can make direct use of the data.

The *Tuomas* system, which was originally designed for summary proceedings, is now used for all types of civil cases and about 200 standard documents used by the courts have been integrated in the system. It is also used to notify the Population Register System of various data relating to divorce, child custody and adoption cases electronically, saving about 30,000 forms a year, and saving the Population Register Centre from having to update its systems manually. A similar positive situation has been developed with regard to the Bankruptcy Register, which is also used by

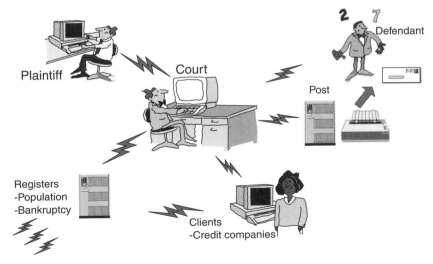

Figure 5.1   *Tuomas* and *Santra* system in Finland

Source: Kujanen and Sarvillina (2001).

credit companies. The updated and automatic sending of relevant information to this registry has eliminated the cumbersome need for the courts to provide this information by telephone.

Sakari, the integrated criminal case management system

Criminal CMS are considered more difficult than CMS for civil cases, due to the fact that there are more actors involved in the transactions with their own ICT tools: the police, the prosecutor, the courts, and the prison department. The *Sakari* CMS manages the caseflow of the prosecutor's offices and the courts, with links to the systems used by the police as well. The *Sakari* design philosophy is the same as that which was applied to *Tuomas*, but more emphasis is put on the information transaction than the case management in court. In other words, it was built around the concept of workflow among different organisations.

The history of *Sakari*, the criminal CMS, is similar to that of *Tuomas* and *Santra*. In 1992, the prosecutor's offices and the district courts were the first to implement a case tracking system,[8] which recorded basic data on the people involved, the suspected crimes committed and related decisions. The data, contained in the investigative report sent by the police, were filed into the tracking system by the prosecutor's staff. These data were also integrated in the tracking system of the district court. It is worth noting that, similarly to the civil applications, this criminal automated tracking system was implemented as a result of the coming into force of a penal reform in Finland, the so-called uniform penalty system. The reform established that all crimes committed by the same suspect would be considered as one single case, and dealt with by just one judge. The application was therefore centralised and registered all cases in progress and suspects in Finland. The prosecutors could share the information regarding a suspect with others, and then decide before which court the case should be filed if the suspect was implicated in separate on-going investigations in different jurisdictions. This application ran on a mainframe with Data Base 2 (DB2), and it meant that all the prosecutor's offices and district courts were equipped with personal computers, a local area network, standard word processing applications, and e-mail.

Sakari is a CMS for both the prosecutor's office and the courts, and it manages case information and the related documents electronically, as well as the editing of the documents needed for the trial.

Sakari allows the transfer of cases electronically from the police to the prosecutor's office and then to the courts, which return the information to the prosecutor's office after the decision, allowing EDI between these three organisations. Therefore, it required a significant effort to change working practices, which was effected with the introduction of a new criminal procedure along with the new CMS.

When the police have completed the pre-trial investigation, the basic information on the case is sent electronically from the police investigative system (*Patja*) to *Sakari*. The information on the case, the suspects, the victim, and a description of the crime, which has been received from the police, is combined in a standard structured document, which the prosecutor can edit or use as it is. A text-bank is also available so that the most frequently used texts and phrases do not have to be rewritten.

The prosecutor and the police also use secure e-mail to send documents and information, such as witness statements. It is worth mentioning that not all the investigation folder is electronic, since some of the investigation material may be available in paper form only (e.g., medical reports), and this will not be scanned.

When a case is filed, *Sakari* lists the cases within the country involving the same suspect to make possible the unification of the different proceedings in just one trial, before a judge.

The prosecutor can access the court's calendar, and correspondence between the court and the prosecutor is, generally speaking, conducted by e-mail. The prosecutor and the court use the same Intranet services so that e-mails are secure, using the same closed and protected network and if necessary encrypted messages. It is also possible to use *Sakari* for passing comments and remarks on the case to the court.

After the court decision, the prosecutor's office will receive the basic information in the *Sakari* system, and the ruling is often sent to the prosecutor by e-mail. The prosecutor can also access the court decision system to obtain information on the sentence. If there is an appeal against the ruling, this can be sent to the court by e-mail, and e-services can be used to correspond with the court of appeal. Therefore, the prosecutor's offices and the courts have access to information from the CMS of the courts of appeal and the Supreme Court (see Figure 5.2).

Sakari is considered a success in Finland. It is recognised that the application has helped to make criminal proceedings quicker and more accurate. Thanks to electronic interchange, case registration, after initial filing by the police, is automatic and the same information is used in all the stages of the procedure. The system has also helped to create a useful exchange of information and practices among the different organisations and actors involved and, in particular, it is a powerful tool for rendering the different practices that sometimes take place in the various offices more uniform.

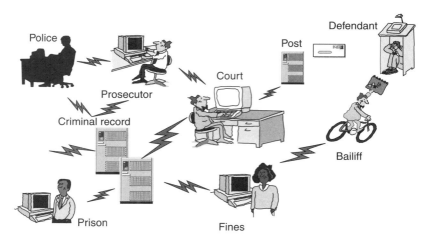

Figure 5.2   The Finnish Sakari system

Source: Kujanen (2007).

It is safe to say that in this case, following the positive experience of the application used in the civil field, coinciding the change in the procedure with the new case management application has helped to legitimate both the law reform process and the CMS.

The initial registration without double or triple filings has reduced data entry errors and helped the support staff to proceed more quickly, thanks also to the fact that prosecutors and judges were using the application themselves to prepare their own documents, thus saving administrative staff time. The process of information sharing to reach agreement on data entry details among the various organisations was long but very fruitful. 'The more the police and the prosecutor agreed on the information, how to describe the criminal act, the points of law and the crime, the less the prosecutors had to alter the information they received from the police investigative system' (Kujanen, 2007, p. 85).

However, it is reported that 'the introduction of *Sakari* was not without problems' (Kujanen, 2007, p. 85). There were technical problems in the beginning, and the application was partly re-written a few years later because of the risks involved in the millennium bug. There also were organisational problems. Using *Sakari* meant that prosecutors and judges had to deal with *structured information*, which meant radically changing their practices of reading and producing unstructured text, or even dictating their documents to be typed up by the administrative staff. *Sakari* was built for use by the prosecutor him/herself and to help the work of the prosecutor.

The introduction of the application was less successful in those offices where the prosecutors and judges did not use it directly but delegated the support staff to do so. The training of the personnel drained a lot of resources and sometimes was described as tedious, but 'The importance of co-operation for all the players in the criminal procedure was a lesson to be learned. It was also necessary to motivate the prosecutors to use *Sakari* and put emphasis on the benefits from the co-operation and the functionality from the integration to the police systems' (Kujanen, 2007, p. 94).

Sakari has been updated on an annual basis. There is a permanent working group made up of representatives of the organisations that deal with the fight against crime (e.g., police, prosecutors, courts and so on). This group manages the development of *Sakari*, defining priorities after a periodic survey of users. The next step will be to move *Sakari* to a web-based service-oriented architecture.

Another application which is worth mentioning is the electronic application that allows public prosecutor's offices in Finland to issue some 300,000 penalty orders[9] (traffic fines included) every year. The entire procedure is fully electronic from the police, through the prosecutor's offices, up to the enforcement agency. This application has also been considered very successful since it frees the police, the public prosecutor's office and the enforcement agency from handling a huge volume of paperwork, which is often to the detriment of more important investigative and enforcement activities. This is a very interesting example, because it shows how technology can make a positive contribution to the functioning of the organisation, particularly when it is used for the functional simplification[10] of highly repetitive, standard procedures.

However, it is also important to underline that

> Sakari in many ways is a product of its time, time before Internet, time with limited technical possibilities and capacity. That in many ways is the explanation of the functionalities of Sakari as more of a case management system using structured information and, compared to a modern system of to-day, less a system supporting document management. (Kujanen, 2007, p. 95)

Since the e-services are now playing a more important role, and most of the case material is already available in digital format (documents, video, audio), Sakari will probably evolve once again to meet the e-service challenge in the near future. Figure 5.3 shows the development of the e-services in Finland.

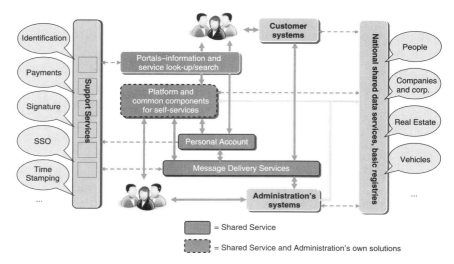

Figure 5.3   The e-services landscape in Finland
Source: Kujanen (2007).

Governance, basic ICT infrastructure and legal framework in Italy

Governance

In Italy, the Ministry of Justice has invested many resources in ICT projects for the judiciary to improve the effectiveness of the justice system, which is in a constant state of crisis (Di Federico, 1998, 2002; Guarnieri and Zannotti, 2006). Unfortunately, the gap between what has been planned and what has so far been put into operation is very wide. There are, in fact, very few working applications currently running in the Italian courts and prosecutors' offices, especially in view of the huge number of projects, and again in comparison with some other European countries (Fabri and Contini, 2001). In Italy, ICT has not yet been the enabler of change that many policy makers expected it to be. Technology has not really affected actual judicial organisational structures (Barley, 1986; Fountain, 2001), the structure of power (Weick, 1990; Garvin, 1993), the procedures, and the overall functioning of the administration of justice.

However, the ICT projects that are currently under way would have not been set in motion without a new policy on technology in the public sector that led to the setting up of the Authority for Information Technology in Public Administration (AIPA) in 1993.[11] The Authority was established to promote, coordinate, plan and control the development of information systems in all branches of the public administration. The ultimate goal was to improve the services supplied by public sector agencies to the general public through the use of ICT. In particular, the Authority was responsible for the strategic coordination of all ICT projects in the public administration, approving the three-year ICT plan that each part of the administration and government agency has to present to the Authority on an annual basis. Other important responsibilities were *regulatory* ones that include the setting of standards for planning, designing and managing information systems together with the setting of quality standards and security policies. Another of the Authority's regulatory responsibilities was to set criteria for monitoring contracts relating to projects carried out within the public sector. The Authority was also to have a significant role in *promoting* ICT, to encourage projects that involved different parts of the administration and to increase the development of the ICT infrastructure. Other responsibilities of the Authority were *financial* ones. The AIPA, through both an *auditing* process and a *cost evaluation* analysis, checked the information technology procurement process followed by different agencies. *Training* and, in general, ICT knowledge transfer within the public sector are other functions undertaken by the AIPA. These latter are mainly pursued through technical publications and the organisation of courses, workshops and seminars. The Authority also acted as an *advisory body* for the government. In this role, the AIPA defined the first technical rules on digital signatures adopted by the Italian government.[12]

In April 2001, a new Ministry of Innovation and Technology was established to further boost the use of ICT. Within the Ministry a National Centre for Information Technology in the Italian Public Administration (CNIPA) was set up, which has taken over the responsibilities of the AIPA, without changing the functions performed in order to assist the public sector in the development of ICT projects. The law that established the AIPA also provided for the creation of ICT Departments within each Ministry, including the Ministry of Justice. The goal was to connect the single parts of the administration with the Authority, and to create a new organisational structure for ICT Departments within the public administration.

The ICT Department of the Ministry of Justice has seen a huge growth in both budget and personnel over the years.[13] Its executive positions have always been held by magistrates.[14] The fact that the executive positions of the ICT Department are held by magistrates should come as no surprise, since it confirms the rule that sees almost all the executive positions in the Italian Ministry of Justice held by magistrates.

From the governance setting just described, it should be clear who is managing, funding, designing and evaluating the ICT projects developed in the public administration and in the judiciary in particular. In fact, each Ministry is in charge of designing, managing, and funding its own ICT projects. The projects have to be proposed in the three-year ICT plan, which has to be presented and approved by the CNIPA every year.

The three-year plan is an important tool for co-ordinating the various initiatives, but the most important one is the mandatory opinion that each section of administration is obliged to obtain from the CNIPA on ICT contracts.[15]

As far as the technological governance of the courts and prosecutor's offices is concerned, it is also important to mention the initiative under-taken by the Judicial Council. This latter, after the setting up of the ICT Department of the Ministry of Justice, established a specific post of *ICT magistrate*. In each of the 26 Italian judicial districts two – with few exceptions – *ICT magistrates*, one for civil cases and one for the criminal area, have been appointed to coordinate, stimulate and evaluate ICT ini-tiatives proposed in their district. The meaning of this decision lies in the judges and prosecutors' perceptions that it is important that it is they who should be responsible for the implementation of ICT in the judicial system. Information and communication technology is definitely considered to be a critical issue in that it is seen as a tool for maintaining the present power structure in the courts and in the Ministry of Justice. Therefore it cannot be delegated solely to managers or ICT specialists, but it must instead receive the fully focused attention of the magistrates themselves.

The implementation strategy adopted by the ICT Department of the Ministry of Justice still follows a *top-down approach*, and it has not really changed even with the establishment of regional offices. The ICT Department of the Ministry of Justice decides on ICT applications, and the use of such applications is mandatory for courts and prosecutors' offices all over the country, without taking into consideration the local contexts in which they are going to be deployed.

Basic ICT infrastructure

As far as the basic ICT infrastructures are concerned, the public adminis-tration has a public network infrastructure (known as *Rete Unitaria della Pubblica Amministrazione* – RUPA), which is moving over to a new infra-structure, known as the Public System of Connectivity (*Sistema Pubblico di Connettività* – SPC). This should increase connectivity performance and be less expensive. This investment should also increase the amount of electronic exchange of information within the public sector, and in particular the use of certified electronic mail (*Posta Elettronica Certificata* – PEC). In this respect, the Government is heavily promoting electronic services that can be accessed by the general public, and the justice sector should not be an exception. However, past experience shows that the problems do not lie in the development of attractive projects, but in making them happen.

All the prosecutors' offices and the courts have personal computers, but not always up-to-date models, a local area network, office software, some Internet connectivity, and a limited number of e-mail addresses. Generally speaking, ICT literacy among judicial and administrative personnel is not very high. It also worth noting that ICT training is mandatory for administrative staff whereas it is on a voluntary basis for judicial personnel.

One problem is that the ICT Department of the Ministry of Justice still seems too weak in its dealings with the ICT vendors.[16] In particular, the Ministry of Justice would still appear to be too dependent on ICT vendors for technical design, implementation policy and monitoring, and developing projects as well as for technical assistance. Even though the ICT Department has recently hired systems analysts and computer programmers, most of the project design along with the information systems maintenance and development is still outsourced. This creates major problems in the interconnectivity among different systems as well as dysfunctional ties with vendors, who tend to play a dominant role in the ICT solutions proposed in order to maximise their profit.

Generally speaking, judicial offices have very little leeway when it comes to customising the software disseminated by the Ministry of Justice, which has overall charge of its design, planning, implementing, monitoring, and developing. Empirical research (Fabri, Contini and Negrini, 1999) has shown how this top-down, centralised approach is a limit to the innovation process. In fact, the initial scope for developing some local applications autonomously by judicial personnel in courts or prosecutors' offices was particularly welcomed, and it generated a sense of ownership and a positive attitude towards technology. This option is now strongly discouraged however by the ICT Department in the attempt to maintain firm nationwide control over applications, and also to prevent security problems.

Not much is known about the ICT infrastructure available to lawyers.[17]

Legal framework

As is the case with most of the legislation, both criminal and civil procedures in Italy are very complex and not inspired by *legal pragmatism* but by *legal formalism*, in other words paying more attention to details rather than procedural outcomes. The regulation regarding the possible use of electronic applications is not an exception and these rules too are very complex, thus adding another layer of complexity to the already existing procedural complexity. It is neither possible nor fruitful to go into detail regarding the cumbersome and never-ending string of regulations that have been introduced in the last ten years to try to make possible the use of electronic documents, particularly in civil procedures, and their exchange mainly between the lawyers and the courts. Here it is sufficient to point out the main stages of the saga. This *legal soap opera* started in 1997, when the Presidential decree nr. 513, 10 November 1997, allowed, theoretically, the electronic exchange of documents – at least this was the aim of jurists introducing the concept of the electronic document – among public sector agencies, and between the public sector and private organisations and the general public with digital signatures,[18] but only after the adoption of the necessary technical specifications and working procedures. The first technical rules were introduced in February 1999 (Decree of the Council of Ministers 8 February 1999). They regulated the use of the digital signature with a Public Key Infrastructure (PKI), and set out rules and standards for establishing certification authorities. Then the rules were changed with the Legislative decree nr. 10 of 2002, which incorporated the provisions of European Directive 1999/93/CE. On 13 February 2001, with the Presidential decree nr. 123, the regulations for the use of electronic applications in civil proceedings were set up. In addition two laws affected electronic transmission: the Presidential decree 196/2003, known as the 'Privacy Code', and the Law 15/2005, which dealt with administrative procedures relating to electronic transmissions. March 2005 saw the coming into force of Legislative decree nr. 82, known as the 'Code of Digital Administration', which contains most of the previous dispositions, while Legislative decree nr. 40, of 2 February 2006 also introduced the option of sending documents to the courts by certified mail, generating some problems of consistency with the previous regulation specifically designed for the project known as *Civil Trial OnLine* (TOL, in Italian known as *processo civile telematico* – PCT). In the meanwhile, throughout the drafting of these main regulations, there has been a plethora of ministerial regulations (e.g., Ministerial decree nr. 264 of 27 March 2000; 14 October 2004 regarding technical rules for electronic transactions; 24 May 2001 on the management of *registries of action*; 15 December 2005 on Document Type Definition – DTD) which attempt to match the existing law with the electronic applications and the day-to-day operation of the judicial offices. The product of this mess of norms is a very complex legal framework, not without inconsistencies, which the same jurists find it difficult to work their way through. It is safe to say that this jungle of norms on electronic transmission replicates the complex paper judicial proceedings that sadly make the legal system in Italy famous for being one of the slowest and least efficient in Europe. It should also be emphasised that civil proceedings in Italy are characterised by different kinds of procedures, depending on the type of case. For example, there are different procedures to be followed by the parties if the case involves employment law, or forced sales, or divorce, or summary proceedings for injunctive orders (i.e., money claims) and so on. This flourishing of different kinds of procedures is certainly another factor of complexity in designing ICT tools. These difficulties have created major problems both in the design and implementation of the applications, with particular reference to electronic transactions.

An unsatisfactory return on investment: ICT applications in the Italian justice system

This paragraph will briefly describe some of the many applications that have been planned and, in some cases, implemented in the Italian judicial system.[19] This brief description will show one of the problems of the development of ICT in the Italian judiciary: the excessive fragmentation of these projects, which generates problems both in financing and managing them. Special attention will be paid to the project known as *Civil TOL* (*Civil Trial OnLine*),[20] which is – on paper – a nice project. It is a classic example of how too much normative and technological complexity can undermine a good idea.

The ministerial criminal case tracking systems and promising local applications

If, on the one hand, in recent years ICT projects have certainly exploded onto the Italian judicial scene, on the other hand, the main problem is still the implementation of these numerous projects, which in many cases are stuck in a feasibility study or an everlasting piloting stage.

The projects involve criminal and civil business as well as the administrative operations of both courts and prosecutors' offices, along with the Ministry of Justice. This section briefly describes some of these projects (Carnevali, Contini, Fabri and Velicogna, 2007) to provide some examples of what has been planned and implemented so far.

In the criminal area, it is worth mentioning the case tracking system (know as *Registro Generale* [Re.Ge.]), which is currently running in all of the 165 courts of first instance, as well as in the attached prosecutor's offices and in the 26 courts of appeal. The software is a typical automated case tracking system based on a client-server architecture. The software allows limited data interchange between the courts and the attached prosecutors' offices. It was designed to be, and it is still, an automation of the handwritten paper docket, in other words a register of actions in the life of a case from the initial criminal complaint to the final sentence. In some prosecutors' offices, where the caseload is very high, data entry can also be carried out by optical acquisition of the criminal complaints. Re.Ge. was designed as a *perfect functional equivalent* (Contini, 2000, p. 261) of the previous paper docket, it automated the *status quo*, and was never planned to be a real CMS or an informing technology (Zuboff, 1988). It was not designed to help judges and prosecutors in their decision-making process, even if in some limited cases, empirical research (Fabri, Contini and Negrini, 1999) has shown how court personnel have tried to increase its potential. For example, some typical database functions were used to automate the production of standard judicial documents, as well as a smart use of the database which allowed some prosecutors to develop the investigations into frequent crimes such as car theft. Since its initial implementation there have already been several versions of the same software both to meet the end-users' demands and to meet the numerous changes in the law that have been a hallmark of Italian criminal law since 1989, when the code of criminal procedure was re-drafted. As of today, the tracking systems are very outdated, and courts and prosecutors' offices are finding it extremely difficult to manage them. The Ministry of Justice has been working to replace Re.Ge. with a web-based application, with functions closer to a CMS rather than a mere case tracking tool. The new application is in its piloting stage and is scheduled to be released to the courts in April 2008, but given the record of delay in the Ministry of Justice it is doubtful that this will happen.

There are also some pilot projects in Italy for transmitting crime reports and related documents from the police to the prosecutors' offices by electronic means. At this stage they are piloting the transmission of .pdf files only. Electronic filing, which will mean that documents can be transmitted and included in the prosecutors' data base, thus avoiding double digitalisation, is still to come.

The second system which is actually running is the application used by anti-mafia prosecutors. Italy has a special unit of prosecutors which has a central bureau in Rome (*Direzione Nazionale Antimafia*) and 26 district prosecutors' offices (*Direzione Distrettuale Antimafia*), which correspond to the 26 districts of court of appeal. These anti-mafia units use a specifically designed Standard Query Language (SQL) database (known as Information system for the Italian national anti-mafia bureau [SIDNA] and Information system for the italian District anti-mafia bureau [SIDDA])[21] which classifies the information collected by the prosecutor's office and then should help prosecutors in their investigative work through a retrieval system. The application has been implemented in all of the 26 district offices and in the central Rome bureau where all the information regarding mafia crime is processed. Communication between the local units and the central bureau is still one of the major problems of the system as it is. On many occasions important information is not transmitted to Rome from the regional offices in order to preserve the absolute secrecy of the information. In addition, the data entry process, and its indexing, is performed manually mainly by police forces, and therefore it is extremely cumbersome and costly. As far as we know, evaluation of the actual use of the system by public prosecutors is not available, while it is sorely needed since its basic architecture will also be used by Eurojust, the European Public Prosecution Authority (Fabri, 2007, p. 22).

Recently, an upgrade of the very outdated National Criminal Record System (*Casellario Giudiziario*) has been introduced. The system was designed to file electronically all the data relating to a conviction and keep track of both convictions and formal indictments of defendants nationwide.[22] The application should solve the serious problem of delay in filing convictions, but in this case too the Ministry of Justice has no plans to evaluate the application after its implementation. The application is also intended as part of a European project for the exchange of criminal records, which is in the pilot stage at the time of writing, and includes France, Germany, Spain, Luxemburg, Belgium and the Czech Republic.

The most interesting developments regarding specific ICT applications are probably taking place in two prosecutors' offices. In one case, semantic knowledge management technology has been used in a complex investigation with thousands of documents and unstructured data. The application (know as *Beagle*) looks extremely promising and has been very effective at the local level. It is hoped that the Ministry of Justice will look carefully into the project, which could have a very positive impact in complex investigations such as organised crime and terrorism. In another case, carried out in the Public Prosecutor's Office in Lecce, in the South of Italy, an interesting evolution of the CMS has been developed, creating a web-based workflow application for managing and retrieving all the documents handled by the public prosecutors. The core of the application is the digitalisation of the public prosecutor's files, which are intended to contain all the documents produced during the investigation (police reports, wiretapping records, phone numbers, data available from the case tracking system etc.) in electronic form. It will also allow electronic access to other data bases (e.g., criminal records, prison records, personal records, land records and so on) which might be of use to the investigation team. The application will have a search engine to allow traditional full text document retrieval, and can be used as a knowledge management tool to generate points for investigation. In addition, the application has a crawler which can search the local newspaper and will allow users, if requested, to share the information with other public prosecutors within the office, who could then carry out a related investigation. The application has been designed to use open source software as far as possible.

In the area of civil procedures the project known as *Civil Trial OnLine* is draining resources

In the area of civil procedures all the courts, both of limited and general jurisdiction, have case tracking/management systems (known as CMS for Civil Procedures Developed for the Italian Courts of General Jurisdiction [SICC]) with limited workflow capabilities. In some courts, it is used as an electronic repository of first instance rulings (known as Polis). These rulings, as well as limited access to the state of the proceedings, are available in some courts on the web for remote access by lawyers (known as Polis web) through digital signature and smart card. However, this is a prime example of how the most serious difficulty in the development of these systems is not technology, but the difficulty in getting judges to change their working practices so that rulings can be stored on the data base, and to change the organisational workflow. The use of both applications has, however, been very limited. The application should be progressively extended to the other courts and be connected to the CMSs but, once again, the step between the pilot stage and the actual dissemination of the software inevitably seems to be very problematic in the Italian context.

Several other applications, which cannot be mentioned here in full, have been developed but it is not always clear at what stage they really are and, above all, what sort of return there will be on the investment.

As mentioned, the ambitious *Civil TOL*, for which Polis and in particular Polis web were supposed to be the test beds, merits special attention.

After more than €12 million was spent over six years,[23] at the time of writing the tangible results of the *Civil TOL* are, *de facto* (a) the numerous regulations introduced to manage electronic document exchange, which requires certified e-mail, digital signatures, encryption of messages, authentication of the parties, a secure access point and a central dispatcher, and (b) a limited e-filing system of injunctive orders, which is only used in one city (namely Milan) after it was piloted in another five out of 165 Italian courts. However it is not running in these five other courts. A Government bill, presented to Parliament in May 2007, states that the use of this application by lawyers will be mandatory for injunctive orders, forced sales, and social security cases by 2010. It is doubtful that the use of technology in the Italian judiciary enforced by law will however produce the expected positive results. The project relies on the use of digital signatures becoming commonplace and is very complex from the technological, normative and organisational perspective. As it has been designed, it will be – and is already – one of the most expensive failures of the ICT history of the Italian justice system. The Directorate on Information Technology of the Ministry of Justice has sunk, and it is still sinking, most of its resources into this project. The goal is now much less ambitious than it was a few years ago, but it is still their most heavily promoted project and receives much support from Ministry executives, notwithstanding the very poor results achieved so far.

The initial idea remains the same: to allow electronic access and transaction in the courts and between the courts and the lawyers in order to improve the service provided. Figure 5.4 summarises the main architecture of the *Civil TOL*.

In brief and without going into too much detail, the *Civil TOL* workflow has been planned as follows. Expert witnesses and lawyers will access the courts through a validation process carried out using a smart card with a digital signature through the Access Point, which will be set up and

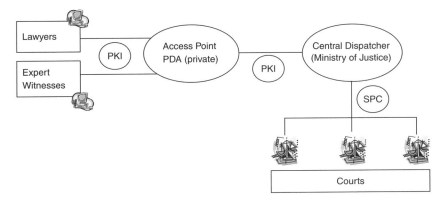

Figure 5.4   The basic architecture of the *Civil TOL* in Italy

Source: Adapted from the website of the Italian Ministry of Justice. www.giustizia.it; visited 20 March 2008.

managed by a service provider (e.g., the lawyers' associations or private companies), authorised and periodically monitored by the Ministry of Justice. This Access Point (PDA) delivers the files to the Central Dispatcher managed by the Ministry of Justice electronically. The Central Dispatcher provides time stamps for the files and delivers the electronic documents to the local court. The Access Point and the Central Dispatcher will use the Public System of Connectivity (SPC) for their electronic transactions. Then the local courts will manage them with their case tracking/management system (SICC) for the case handler. All communication between the court and the lawyers (e.g., summons), or access to court's documents relating to the case will be via the same electronic path, through a certified mail box made available to the lawyers by the service provider who manages the Access Point. In order to produce a legally binding electronic document the lawyers must sign it with a digital signature and use another digital signature to transmit the documents to the courts. Documents will be produced through a DTD set up by the Ministry of Justice.[24]

Initially the ambitious project was going to be used for all types of civil suits, and in several three-year plans the Ministry of Justice stated that, thanks to the *Civil TOL*, 'there will be an acceleration in the settlement of the civil suits by at least 20 per cent and a general increase of efficiency of administrative services by 30–40 per cent?' (Ministero della Giustizia, 2007, p. 1). So far, this is an objective achieved on paper only.

Finally at the end of 2006, the very first running application which formed a part of the wider *Civil TOL* project was actually set up in the Milan court of general jurisdiction. As mentioned earlier, the application is limited to injunctive orders (i.e., money claims). There are some positive statistics from the Milan court regarding the results of this first implementation[25] but, as far as it is known, there is no independent evaluation of the functioning of the application. This is a typical problem that constantly resurfaces regarding the investment in ICT in the Italian judiciary.

There have been a host of problems, some technical and some organisational, in the development of the project, which cannot be described here in detail. However, just to mention a few, the interfaces to be used by the judges and by the lawyers, both initially proposed by the Ministry of Justice, were complex and not user-friendly. Access to the technical details in the possession of the Ministry of Justice and its software developer was very limited, so that other software houses could not develop their own interfaces, which would then stimulate the adoption of the application by lawyers. Partially related to this latter problem, and because of the related costs against a doubtful return, the various lawyers' associations have not yet set up electronic access points, slowing down the possibility of testing the e-filing software in different contexts.

Recently, the ICT Department of the Ministry of Justice seems to have changed its strategy slightly, looking for solutions to the many problems in the implementation of the application. For example, in January 2007, it announced a new DTD schema for electronic documents to try to 'simplify document preparation'. The document will be in pdf form and digital signatures will be used, not to sign an individual document but to 'sign the envelop' used to send the document, and an Extended Markup Language (XML) file will be available in an attachment to be used by the courts. In addition, more attention is being paid to the involvement of software houses in the subsequent steps in order to allow them to develop the applications for lawyers. So, there is more attention both to the functional simplification of the cumbersome project and to the involvement of the lawyers, but the legal, technical and organisational complexity will need a tremendous effort to try to heave the project out from the quicksand.

What did work and what did not work, in the assemblage of e-services in Finland and in Italy

The two stories that have been told depict two very divergent ways for proceeding in the development and implementation of ICT application in the justice field. On the one hand, there is the case of Finland, where, in sum, procedural law is seen and has been used as an enabler of technology. This is quite the opposite of the case of Italy, where technology is seen as an enabler of the law. The different governance settings, strategies and perspectives of the ICT decision makers have certainly contributed to the very different outcome in the development of e-services.

In Finland the success story of the CMS and EDI is an illustration of how procedural reform can be designed to support the benefits that technology can bring to the judicial process. Procedural reform and the Act on electronic data exchange in the public administration were drafted with the technological challenge in mind. Applications were built within a regulation framework that enabled the technology to improve the work carried out by all the players in the judicial field and thus to improve the functioning of the administration of justice as a whole. The law has been instrumental, in some parts, in allowing the ICT tools to match the procedural complexity. The *pragmatic and instrumental* approach used in Finland seems more effective for coping with one of the biggest challenges for successful ICT implementation, which is mobilising the organisation for the changes that this implementation will require. The governance structure and strategy, which was functional and included all the actors in the justice field from the start, has also helped the effective and quite rapid development of the applications. Good results have been obtained by starting from simple projects that can add some value to the judicial work immediately, and then building on that success.

As has been described in Finland, the integrated civil and criminal e-filing and CMS based on a proprietary internal network has been running since 1993, without using a Public Key Infrastructure (PKI) yet, and they are now upgrading their systems to a web-based one. As mentioned, the lawyers' association manages a secure nationwide e-mail service (through a Secure Sockets Layer, SSL3) to all of its 2,000 members. Quoting the Chief Information Officer of the Finnish Ministry of Justice: 'The idea is, that if the system is secure in banking, it is sufficient to guarantee security in judicial correspondence.'[26]

Finland is a prime example of how information and communication technology can have a positive effect in improving services in the administration of justice and facilitating access to justice, without a complicated PKI infrastructure. They are also developing their comprehensive e-services for all cases and procedures (e.g., legal aid applications) without using a PKI infrastructure, which makes e-services both more costly and more complex to manage.

There are quite a few key points in the successful Finnish case. One of them is certainly that the introduction of the ICT applications, both civil and criminal, has taken place hand in hand with major procedural reforms. It is worth noting that the procedural reforms were directed towards simplifying the proceedings in order to make the exchange of documents through ICT applications easier. It is safe to say that a *functional simplification* of the transactions was introduced to better fit with the limits of the technology. For example, it is not necessary for the plaintiff to present the court with an invoice on which money is owed or other documents as long as they are specified in the application.

In Finland, the *Sakari* CMS was designed and developed for the whole criminal workflow and it was introduced along with a major change in criminal procedure, which made the electronic flow of information among the different criminal agencies easier (Kujanen, 2007, p. 25).

It also has to be emphasised how their successful applications have benefited from the involvement of the users, from training, and strong commitment and leadership on the part of the executive officers.

In particular, training was fundamental since in *Sakari* it is possible to write a decision or to send a summons, using documents already available in a data base. The editing of these documents is supported by *Sakari* and the prosecutors and the judge have to work with it. A lot of training was involved in introducing the new way of working, since some judges and prosecutors had been used to dictating their decisions to administrative staff.

Other key points to be singled out are the cooperation between the Ministry of Justice and the Ministry of the Interior, which is responsible for police forces, as well as the co-operation of debt-collection agencies first and then of the lawyers' association, an aspect that has been noticeably absent in the Italian case, where it has not been considered that, without the involvement of lawyers, e-services cannot take off.

It is also important to emphasise that a key point reported in the Finnish case study was the difficult but fundamental training and persuasive pressure was used to motivate judges and prosecutors to use the ICT applications themselves. If this had not happened, the applications instead of being perceived as a success would have probably been a failure.

In Italy, the two most important applications developed so far, the CMS in the criminal area and the *Civil TOL,* have been developed in accordance with the existing procedural law, which has not been modified to accommodate what technology can realistically do.

The case of the *Civil TOL* is a clear example of how ICT complexity, along with rigid procedures and a formalistic legal approach can undermine the design and the development of a successful application. Technology has been, and probably still is, viewed by the designers and policy makers of the ICT Department of the Ministry of Justice as a tool for enforcing the procedural and authority rules inscribed in the *law in book* (i.e., the code of procedure), without considering that if justice is delivered with inordinate delays in Italy, a significant reason for this is actually due to its very complex and muddled procedures. In addition, they saw that through the technology they would be able to standardise the different procedural practices that take place in the day-to-day-operation in courts (*law in action,* Pound, 1910), without considering the importance of the context-specificity of the technology, particularly in the implementation phase. In so doing, the application did not fit in with the different practices, thus creating even more rigidity and negative reactions on the part of the users.

When it was clear that it was almost impossible to replicate the very complex civil procedure in an ICT tool, there was a flurry of regulations in order to try to adapt the applications that had been developed to the procedural law. This contributed to the creation of even more complexity and difficulties in the implementation process.

While in Italy there has been an attempt to regulate all the possible nuances of electronic court transactions in detail with the introduction of yet more regulation, in Finland procedural law has been amended to facilitate the use of the technology and increase the number of electronic transactions (Fabri and Contini, 2003).

To regulate in advance all the possible situations created by the use of an ICT application is a considerable constraint on the process of innovation. This is what is happening in Italy, where a *re-engineering and regulative* approach has been adopted. Much frustration is being experienced and resources are being wasted because *re-engineering* the entire work process is very attractive on paper but extremely difficult in practice. Usually, these projects of gigantic proportions – the Italian *Civil TOL* is a prime example – with goals that are, for the time being at least, too ambitious, have to deal with complexities that are too great and this leads to failure, draining of a lot of resources and with disappointing results when the application is put into practice.

Finland has obtained some good results with ICT so far, focussing on the cost-efficient delivery of e-services to their customers, seeking to make progress in practical terms so as to establish credibility and avoiding pipe dreams. Acting in haste and aiming for rapid change by means of technology is a big mistake. A *pragmatic and incremental* approach has also been taken towards regulation, which, generally speaking, has followed ICT applications, once tested, and not *vice versa*.

These two cases show how technology can present a great opportunity of support to the judicial process and a stimulus for revising old and dysfunctional practices but it is not a *plug and play* tool. It needs to be carefully cultivated,[27] nurtured, and the institutional governance setting within which it has to be assembled needs to be taken into consideration (Harrington, 1991), if it is to produce positive organisational results. The greatest obstacle to progress is only in part the maturity of technology; to a greater degree it is the capacity of institutions and organisations to make the changes in actual working practices and attitudes (Weick, 1990; Ciborra and Lanzara, 1994; Orlikowski, Walsham, Jones and DeGross, 1996; Ciborra, 2002; Avgerou, Ciborra and Land, 2004) which are necessary in order to reap the potential benefits that the technology can bring.

Notes

1. The importance of using ICT tools is noted in various documents of European institutions. Recently, see the draft conclusions of the Council of the European Union on E-justice, 5 June 2007; future developments of E-justice discussed during the informal meeting of Justice and Home Affairs Ministers held in Lisbon, 1–2 October 2007; Opinion nr. 1 (2007)

of the Consultative Council of European Prosecutors of the Council of Europe on 'Ways of improving international co-operation in the criminal justice field', available at: www.coe.int/t/dg1/legalcooperation/ccpej; visited 5 March 2008.

2. The term *governance* is used in many ways and with different meanings in the literature, see Kooiman, J. (1999), Rhodes, R.A.W. (1997). I use it as a term to briefly describe the main institutions, players, structures of authority, and rules that govern ICT in the justice domain.

3. In particular, the *European Research Seminar on Court Technology* funded by a grant from the Grotius Programme of the European Commission was organised in 2000. Some of the findings of this research were published in Fabri, M. and F. Contini (eds) (2001). The research project *Judicial Electronic Data Interchange* was carried out in 2002, and the findings were published in: Fabri M. and F. Contini (eds) (2003). Research on ICT for the Public Prosecutor's Office (2005–2007), which had financial support from the AGIS Programme of the European Commission, Directorate General Justice and Home Affairs, whose findings were published in: Fabri, M. (ed.) (2007). For more details about these researches please visit: www.irsig.cnr.it/JAM. Visited 31 March 2008.

4. Special thanks go to Kari Kujanen, Chief Information Officer of the Finnish Ministry of Justice, for his help and patience in answering my questions.

5. This section on Finland is mainly based on interviews and the fundamental contribution of Laukkanen (2000); Kujanen and Sarvillina (2001); Kujanen and Marttila (2003, 2007).

6. The same *solution* has also been used in the case of 'Money claim online' in England and Wales (Timms, Plotnikoff and Woolfson, 2003, p. 176); see also Chapter 7 in this volume.

7. There are about 2,000 lawyers, 900 judges and 350 public prosecutors in Finland for a population of just over five million people.

8. A case tracking system is a simple automated docket, which registers the basic data and steps of a case in an electronic data base. It has developed into a CMS, which can be defined as an application that manages the case workflow and related documents. The most evolved electronic CMSs provide e-filing and electronic transaction between organisations and parties.

9. Penalty orders are defined as summary procedures, meaning a special procedure for petty crimes where only fines are imposed by the prosecutor. These fines, as well as those imposed directly by the police, can be opposed and then brought to court.

10. 'Functional simplification coincides with the identification of an operational domain [...] Functional simplification refers to the reduction of an initial complexity of a particular domain accomplished by the reduction of the number of variables and interactive sequences involved', see Kallinikos (2006, p. 33; 2005).

11. The Authority for Information Technology in the Public Administration (AIPA) was created by Law nr. 39 of 1993.

12. Presidential decree nr. 513, November 1997: 'Regulations establishing criteria and means for implementing section 15 (2) of Law 59, March 1997, concerning the creation, storage and transmission of documents by means of computer-based or telematic systems'.

13. The Department now has more than five hundred people and it has 13 regional offices Coordinamento Interdistrettuale Sistemi Informativi Automatizzati (CISIA) spread throughout the country.

14. In the Italian justice systems, the word 'magistrate' is used for both judges and public prosecutors, who are both considered part of the Italian judiciary. Their status (recruitment, promotion, transfer, disciplinary decisions) is managed by the Judicial Council (*Consiglio Superiore della Magistratura*).

15. The opinions are generally mandatory for contracts over €160,000, even though it really depends on the kind of contract. The opinion can be: positive, positive under certain conditions, or negative.

16. In this regard, it is worth mentioning that all the public administration sectors are strongly encouraged to use a special government agency for e-procurement (CONSIP) (Presidential decree nr. 101, 4 April 2002). See: www.consip.it and www.acquistinretepa.it. Visited 20 March 2008.

17. It is worth noting that, even though numbers are quite difficult to interpret, there are more than 160,000 lawyers in Italy, of whom about 100,000 are thought to be actually practising law in the courts. The lawyers' offices, generally speaking, are still rather small organisations, and their organisational structure cannot really be compared to that of large law firms. In addition, lawyers are organised in fragmented local associations represented *pro quota* in a nationwide association (*Consiglio nazionale forense*). This is another aspect of the institutional complexity of the Italian justice system, since there is not really one single, strong institutional body to represent lawyers. There are about 6,500 judges in Italy and about 2,700 public prosecutors, for a population of about 56 million people.

18. Digital signature means the result of a computer-based process (validation) implementing an asymmetric cryptographic system consisting

of a public and a private key, whereby the signer asserts, by means of the private key, and the recipient verifies, by means of the public key, the origin and integrity of a single electronic document or a set of such a documents. Presidential decree nr. 513, 10 November 1997, 1/b

19. For more information see: Carnevali, Contini and Fabri (2006); Velicogna and Ng (2006).

20. A more appropriate translation would be *civil proceedings online*, since rather than using electronic means for the trial itself, the goals are the exchange of documents and communications in civil proceedings by electronic means.

21. SIDNA stands for '*Sistema Informativo Direzione Nazionale Antimafia*', 'Information System for the National Antimafia Bureau'. SIDDA stands for '*Sistema Informativo Direzione Distrettuale Antimafia*', 'Information System for District Antimafia Bureaux'.

22. The need to keep track of defendants who are formally indicted was introduced by the 1989 code of criminal procedure. Making this information available to all the courts and prosecutors' offices in the country is still a major problem.

23. These are the official figures released by the Ministry of Justice. For the *Civil TOL* the Ministry spent about €5 million in 2003, about €4 million in 2004, and about €5 million in 2006 (about 84 per cent of the investment in ICT projects in the civil area).

24. For more details about the *Civil TOL* see Jacchia (2000); Zan (2004); Brescia and Liccardo (2005); Intravaia (2006); Taddei Elmi (2007).

25. In 2007 about 11 per cent out of about 40,000 injunctive orders were filed electronically, retrieved 20 March 2008 from www. processocieletelematico.eu/2008/01/relazione-sullincontro-di-milano.html.

26. Interviews with Kari Kujanen, Chief Information Officer, Finnish Ministry of Justice, March 2008.

27. In brief, the idea is that ICT projects and running applications have to be cultivated like plants to provide them with opportunities for growth and to produce good results. See Dahlbom and Mathiassen (1993); Ciborra (2002); De Marco and Sorrentino (2007).

References

Avgerou, C., Ciborra, C. and F. Land (2004) (eds), *The Social Study of Information and Communication Technology*. Oxford: Oxford University Press.

Barely, S. (1986), 'Technology as an Occasion for Structuring: Evidence from Observations of CT Scanners and the Social Order of Radiology Department'. *Administrative Science Quarterly*, 31, 78–91.

Brescia, S. and P. Liccardo (2005), 'Processo Telematico'. *Enciclopedia giuridica*, Volume XXIV Roma, Istituto Poligrafico.

Carnevali, D., Contini, F. and M. Fabri (2006) (eds), *Tecnologie per la giustizia*. Milano: Giuffrè.

Carnevali, D., Contini, F., Fabri, M. and M. Velicogna (2007), 'Technologies for the Prosecution Offices in Italy: the Tension between Legacy and Creativity'. In Fabri, M. (ed.), *Information and Communication Technology for the Public Prosecutor's Office*. Bologna: Clueb (229–281).

Ciborra, C. (2002), *The Labyrinths of Information*. Oxford: Oxford University Press.

Ciborra, C. and G.F. Lanzara (1994), 'Formative Contexts and Information Technology. Understanding the Dynamics of Innovation in Organizations'. *Accounting, Management and Information Technology*, 4 (2), 61–86.

Contini, F. (2000), 'Reinventing the Docket, Discovering the Database'. In Fabri, M. and P. Langbroek (eds), *The Challenge of Change of Judicial Systems. Developing a Public Administration Perspective*. Amsterdam: IOS Press (253–267).

Dahlbom, B. and L. Mathiassen (1993), *Computers in Context: the Philosophy and Practice of System Design*. Oxford: Blackwell.

De Marco, M. and M. Sorrentino (2007), 'Sowing the Seeds of IS Cultivation in Public Service Organisations'. *Journal of Information Technology*, 22, 184–194.

Di Federico, G. (1998), 'Prosecutorial Independence and the Democratic Requirement of Accountability in Italy. Analysis of a Deviant Case in Comparative Perspective'. *British Journal of Criminology*, 38 (3), 371–387.

Di Federico, G. (2002*)*, 'L'indipendenza della magistratura in Italia. Una valutazione critica in chiave comparata'. *Rivista Trimestrale di Diritto e Procedura Civile*, anno LVI, n. 1, 99–128.

Fabri, M. (2007) (ed.), *Information and Communication Technology for the Public Prosecutor's Office*. Bologna: Clueb.

Fabri, M. and F. Contini (2001) (eds), *Justice and Technology in Europe: How ICT is Changing the Judicial Business*. The Hague: Kluwer Law International.

Fabri, M. and F. Contini (2003) (eds), *Judicial Electronic Data Interchange in Europe: Applications, Policies and Trends*. Bologna: Lo Scarabeo.

Fabri, M., Contini F. and A. Negrini (1999), *Progettazione organizzativa e information technology nell'amministrazione giudiziaria italiana.* Bologna: Lo Scarabeo.

Fabri, M. and P. Langbroek (2000) (ed.), *The Challenge of Change for European Judicial Systems, Developing a Public Administration Perspective.* Amsterdam: IOS Press.

Fabri, M. and R. Woolfson (2001), 'ICT in European Justice Systems'. *7th Court Technology Conference*, Baltimore, MD: National Center for State Courts.

Fountain, J. (2001), *Building the Virtual State: Information Technology and Institutional Change.* Washington, DC: Brookings Institution Press.

Garvin, D. (1993), 'Building a Learning Organization'. *Harvard Business Review*, July–August, 78–91.

Guarnieri, C. and F. Zannotti (2006) (ed.), *'Giusto processo?'* Padova: Cedam.

Harrington, J. (1991), *Organizational Structure and Information Technology.* London: Prentice Hall.

Intravaia, D. (2006), 'Processo civile telematico: disciplina normativa e infrastruttura tecnologica'. In Jori, M. (ed.), *Elementi di informatica giuridica*, Torino: Giappichelli (213–272).

Jacchia, M. (2000) (ed.), *Il processo telematico. Nuovi ruoli e nuove tecnologie per un moderno processo civile.* Bologna: Il Mulino.

Kallinikos, J. (2005), The Order of Technology: Complexity and Control in a Connected World. *Information and Organization*, 15 (3), 185–202.

Kallinikos, J. (2006), *The Consequences of Information. Institutional Implications of Technological Change.* Cheltenham, UK: Edward Elgar.

Kooiman, J. (1999), 'Social-Political Governance: Overview, Reflections, and Design'. *Public Management*, 1 (1), 67–92.

Kujanen, K. and R. Marttila (2003), 'Judicial Electronic Data Interchange in Finland'. In Fabri, M. and F. Contini (ed.), *Judicial Electronic Data Interchange in Europe: Applcations, Policies and Trend*s. Bologna: Lo Scarabeo (203–209).

Kujanen, K. and R. Marttila (2007), 'The Positive Interplay between Information and Communication Technologies and the Finnish Public Prosecutor's Office'. In Fabri, M. (ed.), *Information and Communication Technology for the Public Prosecutor's Office.* Bologna: Clueb (75–101).

Kujanen, K. and S. Sarvillinna (2001), 'Approaching Integration: ICT in the Finnish Judicial System'. In Fabri, M. and F. Contini (eds), *Justice and Technology in Europe: How ICT is Changing the Judicial Business.* The Hague: Kluwer Law International (29–43).

Laukkanen, S. (2000), 'The Challenge of Information Society: Application of Advanced Technologies in Civil Litigation and other Procedures,

National Report of Finland'. Retrieved from ruessmann.jura.uni-sb.de/ grotius/Reports/Finnland.htm#<4T. Visited 25 November 2007.

Ministero della Giustizia (2007), 'Piano Triennale per l'Informatica 2007–2009 della Giustizia'. Retrieved, from www.giustizia.it/ministero/ struttura/pt2007–2009.htm#d311. Visited 20 March 2008.

Orlikowski, W., Walsham, G., Jones, M.R. and J.I. DeGross (1996) (eds), *Information Technology and Changes in Organisational Work*. London: Chapman & Hall.

Oskamp, A., Lodder A. and M. Apistola (2004) (eds), *IT Support of the Judiciary*. The Hague, NL: Asser Press.

Pound, R. (1910), 'Law in Books and Law in Action'. *American Law Review*, 44 (12).

Rhodes, R.A.W. (1997), *Understanding Governance*. Buckingham, UK: Open University Press.

Taddei Elmi, G. (2007) (ed.), 'Il Processo telematico'. Special issue, *Informatica e Diritto*, XVI (1–2), Napoli: ESI.

Timms, P., Plotnikoff, J. and R. Woolfson (2003), 'Judicial Electronic Data Interchange in England and Wales'. In Fabri, M. and F. Contini (eds), *Judicial Electronic Data Interchange in Europe: Applications, Policies and Trends*. Bologna: Scarabeo (171–184).

Velicogna, M. and G.Y. Ng (2006), 'Legitimacy and Internet in the Judiciary: A Lesson From the Italian Courts' Websites Experience'. *International Journal of Law and Information Technology*, 14, 370–389. Retrived from ijlit.oxfordjournals.org/cgi/raprint/14/3/370.pdf. Visited 30 May 2007.

Weick, K. (1990), 'Technology as Equivoque: Sensemaking in New Technologies'. In Goodman, P., Sproull, L. and Associates (eds), *Technology and Organizations*, San Francisco, CA: Jossey Bass (1–43).

Zan, S. (ed.) (2004), *Tecnologia, organizzazione e giustizia. L'evoluzione del processo civile telematico fascicoli e tribunali: il processo civile in una prospettiva organizzativa*. Bologna: Il Mulino.

Zuboff, S. (1988), *In the Age of the Smart Machine*. New York: Basic Books.

CHAPTER 6

Aligning ICT and legal frameworks in Austria's e-bureaucracy: from mainframe to the Internet

Stefan Koch and Edward Bernroider

Introduction

The use of ICT in the Austrian judicial system can be described as widespread. Currently, a plethora of different benchmarking studies have been published ranking different countries according to their e-government readiness or maturity, but they are inconclusive, so no results are given here. For discussion of these studies, see for example Lee, Tan and Trimi (2005) or Ostermann and Staudinger (2005). An overview of the technologies in use, which also covers the general organisation of the judicial system in Austria, can be found in Bauer (2001).

In order to analyse the use and continual evolution of ICT and draw lessons from it for an international readership, two projects are analysed in this paper. These are firstly the Legal Information System (LIS), an electronic database on Austrian law available to the public, along with the eLaw application, which serves as a workflow and document management system used within the administration in the process of producing new laws or regulations, and the electronic communication system. Electronic government information repositories are growing in number, use, and diversity and can be seen as one manifestation of the emergence of e-government (Dawes, Pardo and Cresswell, 2004).

The second case, ELC (Electronic Legal Communication, known in Austria as ERV *Elektronischer Rechtsverkehr*) constitutes a means of transmitting petitions (e-filing) to the courts, and is also used for receiving decisions or other documents from them. Using the categorisation of e-government practices as proposed by Lee, Tan and Trimi (2005), the LIS constitutes a government-to-citizens (G2C) application, with the underlying eLaw system an example of a government-to-government (G2G) system. The ELC system consists of a mix of G2C and a mostly government-to-businesses (G2B) application, while also aiming for internal government efficiency and effectiveness (IEE).

The main objective of this research paper is to analyse these two major ICT developments in justice by focusing on the historical development process of each application, highlighting and discussing major events and decisions together with the reasoning behind them. In addition, the objectives include an assessment of application usage in legal practice from multiple viewpoints including project sponsors, developers, administrators, and users/operators. Among the users we have included, in particular, Austrian citizens. This viewpoint is essential in order to be able to determine the success or failure of an application, and also any reasons for this.

Methodology

Data collection

We adopt a case study methodology (Yin, 1981; Benbasat, Goldstein and Mead, 1987; Stuart, McCutcheon, Handfield, McLachlin and Samson, 2002), and use two similar cases. Basic to this research approach is the assumption that an applicable theory does not exist or cannot be applied, for example, cause and effect relations such as the time dependent relationship between technology development, introduction, and on-going diffusion. Furthermore, the case-based approach should allow for the development of an understanding of the subject in hand, and the development of theories based on this. Therefore, a grounded theory approach (Glaser and Strauss, 1967; Strauss and Corbin, 1990) is followed in this research.

This research approach was based on a process-oriented case-based research methodology (Stuart, McCutcheon, Handfield, McLachlin and Samson, 2002) comprising the following steps (the dissemination step is not relevant in this context and was therefore excluded):

1. Literature review and formulation of research questions,
2. Instrument development,
3. Data gathering,
4. Data analysis.

The first step involved the search for relevant literature covering both of the two major ICT developments in justice, the Legal Information System and the Electronic Communication System in Justice-related Communication. This led to the development of the body of knowledge and understanding needed to specify and revise the research questions in the context of the research areas set out in the previous section.

The second step was the development of the research instrument and the selection of field sites. This included the development of the study protocol and questionnaire. The study design had a clear focus on the continual evolution and development of ICT and the alignment with its environment, yet provided flexibility, and complied with validity requirements. The site selection considered specific entities in order to comply with the given investigation objectives, that is, they include both application owners and users.

To collect data on developers' and maintainers' viewpoints the following interviews were conducted: for the LIS, Helmut Weichsel from the Austrian Federal Chancellery (e-Government – Program- and Project-management) was interviewed. As regards ELC, Thomas Gottwald from the Ministry of Justice (Department for Legal Informatics – *Rechtsinformatikabteilung*) provided the necessary information.

To collect data on user perspectives six interviews (three for each case study) were carried out. Two different functions for the interview partners were defined since the perceptions of the technologies will be different depending on the role of interviewee. Two interviewees were professional lawyers, while the third interviewee was an Austrian federal judge. All interviews were conducted in February 2006.

The third step involved analysis of different data sources such as the written and taped records of the interviews and documents supplied by the target organisations.

The challenge of the fourth step was to arrive at a conclusion from the data gathered. It comprised the search for and identification of patterns, conceptual observations, critical exogenous factors, and so on. For example, Brüggemeier, Dovifat and Kubisch (2005) proposed a micro-political arena-based approach for analysing the innovation process in electronic government applications. They differentiate four separate areas, those of inception, conception, implementation and routinisation, and several external factors influencing the project. In particular, within each area, the actors, their constellations and power structures were analysed. The electronic government case studies analysed in this paper are well matured strategies that were analysed from the government and user perspective. For the latter, the popular DeLone and McLean (D&M) IS success model (DeLone and McLean, 1992) can be used. It constitutes a comprehensive multi-dimensional approach to assessing the success of Information Systems (IS). Given its focus on IS together with its popularity, it was adopted for assessing the electronic government cases reviewed in this article. More information on the assessment model is given in the next section.

Applied evaluation model

For assessment from the user perspective, a model was needed that could account for the many facets and perspectives of Software and Information System (IS) based technologies. For this purpose a model was needed that could provide a holistic picture of adoption success achieved, rather than a model that concentrated on the rationale behind technology adoption. Information systems success is a central topic in IS literature. A widely adopted model in IS success research has concentrated on the multi-dimensional and interdependent nature of IS success, namely the DeLone and McLean (D&M) IS success model (DeLone and McLean, 1992), which the authors revised ten years later (DeLone and McLean, 2003). The authors explicitly acknowledge the complexity that surrounds the identification and definition of the concept of IS success. They review the large number of studies on IS success and present a comprehensive and integrated model. The purpose of the original model was to synthesise previous research involving individual measures into a coherent concept. The postulated model was grounded on the communication research of Shannon and Weaver (1949), the information influence theory of Mason (1978), and empirical IS-related research studies. They identified six main dimensions for categorising various measures of IS success and postulated that they were interrelated rather than independent: (1) 'system quality' (2) 'information quality' (3) 'use' (4) 'user satisfaction' (5) 'individual impact' and (6) 'organisational impact'. Based on a large number of research contributions which have appeared since the original model was published (with references in nearly 300 articles in refereed journals), the authors revised their concept. Quality was postulated as three-dimensional construct ('information, systems, and service quality'), each of which was to be measured and controlled separately. These quality dimensions will singularly or jointly affect subsequent 'use/intention to use' and 'user satisfaction'. Additionally, the amount of use can affect the degree of user satisfaction as well as the reverse being true. Use and user satisfaction are direct antecedents of individual impact; and the impact on individual performance will eventually have some organisational

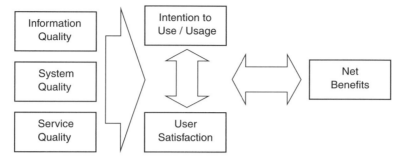

Figure 6.1   The (updated) DeLone-McLean (D&M) model

impact. As a result certain (positive or negative) 'net benefits' will be seen (DeLone and McLean, 2003) (see Figure 6.1).

For this study of IS implementation and success, an assessment of adoption and usage as well as strengths and weaknesses was needed. It was necessary both to evaluate the quality of the applications, and adoption together with resulting benefits. The best system, if not utilised, will not yield any benefits for the organisations implementing it. Important social actors in this stage comprise end-users, technical administrators, and business and IT management personnel. All of these are captured by the dimensions considered in the DeLone and McLean (updated) success model, although the authors specifically focused on decision makers as users of IS systems. The model's multi-dimensional approach, which fits perspectives together with popularity, justifies its usage for this research project. Consequently, it should be possible to compare or validate findings in related research.

The notions of information infrastructure and of installed base, in particular, are useful for taking a deeper look at ICT development processes. Both can be seen as facilitating or constraining factors, directly or indirectly influencing various dimensions of the model, in particular 'use/intention to use' and 'user satisfaction'. The concept of installed base covers the existing technical (for example hardware, software, and data) and organisational (for example human resources and skills, management practices, and legal arrangements) set-ups. In particular, facilitating conditions and top management support were identified as critical to Information Systems success based on measurements with constructs from the DeLone-McLean model (Sabherwal, Jeyaraj and Chowa, 2006). Infrastructure openness implies that ICT needs to accommodate a growing number of heterogeneous actors and technical artefacts. Consequently, in the case analysis these facilitating or constraining factors will also be considered in conjunction with the measurements provided through the DeLone-McLean model.

Legal Information System (LIS)

Description

The Legal Information System (LIS) of the Federal Government, or *Rechtsinformationssystem des Bundes* (RIS), is an electronic database of Austrian law. It is coordinated and operated by the Austrian Federal Chancellery. It is a tool for carrying out searches of case law and documentation of court practices, and also for locating sources of the law and the literature.

The main sources making up the contents of the LIS are:

- The Federal Law Gazette: Since 2004 the legally binding Austrian Federal Law Gazette has only been published in the Austrian Legal Information System (in a variety of formats), with a database providing access to older issues in legally non-binding form from 1983 to 2003 in HTML-format and from 1945 to 2003 in PDF-format.
- Draft bills, Government bills: These databases (2002–03 and from 19 December 2003) contain draft bills originating from Austrian ministries, and government bills.
- Federal law: This database covers Austrian federal law (some 99 per cent). Amendments are incorporated as soon as they are promulgated so that the database always contains the applicable version of a document (one document equals one section or one article or one annex). In addition to the applicable version, many norms also offer the opportunity to access previous versions, making it possible for the user to reconstruct the development of the regulation.
- State (regional) law: This database contains the law of the nine different Austrian States (not all States include their previous versions as well).
- The State Law Gazette: This database contains all issues of the State Law Gazette in their original versions from seven out of the nine Austrian Provinces (with start dates ranging from 1995 to 2001).
- Municipal law: This database contains the law of some Austrian municipalities in five different states.
- European Community Law: European community law includes data from The Office for Official Publications of the European Communities. This CELEX database contains treaties, external relations, secondary legislation, complementary legislation, preparatory works, case law, national measures, Parliamentary questions, Official Journal C-series and EFTA documents.

- Case-law documentation: The databases contain both the legal maxims and the full text of the rulings of various courts. These include the Constitutional Court (nearly all rulings since 1980), the Administrative Court (nearly all decisions since 1990 and significant rulings from previous years), the Supreme Court, Independent Administrative Tribunals (selected rulings since 1991), the Independent Federal Asylum Board (selected rulings since 1998), the Environmental Senate, Procurement Review Authorities (including the Federal Public Procurement Arbitration Body since 1997 and the Procurement Review Authorities of Salzburg and Vienna since 2004), the Data Protection Commission, the Federal Communications Board, the Appeals Tribunal and the Supreme Disciplinary Commission (both covering case-law on disciplinary matters and matters pertaining to employee transfers in the Federal Government since 1999) and the Supervisory Tribunal for Employees' Representation.
- The 'norm list' of the Administrative Court: This list of standardised, synonymous quotations of regulations is edited by the Administrative Court and is an index of admissible norm specifications in the form of abbreviations (by letter or short titles) for the case-law documentation of the Administrative Court.
- Decrees: Selected decrees and regulations enacted by the Austrian ministries. These generally specify aspects of federal law, or contain implementation procedures.
- Decrees of the Federal Ministry of Justice: Selected decrees and regulations from the Austrian Federal Ministry of Justice.
- Austrian laws in English: This database contains selected Austrian laws in English translation.

The system is freely available to the public using a web-interface and can be found at http://www.ris.bka.gv.at/ (visited 28 August 2008); any commercial use of the data requires the approval of the Federal Chancellery or the State government or court concerned.

The LIS makes use of full text retrieval software, thereby allowing the user to search for any term. As the documents stored are divided into categories (for example section, article, norm, legal principles) it is also possible to focus the search on a specific category, thus reducing the number of hits.

A relatively new system, eLaw (*eRecht*) is of interest in this context as well, as it serves as a source of information for the LIS. It serves as a workflow and document management system which is used within the administration in the process of producing new laws or orders. Not all employees have the necessary clearance to access this system through their respective intranets; communication channel security is handled through SSL-connections with username and passwords. Currently, ten different workflows are implemented, depending on which type of law or order is involved. For example, the process steps for the workflow pertaining to a new federal law are:

1. Creation of a new project by Ministry,
2. Expert and NGO survey (not mandatory),
3. Application to the Council of Ministries,
4. Formal application of the Government,
5. Process in Parliament (handled within a separate system),
6. Decision by Parliament,
7. Certification,
8. Publication in the Federal Law Gazette (that is LIS).

The process of creating and changing documents is aided by macro-supported templates. Automatic checks on whether the relevant templates and forms have been followed are also implemented. This ensures strict differentiation between meta-data and text, and allows for conversion in different formats such as PDF or XML, and electronic signatures.

The document management functionalities offered include check in/check out version control and change protocols. The workflow also supports e-mail sending of documents, digital signatures and user management.

History and development process

The development process of the LIS is a very long one, encompassing several versions, including two major ones, over the course of roughly 30 years. Not all data is therefore available on all the versions. In general, most of the development work was carried out in-house by the Federal Chancellery, sometimes with the aid of external software development companies. The Federal Computing Centre (*Bundesrechenzentrum* – BRZ) is an independent limited company owned by the Austrian Government represented by the Ministry of Finance and is responsible for many e-government initiatives in Austria. However, in terms of the LIS, the BRZ was not involved in the development cycles, mostly because of small initial project size and in order to reduce overheads.

The implementation of the very first version of the LIS began in 1972, as an IT trial project incorporating constitutional law. Project partners were the Austrian Federal Chancellery, which is still responsible for the LIS, and IBM. A major decision regarding the LIS occurred in 1983, when the ICT-department and the Constitutional Service, both within the Austrian Federal Chancellery, decided to develop an internal law information system. They therefore provided the initial impetus for the systems, and also acted as main sponsors later on. The Constitutional Service has remained project leader up to the present day. The main goals for these first implementations were increases in efficiency and time saving within the administration. Accordingly, the initial contents comprised laws governing public employees and the Constitution. In October 1986, the Government endorsed the project and formally decided on the implementation of a comprehensive LIS.

Until the next major step in its evolution, the LIS was a strictly internal application for the public administration, with the ministries joining in with the Federal Chancellery over time. Citizen access to the system was provided later on but only a very limited number of notaries or lawyers actually took advantage of the opportunity of accessing services, which were only available using mainframe connection. This changed in June 1997, when the Federal Chancellery decided to make substantial parts of the LIS available on the Internet to the public. While this step constituted a major change in user focus, a major technical revolution occurred at the same time: in a pilot study from Autumn 1996 onwards, and productive until Spring 1997, a new version based on Internet technology (Callable Personal Librarian – CPL – Fa. AOL/PLS, AIX, MS, Java Scripts; .net, XML and Style Sheets) was provided. Before that, and until the end of 1999 in parallel operation, a mainframe version had been operating. The main reasons for this step were both of a technological nature, foremost the Y2K problem, and also organisational, as the change in user group necessitated an update. The mainframe version was implemented on IBM/Hitachi with IMS, STAIRS and PL/1, without any potential for graphics and with a cumbersome user interface. Currently, two versions still exist, but without major differences in contents, and no difference in technology: an Internet version for the general public and an Intranet version for the public administration. The difference is in access to a single database (*Rechtsdatenbank* – RDB) with associated costs. Contents-wise, what is offered by the LIS has expanded during the whole time of operation up to the current situation, with an important change in 2004. From 2004 on, the legally binding Austrian Federal Law Gazette has only been published in the LIS. The main reason for opening up the systems to the general public was to offer comprehensive law information for free. This aim is also codified in several laws (see for example § 13 BGBlG 2004, IWG BGBl nr. I 135/2005 of 18 November 2005, and also the PSI-directive of the European Union – 2003/98/EG / CELEX-nr.: 32003L0098). In addition, services supplied by private companies to provide citizens with additional information in the form of commentaries or articles were envisaged. Currently, a new version is being planned. One aim is to switch to XML-technology. In addition, there will be a further increase in the contents offered.

Two major versions of the LIS can be differentiated: The mainframe version, which was in operation until 1999, and the Internet version, operational since 1997. The differences between these are twofold: in terms of user focus and technology. The main impetus for starting the development of the Internet version was the Y2K problem with the former version. At this point, it was decided that the switch to a new platform, especially in view of the associated costs, should benefit the population as a whole, and that the new possibilities afforded should be used to grant all citizens access to the LIS. It has to be said that this decision at the time constituted a bold move. The subsequent widespread Internet access within the population was far from certain at the time of this decision in 1996, but this assumption has been proven to be correct. Unfortunately, the costs of this new version could no longer be quantified with precision, but are probably of the order of approximately €100,000. Operational costs are not quantified either, but are estimated to be low. Within the Vienna office, and the backup computing centre in St. Johann, two members of staff are responsible for the LIS, but they have other duties as well, for example maintaining servers.

Users were not involved to any great extent during the development process. When the mainframe version was designed, some attempts were made to contact users in the public administration, that is different ministries, but their wishes were mostly incongruent. The user interface in particular was designed without any user consultation. On the other hand, all organisations providing input to the system were contacted in order to specify the necessary interfaces. For the second major version, the new prospective user group, that is citizens, were not involved in any way, neither in terms of needs analysis, nor user testing. As described below, this may be one reason why it is mainly staff from within the administration and people with law-related jobs who use the system.

Several times during the process of evolving the LIS, new regulations and/or laws were necessary, most notably to enable the legally binding publishing of new federal laws. The second major step was when eLaw was designed: the Council of Ministers decided to adopt the system in all ministries, making it a compulsory step in the process of introducing new laws. In both cases, the initiative came from the Federal Chancellery, with the

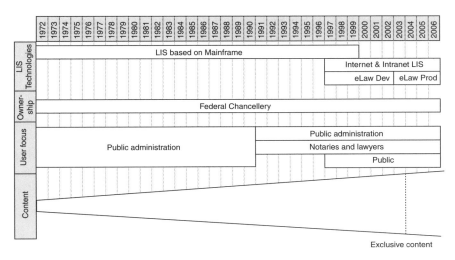

Figure 6.2   Overview of LIS development over time

Constitutional Service responsible for negotiations with the Government. The talks concerning the publication of new laws in the LIS had started with a former government in 1999, but could only be completed after a new government has settled in, and it came into effect in 2004 (Figure 6.2).

In contrast to the LIS, the history of the eLaw application started much later. It commenced with an initiative from the Government in Spring 1999, motivated by the search for possible cost reductions, and it was also initiated by the Constitutional Service. The main idea at that time was to establish a purely electronic production process for laws, regulations and other judicial material, from inception until publication on the Internet. The idea of open networks and the Internet vision was anticipated from the start, as recommended as the basis for a global information infrastructure at the time (Perritt, 1996). Two projects within the social security system, the documentation covering social security laws and the publishing of the official bulletin of the Austrian social security system (see also § 31 Abs 9 ASVG), served as reference projects. In 2001, a project team at the Austrian Federal Chancellery was set up with members from the Constitutional Service, the ICT department, the service for the Council of Ministers and the Parliament. The Government decided in June 2001 and March 2002 to go ahead with the electronic production process. Training programmes and tests were started in 2002, and in 2003 trials and parallel operations began. Since 2004, as mentioned above, the legally binding Austrian Federal Law Gazette has only been published in the LIS ('*Kundmachungsreformgesetz 2004*', Art 49 B-VG and BGBlG 2004). The new development provides sound management of flow and storage of government information, which has been criticised in other countries (Koga, 2003).

The main aim of the eLaw project was to ensure comprehensive electronic support for the production process, thus reducing the likelihood of error, enabling version control, ensuring conformity to standards, allowing for meta-data to be stored with objects, and providing for electronic signatures and easy publication on the Internet within the LIS system. In addition, cost reductions were envisaged in the areas of printing and paper, postal services and archives. Transparency and enhanced service to the citizen were also cited. Nevertheless, in the discussions with the Government regarding the necessary regulations, the promise of possible cost reductions in particular was deemed to be a very decisive factor.

Adoption and evaluation

The adoption of the LIS has grown considerably during its lifetime. Of course, opening access to all citizens has had a major impact on these figures, with an increase in contents and publicity over the years compounding this effect. Currently, all access is through the Internet version, so adoption rates are calculated based on web server log file analysis, with all the associated problems. In addition, the style of analysis and the criteria used have changed over the years. It is not possible to differentiate between user groups with these techniques, but analysis of access to different contents is feasible.

The current rate of access is about 4.5 to five million per month, with 4.6 million in January 2006. This has grown from a mean rate of 3.5 million accesses per month in 2003 (when a change in log file analysis occurred). The main area of interest is federal law. Regarding structure of the user group, this can only be inferred from the e-mail feedback, resulting in self-selection problems. Roughly half the usage comes from within the public administration, the other half from citizens. Within the citizen group, a majority was characterised, again based on e-mail correspondence, as being from different sectors of the legal profession, including lawyers, notaries, and the legal departments of large companies.

The results from the interviews showed that the LIS is used regularly and that users are satisfied with the system, giving it a good to average rating. During the interviews, a rival system, namely the Rechtsdatenbank (RDB), was mentioned: it can be used to support the same tasks as the LIS. In practice, user satisfaction with RDB is higher but usage rates are lower because of the costs involved in using RDB.

Based on the analysis above, the LIS can be deemed to have been a successful project. It has served well both as an internal tool for increasing the efficiency of the public administration, and also as an information channel for citizens. That the pure front-end provided by the LIS in the past has been extended in the context of the eLaw project, so that an integrated system now covers the whole production process of judicial materials, is also positive. This will lead to increased efficiency, cost reductions and above all to a reduction in error.

As a further positive factor, the development of the Internet was correctly predicted, although at the time of decision this was not clear. Following this prediction, the release of the LIS was based on Web technology, which at that moment was a relatively bold move but it paid off later.

On the downside, a lack of user consultation in the development process has been observed. In particular, for a system aimed at the information needs of a large and heterogeneous group of people, that is the whole population, the user interface needed to be designed to afford a number of different ways of accessing the data. For example, Marchionini, Haas, Zhang and Elsas (2005) describe problems in designing a user interface for citizens accessing government statistical data. In the LIS, the user interface does not offer much leeway in this respect. It could be assumed that the fact that the user group is mostly from the administration or citizens within legal professions stems at least partly from this failure to include different user groups in the development process. The provision of a more intuitive user interface and different ways of presenting the information might expand the user group at least to some degree.

As a general observation, the quantification of benefits from introducing the system, which would be most apparent within the public administration, is missing. This information would be necessary to guide further development efforts, and to evaluate the effectiveness of the system and its approach. The benefits of e-government systems in particular have only scarcely been quantified. An overview of exemplary projects together with a process-oriented evaluation method can be found in Wolf and Krcmar (2005).

The results from the user perspectives were very consistent. In general, information quality is very good, but there are deficiencies in particular in the areas of coverage and partially in the area of completeness. The contents provided by the LIS do not cover all the needs of two of the three users who were interviewed. This in particular concerns the need to consult older juridical cases which are not included in the LIS (completeness) and certain information required which does not fall within the juridical context provided (coverage). Again, users rely heavily on the above-mentioned rival system RDB if they fail to receive the necessary legal advice from the LIS. On the other hand, one interviewee stated that the system is perfect given its intentions. It provides the expected juridical contents. This hints at a possible gap between the intentions of the system and the actual needs of some users. Although no liability is accepted for the correctness and completeness of the LIS by the Austrian Federal Chancellery, users do not question consistency, reliability, updating, and accuracy of information retrieval results.

Good system quality was also reported by the users. Usability, availability and response times constitute key strengths, while functionality, query potential and adaptability can be seen as (relative) weaknesses. The LIS presents itself as a non-adaptable system, and therefore received the lowest rating in this category. However, adaptability was also regarded as not being important. One interviewee in particular stated that changes in the output format of the information presented are neither needed nor desired. All juridical information provided should follow the same style guide, different output formats might even be harmful to communication or coordination between different users of the system. Although the LIS makes use of full text retrieval software, giving the opportunity to search for any term, functionality and query potential were assessed as being average.

For the third category in the quality domain of the D&M model which has been applied, namely service quality, no information could be obtained. The system is used without service agreements with the provider. Hardware or software problems within local installations are serviced by in-house or contracted specialists and cannot be attributed to the LIS operation. Downtimes of the LIS service itself could not be assessed in all the interviews.

The evaluation of the net benefit shows that in general, the effects of the LIS on the individual as well as on the organisation itself are rated as being very positive. Time and cost savings are considerable. Apart from one interviewee, the effectiveness gains were also assessed as being very significant. The results in the other two dimensions assessed are consistent across all three entities.

Analysis

To follow up on the discussion above, several points from the LIS case can be generalised. It would seem interesting that both a technical and a user focus were adopted at the same time. Because the technology was outdated and especially given the Y2K problem, a new version became necessary, and it was used to open access to the system to the general public. The reasoning that in view of the costs incurred it should be beneficial to all citizens is an important argument, which is also echoed in the X and BSD open source software licence, where it was argued that as the software was funded by grants from the US Government, the citizens had already paid for the software with their taxes and thus were granted permission to make use of that software as they pleased (Perens, 1999). Forecasting Internet penetration in the whole population and following through with this decision was a bold move and proved successful. Naturally, this success cannot be generalised, but in e-government systems too, the technological base needs to be up-to-date, especially if a system is expected to grow and evolve over time, as the LIS has done. We see in this case that the technological possibilities have shaped the legal framework. The laws necessary for the system to take effect were drawn up and passed.

The development process was also particular in that the impetus came from within the administration, which seemingly knew best what efficiency potentials could be realised with such a system, and later on with the eLaw application covering the whole production process. The Government itself, and the necessary laws, followed afterwards. User involvement during development was low, but, in particular, if an information system for the general population is envisaged, involvement should in general be more extensive, and cover various aspects of user interface design, for example task analysis, user testing and so on. This emphasises that opening up a network or application is not only – or even mainly – a technological problem, but may come to have repercussions on the way of doing things, and the way of looking at things behind, and beyond, the application.

From the user perspective the LIS was assessed as a very important, regularly used legal advice system with significant impact on working behaviour as well as on individual and organisational work efficiency and effectiveness. Information and system quality are very good, with minor quality shortfalls grounded in the areas of information completeness and coverage, and also query potential. The rival legal advice system RDB was regarded as having the edge in all three aspects. However, since the LIS achieves its aims in terms of information coverage in the targeted juridical areas, it would be wrong to criticise coverage and completeness from the system design perspective. An important conclusion is the open design, free usage and good usability of the Internet-based information retrieval system on which the LIS is based.

Electronic Legal Communication (ELC)

Description

The ELC-system is a means of transmitting petitions to the courts, and also for receiving decisions or other documents from the courts. Currently, only petitions concerning the Land Registry are excluded, and those concerning the Companies Registry are limited to annual financial statements. The primary and most important applications are money claims and requests for enforcement in civil matters (e-filing). This form of communication with the courts is legally equivalent to conventional filing, and therefore is not to be confused with faxing or sending a simple e-mail. Descriptions of the system and its savings potential can also be found in Bauer (2001) and Gottwald and Viefhues (2004).

To use the system, both customised software and the necessary hardware, together with a connection and an Austrian bank account are needed. Each participant has a unique identification code, which is allocated by the Chamber of Notaries and Lawyers for this user group, and the Ministry of Justice for others. The interface specification for ELC is publicly available and can be downloaded from http://erv.telekom.at/. The software for using the system can be developed by the user, and the functionality is included in most standard software systems for law firms, for example ADVOKAT (Greiter & Greiter), jurXpert (ACP IT Solutions GmbH), MedixERV (Medix Informatik GesmbH), PARAGRAPH (Progressive Software Design), POWER ANWALT (Uhrwerk), R/WIN (Stampfl & Co KEG), WinCaus (EDV2000) or WinMEX (EDV-Technik Went).

Using the specified interface, petitions are transmitted to the sole transmission agency (clearing house) available, Telekom Austria AG, which forwards these once a day at midnight to the Federal Computing Centre (*Bundesrechenzentrum* – BRZ). The BRZ then forwards the files to the courts, where they are catalogued, printed and given to the judges. An acknowledgment is sent to the petitioner with data including case number, via the same channels. Data are transmitted asynchronously at a speed of 2,400–14,400 bit/s in ASCII/German code.

History and development process

ELC was introduced in 1990, based on the initiation of a claims process and ICT-based entry into the register (e-filing). First, lawyers, notaries, the Federal Law Office of the Republic of Austria and other institutions were offered the possibility of electronically filing legal actions which result in an order of payment which takes effect on condition that no objections are made. The project originated from within the Ministry of Justice, at the highest level of the administration. The software development itself was carried out by the Federal Computing Centre (Bundesrechenzentrum – BRZ), with the participation of Radio Austria acting as clearing house. Interestingly, the costs were mostly borne by Radio Austria (now Telekom Austria AG, at that point state-owned), which refinanced these through the volume of transactions later on. It should be noted that the Chamber of Lawyers was included in the project right from the beginning. The system is operated by the Federal Computing Centre. The Ministry of Justice is not involved in any technical aspects.

For the ELC-system to fulfil its function, several changes in laws and regulations were necessary. These were drawn up by the Ministry of Justice in all cases and were signed by the Minister. In the case of laws, the Minister forwarded them to Parliament. It was noted in an interview with the Ministry of Justice, that '*we drew them up as we needed them*'. The most important change concerned the Court Organisation Statute passed in 1990 (§ 89a Abs 1&2, § 89b-e), which contained the main regulations regarding among things e-filing, contents, relevant dates and warranty. Various orders or ministerial decrees were also issued by the Ministry of Justice, including most importantly a decree on ELC in 1995, which contained detailed descriptions of e-filing, regulations on the transmission agency, security and identity and interface descriptions. There were also changes to several decrees dealing with forms to be used in the judiciary system (*ADV-Formverordnung* AFV 2002, 3. *Formblat-Verordnung Formblatt-V*), as well as changes to the law governing court fees, the regulations regarding deposits and withdrawals (*Abbuchungs- und Einziehungsverordnung AEV*), changes to the regulations concerning lawyers (including the Austrian Lawyers Organisation Statute) and minor changes to the code of commercial law, the code of criminal procedure and financial penal law (HGB, StPO, FinStrG).

Until 1994, this service had only been available to lawyers, notaries and the Federal Law Office of the Republic of Austria acting as representative for the regional authorities. Since then, public law bodies and certain organisations subject to government supervision such as banks and insurance companies have been included. Since 1999, any law firm has been required to have the necessary technical facilities to support the system (amendment of the Austrian Lawyers Organisation Statute of 1 February 1999), and, in accordance with the new budget law, their agreement to be able to receive documents from courts is not solicited. At the same time court fees were reduced for any proceedings dealt with electronically, and the tariffs for lawyers were increased. In Austria, the costs of court proceedings are paid by the losing side. Also, since 1999, decisions and other documents from the courts have been transmitted electronically, unless explicitly requested otherwise. After several years of operation, the system was made available in its entirety to all citizens in 2000, but the need for using a customised software package has limited the uptake by the general population. Since 2001, the possibility of transmitting annual financial statements to the Companies Registry has been offered.

As the technical base of ELC is no longer up to date, a major redesign known as webERV is under way. This will introduce an Internet technology-based interface with interactive forms relying on XML for data transfer. According to the development roadmap, WebERV should eventually replace traditional ELC by the end of 2009. This will eliminate the need for customised software and open up the system more fully to the general public. Different forms of payment such as credit cards will also be accepted. Communication between law firms will also be included, together with the possibility of filings for the Land Registry and the Companies Registry. The use of digital signatures and citizen cards will provide another means of identification. Finally, the European initiative for a common claims process will be used to promote internationalisation, which in previous attempts has failed. For the near future, a slow migration is planned with both versions operating in parallel until 2009. As a further enhancement, the aim is to integrate notary work fully in the ELC-system. In particular, the drawing up and authenticating of deeds using electronic signatures will be offered, together with authentication by courts. This should also lead to the establishment of electronic document archives that allow for the continuing storage of documents, increased security and easier transfer and access (Figure 6.3).

One of the main aims of introducing the ELC-system was to open the process to external customers, thus speeding up proceedings. They would have both the necessary information readily available, and would also be able to initiate new actions by submitting claims or similar petitions. The strategy pursued was to aim for access for lawyers, who traditionally act as middle-men or intermediaries between citizens and the judicial system. In most cases, citizens do not approach the courts in person, but act through or with the help of a lawyer. Therefore, it was deemed more feasible to have lawyers brought into the network, and by facilitating their work to generate benefits for the wider public. Therefore, a win-win situation for lawyers had to be created, which was achieved by using financial incentives. On the one hand, possible efficiency increases within law firms were

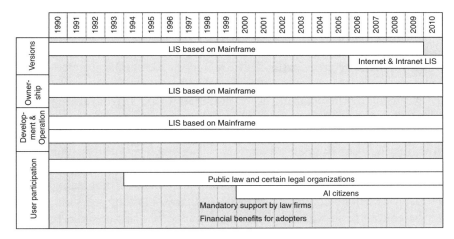

Figure 6.3   Overview of ELC development over time

publicised, and some of the savings benefiting the Government were to be passed on to the law firms together with changes in the tariffs. As a result of the tariff reform, increased income is achieved by law firms if their transaction volume exceeds 15 petitions per month. For the courts, the initial recording of a default action or a motion for execution is no longer necessary, as data can be transmitted electronically without a change of medium and is thus more rapidly available for processing, and also more accurate. As yet, no petition has been lost, and everything can be reconstructed using the log facilities of the ELC-system. Most problems result from incorrect user inputs.

Adoption and evaluation

The adoption of ELC is still very much limited to the judicial sector. In 2003, about 4,750 members were using the ELC system, out of which law firms numbering about 4,400 clearly constituted a majority. This is in accordance with the strategy adopted. As of 2005, 95 per cent of the 4,900 users are law firms. Interestingly, adoption and usage do not depend on the size of the law firm, but are reported to depend on the individual preferences of lawyers.

In 1999 about 700,000 default actions (70 per cent of these claims) were filed electronically. In the year 2004, about 2.1 million actions were filed with the courts, and about 4 million decisions and other documents were transmitted by the courts themselves (most of these being case numbers).

In 2003, out of 855,000 civil law suits, 85 per cent were submitted electronically, and out of 1.23 million enforcements, about 60 per cent were initiated electronically. The latter number is expected to rise considerably when the social security system is fully integrated into the system.

Regarding adoption rates, the installed software and hardware base and the provision of financial incentives are seen as marking a turning point. After the court tariffs were lowered and opportunity for lawyers to make additional profits was opened up, adoption rates increased rapidly. At that time, in 1995, enforcement orders were also added as an important functionality. Currently, a similar problem is being encountered with notaries, who, although equipped with computers, are not technologically up-to-date. It has been noted that if a PC is more than about four years old, it will not be able to cope with the requirements of ELC, and this is a problem within that particular user group.

Currently available figures on time and cost reductions are favourable. The time saved for recording an application for the first time in civil and enforcement proceedings is estimated at 7.5 minutes per case, which translates into savings of almost €2.25 million (although the method for arriving at this evaluation is unclear). This amount could increase to up to €3.63 million, if the system involved a larger proportion of proceedings. If 75 per cent of enforcement applications (approximately 1.4 million) were filed electronically, there would be a savings potential of 78 jobs in court offices, and a further 93 if more intensive utilisation of the mailing facility could be achieved. The reduction in postal costs is estimated as €2.5 million (as of 2004). As regards the registrars (Rechtspfleger), a simplified procedure for enforcement orders will lead to a reduction of 67 jobs. The number of bailiffs could be reduced by approximately 37 as a result of the automated service, voluntary payments, and a greater reliability as regards addresses. All in all, this will lead to a reduction of a quarter of all staff working in the field of enforcement proceedings. In addition, in 2003, €2 million was saved in mailing costs (Bauer, 2001; Verfahrensautomation Justiz, 2003).

Due to the hidden functionality that ELC provides in diverse applications, the assessment of system features from the user perspective is less extensive than for the first case study. Once the user has posted the document electronically, s/he is not involved in further interactions with the underlying technology.

The evaluations provided in user interviews showed that ELC is used regularly and that users are satisfied with the system to a high degree. Only the two lawyers were able to provide assessments of the technology. The Austrian federal judge is not involved in ELC, since all documents are received by the central administration and subsequently distributed in a traditional paper format. This media disruption can be regarded as a major flaw in the adoption process of a totally electronic workflow system. It should be noted that actual usage (and intention to use) cannot be regarded as suitable success indicators for systems or technologies that contain mandatory elements, as is the case for ELC in law offices, which are obliged to have the technology available. This regulation obviously has a major impact on the adoption process.

ELC is not an application in itself but rather a means of communication and this can be seen both as a strength and a weakness. On the one hand, there are no costs in developing a user interface, and an optimal solution can be selected in the free market. On the other hand, the users of the service – currently mostly law firms – have to choose one out of a set of implementations, which might or might not be an optimal solution and be supported in the long run. This constitutes the main weakness of ELC, namely its dependency on software providers, as can be seen in the following empirical data analysis.

System quality was assessed as being high with relative weaknesses in the areas of usability and availability. The factors considered clearly depend on the ELC implementation used. While one interviewee could not report any quality-related system problems, the other interviewee clearly communicated dissatisfaction with their current system, which had only recently been introduced in their organisation. As a reason for switching to a new, more comprehensive and costly system, the growth of the organisation with new demands on certain system features, in particular in the area of capacity handling, was mentioned.

Service quality is an important dimension for ELC since without a running system no documents can be filed. Here again, two different perspectives can be seen. While one user/organisation reported no problems and is clearly content with their service organisation, the other is not.

Positive net benefits were clearly communicated in both cases, in particular regarding extensive time and cost savings, although costs for acquiring, operating and maintaining the systems were also reported as being high. A cost-benefit comparison was not considered since the use of ELC technology in law firms is mandatory.

Analysis

The strategy employed to generate benefits for the general population using an intermediary, in this case lawyers, has proven to be successful.

The ELC technology was widely adopted in Austria as a result of the combined mandatory and incentive strategy employed. The use of ELC was made obligatory for lawyers but financial incentives were introduced simultaneously. It remains to be seen whether the costs of different types of applications can be justified in other countries, if the contents of these types of application are required to be the same.

The mandatory system meant the technology was widely adopted, but it makes it difficult to draw comparisons with adoption rates in other areas. The costs for adopting ELC are at first sight considerable, since they include hardware and software investment and organisational changes. The possible benefits are extensive, but hard to quantify for the potential adopter. The new development, webERV, based on Internet technology will make it easier for all new users to utilise ELC.

An important pre-condition for ELC adoption is the maturity of the technical processes involved, security issues and their legal foundation. This was achieved early on in Austria through various amendments to the law, in particular to the law covering court organisation (§ 89a Abs 1&2, § 89b-e), and to other regulations (especially on ERV, 1995). We see a distinct shaping of the legal and process framework following on from the technology. Processes, which have already been formalised to a large degree, become even more formalised as a result of the nature of specifying the interfaces and exchanges involved in the implementation of software. As the history has shown, more and more processes are covered, starting with the most formalised and then moving on to less formalised and less frequently enacted processes. The user perspective showed no concerns with security related features. Security features, for example digital signatures and certificates, are pre-conditions for ELC adoption.

The installed base in software and hardware is a turning point for system adoption, an issue that initially concerned law firms and which is currently being encountered with notaries. The webERV initiative should impose less stringent conditions on the technical infrastructure needed and can be seen as a major driver for ELC adoption by users other than law firms.

Discussion and conclusions

In this paper, two case studies on e-justice in Austria have been analysed. We find that both cases have several points in common. Both have a long, evolving history of different versions and configurations, with a change of focus over time. Both have continually and gradually amassed more and more functionalities, with the change in focus being more obvious in the LIS case, with a decisive switch from mainframe to the Internet, and from a closed to open user network. But in the ELC case too, both functionality and the user group have continually expanded. It might be argued that what we see today is that some, successful systems tend to survive and thrive in the process of becoming more and more important and all-encompassing, while other applications dwindle and die. Another commonality between both cases is that they are grass-root projects originating from within the administration, only later being endorsed by Government. Since the main users in both cases, at least of the first versions, were staff from within administration, the projects can be labelled as user innovations (von Hippel, 2005). This term refers to innovations produced by users, who expect to benefit from using a product or service, as opposed to a manufacturer, who expects to benefit by selling it. The main reason for users developing innovations is 'sticky' information concerning their needs and context of use, with stickiness referring to high costs for transferring this information because of its implicit nature or for other reasons (von Hippel, 1994). When it is too difficult or costly to transfer this information, the focus of problem solving may shift to the users. This means that they develop their own solutions, which best fit their precise needs. In particular lead users, who can be defined as being at the cutting edge of an important trend and who have high expected benefits from a solution, have been shown to produce attractive innovations (von Hippel, 1986). In our case studies, the people within the administration have shown lead user characteristics on two distinct occasions: they recognised the possible savings and efficiency increases inherent in applying ICT to their current work early on. This led to the production of a first version of the systems with an internal focus, with the users having benefited from using their innovation. Some users have also been ahead of the trend in recognising the possibilities offered by Internet technologies and opening up networks. This has led to the production of a new innovation, and new versions of the systems, which has been opened up to the public.

After the projects were endorsed by Government, the laws necessary for the system to come into full effect were passed. This shows that in both cases available technological possibilities have had an impact on underlying practices, and even on the legal code. The installed base, the infrastructure and systems available technologically or already in place, played an important role. The organisational components such as routines or the legal code seemed to be less rigid, and have been adapted to the technological necessities.

Both have two general aims, although these were not apparent at the beginning of their lifetime. The first goal was to increase efficiency within the administration, and later the second aim became to provide benefits for the general population. It is important to note that the first effect was the main driver and starting point, especially in getting government backing. Benefits for the general population came in later as a goal, apparently as an afterthought and to this effect, two different strategies were employed, with the LIS constituting an open information system for any number of users and their diverse needs, while ELC uses lawyers as intermediaries for the population, who benefit from faster proceedings. Accordingly, the adoption of the LIS was completely voluntary, and relied on quality and word-of-mouth. Presumably the absence of user involvement at the development stage and thus a limited user interface also led to the result that most users come from legal professions. In the case of the ELC system, a combination of mandatory usage and financial incentives was applied to ensure the adoption by the necessary intermediaries.

From the users' perspective, both technologies were regarded as very important for conducting work in the legal sector. The measurement model clearly demonstrates the success of both projects. With regard to the LIS, the quality dimension was dominated by strengths, while minor weaknesses were detected in the area of data base coverage and query design. The relative weakness regarding contents coverage had already been foreseen, and, as mentioned, a further increase in contents offered is planned. As regards ELC, since it constitutes an interface and communication channel, quality assessment from the viewpoint of a user cannot be separated from the solution employed for utilising the technology (that is the software involved). Therefore, the user perceives ELC quality in terms of the quality of the system into which ELC is embedded. The new WebERV development, which is currently being introduced to the public, will enable a better separation of ELC and its environment. With regard to both cases, both rate of use and user satisfaction are high. Both systems are used on a regular daily basis in the law agencies considered in the research, and also reflect the different needs that emerge in the Austrian courts. The benefits for users and their organisations were regarded as very advantageous, although high acquisition and maintenance costs were reported in the case of ELC (again in terms of the software system that implements ELC). Again, WebERV needs to be mentioned as it will allow filing of legal actions electronically within a web interface with interactive forms relying on XML for data transfer. This will eliminate the need for customised software and open up the system for all users more fully (Table 6.1).

To conclude, both case studies are based on well matured and highly successful technologies in the electronic government sector, which are often cited as best practice reference projects. The technology development

Table 6.1 Key points of evaluation based on both case studies

Key aspects of LIS and ELC

- Highly significant developments with high adoption rates
- Switch from mainframe to Internet, from closed to open user network.
- Attributable as user innovations
- Adaptation of organisational components according to needs

	Pluses	Minuses
LIS specific	• Open information system for any number of users • Quality • User satisfaction	• Absence of user consultation • Limited user interface • Data base coverage and query design
ELC specific	• Successful intermediary adoption approach for faster proceedings • Combination of mandatory adoption and financial incentives • User satisfaction	• Acquisition and maintenance costs for traditional ELC

process was initiated more than 30 years ago in the case of the LIS and more than 15 years ago in the case of ELC, while the necessary environments for both electronic government initiatives were created on the way. Significant advances in the outcomes attained by firms and individuals in both cases were detected, and these clearly disconfirm the often cited productivity paradox in the case of both technologies. It will be interesting to see whether the current focus on opening up the networks further will be sustained in the newer versions of both systems.

References

Bauer, P. (2001), 'A Show Case for the Future: E-Justice in Austria'. In Fabri, M. and F. Contini (eds), *Justice and Technology in Europe: How ICT is changing the Judicial Business.* The Hague: Kluwer Law International.

Benbasat, I., Goldstein, D.K. and M. Mead (1987), 'The Case Research Strategy in Studies of Information Systems'. *MIS Quarterly,* 11 (3), 369–386.

Brüggemeier, M., Dovifat, A. and D. Kubisch (2005), 'Analyse von Innovationsprozessen im Kontext von E-Government'. *WIRTSCHAFTSINFORMATIK*, 47 (5), 347–355.

Dawes, S.S., Pardo, T.A. and A.M. Cresswell (2004), 'Designing Electronic Government Information Access Programs: a Holistic Approach'. *Government Information Quarterly*, 21 (1), 3–23.

Delcambre, L. and G. Giuliano (2005), 'Digital Government Research in Academia'. *IEEE Computer*, 38 (12), 33–39.

DeLone, W.D. and E.R. McLean (1992), 'Information Systems Success: The Quest for the Dependent Variable'. *Information Systems Research*, 3 (1), 60–95.

DeLone, W.D. and E.R. McLean (2003), 'The DeLone and McLean Model of Information Systems Success: A Ten-Year Update'. *Journal of Management Information Systems*, 19 (4), 9–30.

Glaser, B. and A. Strauss (1967), *The Discovery of Grounded Theory: Strategies for Qualitative Research*. New York, NY: Aldine de Gruyter.

Gottwald, T. and W. Viefhues (2004), 'Elektronischer Rechtsverkehr in Österreich – Schlussfolgerungen aus deutscher Sicht'. *MMR*, 12, 792–797.

Koga, T. (2003), 'Access to Government Information in Japan: a Long Way toward Electronic Government?' *Government Information Quarterly*, 20 (1), 47–62.

Lee, S.M., Tan, X. and S. Trimi (2005), 'Current Practices of Leading E-Government Countries'. *Communications of the ACM*, 48 (10), 99–104.

Marchionini, G., Haas, S.W., Zhang, J. and J. Elsas (2005), 'Accessing Government Statistical Information'. *IEEE Computer*, 38 (12), 52–61.

Mason, R.O. (1978), 'Measuring Information Output: a Communication Systems Approach'. *Information and Management*, 1 (5), 219–234.

Ostermann, H. and R. Staudinger (2005), 'Benchmarking E-Government'. *WIRTSCHAFTSINFORMATIK*, 47 (5), 367–377.

Perens, B. (1999), 'The Open Source Definition'. In DiBona, C., Ockman S. and M. Stone (eds), *Open Sources: Voices from the Open Source Revolution*. Massachusetts: O'Reilly & Associates.

Perritt, Jr. H.H. (1996), 'The Information Highway: on Ramps, Checkpoints, and Tollbooths'. *Government Information Quarterly*, 13 (2), 143–158.

Sabherwal, R., Jeyaraj, A. and C. Chowa (2006), 'Information System Success: Individual and Organizational Determinants'. *Management Science*, 52 (12) 1849–1864.

Shannon, C.E. and W. Weaver (1949), *The Mathematical Theory of Communication*. Urbana, IL: University of Illinois Press.

Strauss, A. and J. Corbin (1990), *Basics of Qualitative Research*. Thousand Oaks, CA: Sage.

Stuart, I., McCutcheon, D., Handfield, R., McLachlin, R. and D. Samson (2002), 'Effective Case Research in Operations Management: a Process Perspective'. *Journal of Operations Management*, 20 (5), 419–433.

Verfahrensautomation Justiz (2003), 'Projektabschlussbericht für das Projekt "Redesign – Verfahrensautomation Justiz" '. Bundesministerium für Justiz / IBM Österreich, Wien. Retrieved from www.bmj.gv.at/_cms_upload/_docs/abschluss_vj_redesign.pdf. Visited 29 November 2007.

von Hippel, E. (1986), 'Lead Users: A Source Of Novel Product Concepts'. *Management Science*, 32 (7), 791–805.

von Hippel, E. (1994), 'Sticky Information and the Locus of Problem Solving: Implications for Innovation'. *Management Science*, 40 (4), 429–439.

von Hippel, E. (2005), *Democratizing Innovation*. Boston, MA: MIT Press.

Wolf, P. and H. Krcmar (2005), 'Prozessorientierte Wirtschaftlichkeitsuntersuchung für E-Government'. *WIRTSCHAFTSINFORMATIK*, 47 (5), 337–346.

Yin, R.K. (1981), 'The Case Study Crisis: Some Answers'. *Administrative Science Quarterly*, 26, 58–65.

CHAPTER 7

Institutional complexity and functional simplification: the case of money claim online service in England and Wales

Jannis Kallinikos

Introduction

Objectives and findings

The present chapter reports the investigation of *Money Claim OnLine* (MCOL), a web-based service for issuing money claims and resolving fixed money disputes introduced in the judiciary of England and Wales in February 2002. The service has been widely and rapidly adopted and represents a good example of how ICT-based systems and artefacts can be deployed within justice to assist the management of tasks other than purely administrative ones; that is, tasks that involve transactions between the courts and citizens or organisations.

The investigation focused on the examination of the institutional, organisational and technological conditions that made the conception, development and implementation of MCOL possible and successful. At first glance, the issue emerges as straightforward. The instrumental ability of ICT-based systems or artefacts would seem contingent on the degree to which they have managed to capture the essence of the processes which they are called to bear upon, streamline and codify. User-friendliness is also crucial for web-based services that wish to appeal to the wider public.

Straightforward as these factors may be, they never fully account for the degree to which ICT-based applications are successfully integrated into the operations of such complex institutional systems as that which justice represents. The successful transposition of offline processes to online services is taking place within a dense cultural and institutional context that conditions such innovations in many ways. The present research sought therefore to chart down the complex navigation, as it were, of MCOL in the dense system of rules, codes and regulations, practices and institutions underlying justice in England and Wales. The purpose has been not to map out the detailed process of developing MCOL, but to find out the factors that contributed to the conception or identification of the service and its gradual and successful embeddedness in the justice system of England and Wales.

The conclusions of the investigation suggest three clusters of factors that could be invoked to account for the conception, development and implementation of the service. *First*, MCOL built on technological antecedents that managed massive money claims though an established EDI system. The service of electronic money claims as such antedated MCOL. However, serendipitous technological developments captured by the diffusion of web-based systems and the Internet joined hands with the existing technological solutions for managing bulk claims to make possible the identification of the service. The government's modernisation programme and the political determination to deploy ICT to improve the quality of public services were also instrumental to the development of MCOL.

Secondly, the *Department of Constitutional Affairs* and the *Court Service*, the hosts of MCOL, used with considerable wisdom the key technological strategy of procedural and functional simplification. Money claims, as distinct from other claims, often involve relatively straightforward procedures of dispute resolution. In addition, what was transposed onto an online service was a further streamlined process of money claims cleansed, to a considerable degree, of the judicial intricacies that usually underlie more complex money claims. The online viability of the service was crucially linked to the simplified version of money claims that went online.

Thirdly, online processes crucially depend on and are supported by a rather elaborate system of offline and often culturally and institutionally embedded operations that are easy to overlook or take for granted. The aforementioned procedural and functional simplification is indeed predicated on the ability to buffer the online service or offload from it all those complications that intrude and concede their treatment to the traditional offline process. Without this kind of indirect support provided by the traditional system, MCOL would have been impossible. Such a conclusion contrasts with and challenges a widespread assumption according to which online processes are conceived as substitutes for offline operations.

Methodology

The data and information on which this report is based have been mainly collected through personal interviews and the study of documents. Demonstrations of MCOL and site observations have also provided some information on the routine operations of the system. Some statistics on MCOL compiled by the *Court Service* are used. Personal interviews with key actors involved in the development (Department of Constitutional Affairs and the Court Service) and monitoring (Country Court Bulk Centre and the Northampton Court) of MCOL and the careful study of documents and the procedures associated with money claims constitute the core of the data on which the analysis of MCOL and the conclusions drawn are based.

Interviews were semi-structured. A certain acquaintance with the judicial processes of money claims and the wider issues associated with the involvement of ICT in justice were essential to arrive at a pre-understanding of the wider context within which MCOL is embedded. A semi-structured interview guide was subsequently constructed on the basis of that pre-understanding. Interviews were recorded and transcribed to form together with the study of documents, some statistics and other relevant material the empirical corpus of the investigation. Data collection has by and large conformed to an inductivist procedure. Theoretical ideas were brought in later to assist the analysis of empirical data but they did not essentially interfere during the data collection stage.

It is perhaps worth making clear that the interviews have so far focused on the 'supply' side, that is that part of the judicial system that conceived and implemented MCOL and operates it now. The perception of MCOL by users (for example citizens, lawyers, organisations) and the ways they make use of the service have not been investigated at this stage. The few data I present on user evaluation have been compiled by the *Court Service*.

Structure of the chapter

Following this short introduction, MCOL is presented in the *second section* of this chapter. After some background information, I describe the basic functionalities of the MCOL and provide some indicators on its diffusion. *Section 3* then moves on to considering the technological conditions that made MCOL possible in the first place. As already mentioned, technological antecedents in the form of an already existing EDI system for processing bulk money claims issued by various organisations (for example banks, utility companies) joined hands with the serendipitous diffusion of the Internet to make MCOL a technologically possible and attractive online service. In *Section 4* I describe in some detail the whole judicial process of money claims and show the complex imbrications of offline and online processes currently in practice. In *Section 5* I draw on the other sections and endeavour to present in some detail the major conclusions of the investigation of MCOL.

Money claim online – an overview

ICT in the judicial system of England and Wales

According to Susskind (2000) the major influence in the development of ICT for the civil courts was Lord Woolf's 'Access to Justice' inquiry and its recommendations that were later captured in the White Paper 'Modernising Justice' (Court Service, 1998) by the new Labour Party. The recommendations centre on improving access to justice, reducing the cost of litigation, encouraging alternative dispute resolution procedures and reducing the complexity of the rules and terminology through the deployment of ICT (Timms, Plotnikoff and Woolfson, 2003). Woolf's reforms and later the White Paper 'Modernising Justice' identified 'pre-action protocols setting standards and timetables for the conduct of cases before court proceedings are started' (Court Service, 1998, p. 40). The White Paper identified three distinct categories or, in its own terminology, a system of three tracks to which disputed claims should be assigned, that is:

- *small claims procedure,* which involves small, straightforward claims below £5,000 to be settled by an informal hearing before a district judge.
- A *fast track* for claims between the upper limit of small claims up to £15,000. Claims of this sort will be subject to a fixed timetable, requiring a hearing within 30 weeks. The amount of oral evidence will be strictly limited.
- A *multi track* for cases over £15,000 which often involve a considerable degree of judicial complexity making necessary a higher level of judicial intervention to be directed and controlled by a judge.

It is obvious that simple claims and fast track claims are relatively straightforward. In such cases, ICT involvement may substantially assist the carry over of the related procedures, since regular consultation by any judge may be limited. Failure to meet deadlines on the fast track must automatically trigger appropriate action. ICT involvement in multi-track claims is a much more complicated issue. In cases of this sort, judges need to be more pro-active in the management of cases. To do this effectively, they need to have direct access to case management or e-filing systems or to the outputs of these systems. Lord Woolf's reforms also identified key implementation issues. For example the report recognised that not all judges, agencies and other parties involved will be willing or able to use any new technology to the desirable degree. In this sense, there seems to have been awareness and a wide, albeit often implicit, consensus that there must be parallel systems in use; that is, ICT will coexist with paper-based systems for judicial case management for some years to come (Plotnikoff, Woolfson and Lyons, 2001).

Money claim online

Money claim is a specific *Civil Justice Procedure* that falls under the jurisdiction of county courts. The procedure is enacted by individuals or businesses with the purpose of settling money disputes. The claimant, who is the person that initiates the procedure, claims a specific amount of money from the defendant, the person who allegedly owns the amount. Traditionally money claims involve a court hearing, though simple money claims can be resolved and have been resolved without such a hearing.

Money Claim Online was launched in the period December 2001–February 2002 by the *Court Service*, the executive hand of the *Lord Chancellor's Department* (that is the Department of Constitutional Affairs renamed as the Ministry of Justice in 2005). It is the *Court Service's* first online service and it allows users to issue money claims, request judgment by default or admission, apply for a warrant of execution, respond to a claim and track the progress of their case. As already indicated, a push from the government in December 1998 with the White Paper 'Modernising Government' formed the Courts and Tribunals Modernisation Programme. A major aim of the programme was to initially elicit areas within the justice system where avoidance and early resolution of disputes could be encouraged, and secondly to ensure that the most appropriate form of dispute resolution is selected. Within this context ICT-based systems and applications were conceived as holding considerable promise (Timms, Plotnikoff and Woolfson, 2003).

Money claims was identified as an area that could be essentially supported by an online service for mainly two reasons. First, a large majority of money claims are issued for unpaid invoices from large organisations like utilities, telecommunication and credit card companies and act more as a reminder in order to agree some sort of debt reduction. For this reason, money claims of this sort are settled without having to go through a court hearing. The defendant as a rule acknowledges the debt and pays it. The second, perhaps equally important, reason was the technological antecedents that could support an online service. Approximately 50 per cent of all money claims are issued through the County Court Bulk Centre (CCBC). The CCBC is an EDI system that was developed and implemented by EDS so that organisations that issue large numbers of money claims (for example banks, utilities) can make the process of issuing claims more efficient. A significant goal thereof was to remove the administrative burden associated with simple claims of this sort from County Courts (The first tier of justice).

Customers of MCOL interact with the system through a series of step-driven screens. The welcome screen of the website asks the customer to select between two roles, the role of the claimant and the role of the defendant (Figure 7.1).

During the first four months of its operation MCOL was used to issue approximately 3,000 money claims. This figure climbed up to 21,513 claims

Figure 7.1   Screen for choosing between claimant and defendant roles

in the second year of the service's operation, covering the period from April 2002 to March 2003. During the last two or three months of that year, the issue rate ran approximately at 2,400 claims per month (ca 600 per week). Compared to other county courts, MCOL became after only 16 months of operation the second (by claims issued) claim issuer in England and Wales. Leeds County Court with 26,120 was first for the year 2002–03 (Figure 7.2). In May 2003 user analysis of MCOL performed by the *Court Service* and the *Department of Constitutional Affairs* showed that during these 17 months of MCOL operation, parties issuing fewer than 4 claims accounted for 78 per cent of MCOL actions. Solicitors issued 27 per cent of MCOL claims, a reduction on the January 2003 analysis, which reported a 45 per cent solicitor share of repeat users. This can be compared to the 690,000 paper-based claims issued each year in county courts. Solicitors issued approximately 66 per cent of these claims. MCOL cases represent 3 per cent of the claims not issued through the CCBC. This effectively means that solicitors using MCOL during April-May 2003 accounted for less than one per cent of the national claims issued.

The overall picture is however steadily improving. The current diffusion of MCOL suggests it is on the way to becoming a significant judicial service in terms of the quantity of money claims handled by it. Already during the third year of its operation (April 2003 to March 2004) MCOL managed to

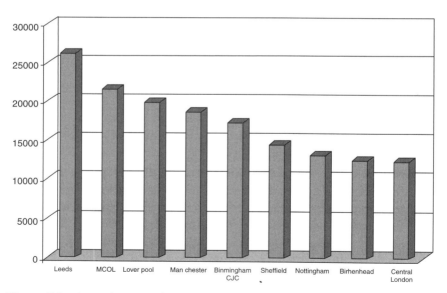

Figure 7.2   Issued money claims by county court in the period from April 2002 to March 2003

climb to the first position among the county courts in England and Wales in terms of money claims issued through it. During that year, 39,589 money claims were issued through MCOL while during the first ten months of the fourth year of operation (April 2004–January 2005) this number rose to 43,938 money claims, suggesting that the service is about to climb over the symbolically significant figure of 50,000 money claims a year. Though it may be premature to draw any definite conclusion at this stage, a closer look over the monthly distribution of money claims during the last eight months of that period (June 2004–January 2005) suggest a stabilisation of money claims issued through MCOL between 4,000 and 5,000, higher for November 2004 (5,182 money claims) and lower for December 2004 (4,062). Also, a closer analysis suggests a relatively even distribution of money claims in terms of money bands with roughly 32 per cent falling within the money band £1,000–5,000 and roughly 60 per cent falling below £1,000. Some of these figures and relationships are depicted in Table 7.1.

User research conducted by the *Court Service* during the first 18 months of MCOL operation showed that customers valued the speed of the service, the instant acknowledgment of registration, the ability to download a PDF version of the claim form, and the fact that they could enter the judgment and enforce it online. The user research also showed that a key reason (29 per cent) for not using MCOL was the lack of access to a credit or debit card; 16 per cent of the respondents indicated that the space for the particulars of the claim was insufficient, 22 per cent did not want to re-key in data from their own ICT systems, and 23 per cent declared that they receive a good service from their local court. Finally the user research indicated that favourites for other online services included court lists, attachment of earning searches, issue of attachment of earnings applications, checking of all claims, issue of PI/unspecified claims, sending e-mails to court, bankruptcy petitions online, possession claims issuing online.

Table 7.1   The development of MCOL

	April 02–March 03	April 03–March 04	April 04–January 05 (10 months)
Number of money claims	21,513	39,589	43,938
Fee bands			
• £0–1,000	59.2%	59.2%	59%
• £1,000–5,000	32.6%	32.5%	31.9%
• above £5,000	8.2%	8.3%	9.1%
Monthly distribution of money claims (average)	1,792	3,299	4,393

Brief as this description is, it nevertheless conveys a picture of the overall context within which MCOL was identified and developed. It also suggests that the service has from its very beginning managed to diffuse and establish itself as a significant online service. Before however continuing to describe its development, a few details about the pre-existing technological set-up and the organisational and administrative context that was associated with it are required to more fully appreciate MCOL.

Technological antecedents – the installed base

The county court bulk centre

The conception, design and implementation of MCOL represent the confluence of several technological developments. Services like MCOL usually ride on existing technological arrangements, even though they may demand their reconfiguration. Its innovative character notwithstanding, MCOL could in this respect be seen as the offspring of the CCBC.

The CCBC is based at Northampton and operates under the jurisdiction of the Northampton Court. Its main operation is to manage bulk money claims, that is multiple claims issued by organisations like banks, public utilities and the like. The EDI system, which forms the very core of the CCBC, was developed and run by Electronic Data Systems Ltd (EDS) and it has been in place for over 15 years. The CCBC accounts for approximately 50 per cent of all the money claims issued each year in England and Wales. The purpose of the CCBC is to relieve county courts of much of the routine repetitive work associated with the issue of straightforward default claims.

Any England or Wales registered company or organisation can become a member of the CCBC so that it can use it for claim issuing. Before 2000, when a new upgrade to the system allowed the companies to connect to the CCBC through a dial-up connection, the process of sending the claims to the CCBC was done through posting of magnetic media. Each organisation could send structured files with the particulars of a claim (such as claim number, claimant, defendant name etc) to the CCBC, which then processed the tapes. When the data regarding claims have been verified, they are sent from the CCBC to the EDS Printing and Posting centre in Washington, County Durham. EDS then prints and posts the claim(s) to the defendant(s). In the year 2000, EDS upgraded the CCBC and created an interface as a Windows RAS dial-up service.

The fact that the system was already in place was essential to the identification and development of MCOL. In essence, MCOL was conceived as the front-end of the CCBC system, which formed the administrative-technological backbone (the back-end) of the entire project. If the front-end could handle and deliver information to the CBCC in a structured format then an important part of the requirements for extending the operations of the system to the public would have been met.

Standards

The developers of MCOL have used the *e-Government Interoperability Framework* as guidance for choosing between the available technological standards. The main thrust of the e-Government Interoperability Framework is the adoption of Internet and World Wide Web standards for all government systems. This approach is designed to be pragmatic and aims to reduce the costs and risk of operating information technology systems while keeping the public sector in step with the global Internet diffusion.

The most significant standards adoption comes in three areas: *Data Exchange*, *User Interface* and *Connectivity*. For the exchange of data the eXtensible Markup Language (XML) was used. For the user interface the e-gif standard denotes the use of Internet browsers (Internet Explorer, Netscape, and Opera). Finally for the network connectivity TCP/IP was chosen (See for example Timms, Plotnikoff and Woolfson, 2003).

Developing MCOL

The first step in the development of the project was for the *Department of Constitutional Affairs* (DCA) to establish the business case alongside a feasibility analysis. Because of the pre-existing back-end (the CCBC), this project was really about providing a user friendly interface to an old EDI system, which would be used by the general public and professionals (solicitors). To establish the requirements the DCA worked with EDS and used screen mock-ups (or user interface prototypes). The role of these prototypes was twofold: first, to serve as an instrument for better requirements elicitation and secondly to demonstrate at various judicial conferences and inside the DCA the shape of the service so that momentum and enthusiasm could be created.

Initially EDS had quoted a two-year timescale for the project. The company intended to develop the system from scratch without reusing existing libraries and software components. The DCA however rejected this and required a much faster development lifecycle. EDS then subcontracted EzGov, a software company owning the *FlexFoundation Library*. FlexFoundation provides the required software libraries for rapidly creating form-driven websites. It provides a form creation package, along with all validation and verification criteria, and the ability to set the specific rules on how to proceed on a multi-step process. FlexFoundation also provides a registration-based user environment, and also a payments engine. By subcontracting the complete project development and management to EzGov, EDS managed to slash the required time from two years to nine months.

EzGov worked with the DCA and created the use cases and user interface prototypes for the MCOL front-end (EzGov, 2003). When the use cases and user interface prototypes had been signed, EzGov went ahead and coded the project. However because EzGov was not responsible for the integration of MCOL with the CCBC, EDS had to integrate the front-end with the back-end. Slight modifications were required in the CCBC system such as changing particular fields so that the CCBC could distinguish whether a claim originated from a tape, a dial-up connection or MCOL.

At the time of development there were talks about whether to use the FlexFoundation user-registration and login system, or to use the *Government Gateway* for user validation. The same decision had to be made regarding payments and how to process them. FlexFoundation had an existing payments engine, while the *Government Gateway's* payments engine was not ready at that time. The DCA discussed these issues with the project manager of the *Government Gateway*. They finally decided to go ahead with the inbuilt functionality of FlexFoundation. The main reason behind this decision was the fact that the project was running on a very tight timescale, and, although the developers from *Government Gateway* were hoping to have the system ready in time, it was deemed that it was a risk not worth taking.

The project managers decided to go for a soft-launch. This meant that after the testing carried out by EzGov and EDS they launched the MCOL service but did not advertise it as yet. On the first anniversary of MCOL a significant enhancement was added to the service. Up to that moment, MCOL fully facilitated the customers making claims but it did not provide any functionality for the defendants. The DCA was encouraged by the judiciary to enhance MCOL so that both parties had the capability of performing their actions electronically, something known in the judiciary as equality of arms. Consequently the DCA worked with EDS and EzGov so that the ability to defend online could be provided. However because of the nature of the CCBC system it was possible to provide defending capability for claims issued not only through MCOL but also for claims issued by the CCBC itself.

Methodology

Prototyping was used as a vehicle for eliciting requirements. User participation in the process was not only limited to the initial stages of requirements elicitation. The DCA worked in close co-operation with EzGov during user interface prototyping. In brief, the life cycle of the project can be broken down into the following steps.

1. Business case,
2. Requirements,
3. Use cases plus wire frames,
4. Coding and initial testing,
5. Integration and implementation,
6. Live testing,
7. Phase two, Enhancements.

During the development process EzGov came across a particular set of problems. EzGov's analysts would construct the use cases for the system. In some cases where they could not understand the judiciary rules and procedures, they would ask for advice. Analysts from the DCA would then ask county courts for their expert advice. However EzGov was getting different answers depending on who was responding. This inconsistency was attributed to the fact that when there is a local system that is doing manual processing there can be variations on the results.

   This situation required intervention from the DCA project manager. The differentiation of answers was holding up the development of the project running on a very tight timescale. The project manager eventually had to decide on what answer would be deemed as correct. He would often distil what he considered a typical answer.

Actors, systems and architectures

A number of different systems and applications work together in order to make the operation of the MCOL service functional. As a means of making the description easily intelligible, these systems will be grouped into front-end and back-end systems. Front-end systems are those in which customers have some sort of direct interaction, whereas back-end systems are those that the customers do not directly interact with. The MCOL website, the front-end of the system, is the central point of interaction with MCOL customers. The MCOL website draws its own information from its own database, the MCOL database. The service is essentially supported by the Credit Card System that enables payment by credit card. The CCBC is the old EDI system located at Northampton. It connects directly to the MCOL database and also to the EDS Printing and Posting system. The accounting system encapsulates all the activities required in order to account for the payments that are made through MCOL. It is done off the CCBC system manually. All these systems must work together to sustain MCOL as an online service.

The main actors involved in the issuing and processing of money claims electronically are the following:

- Customers: Residents of England and Wales and formal organisations.
- EDS: Electronic Data Services is the company that has developed and operated the CCBC system and subcontracted the development of the MCOL system.
- Northampton Help Desk: The MCOL Help Desk at Northampton, which acts as a first line of support.
- CCBC: The old EDI system with which the new MCOL system exchanges information.
- Credit card companies: The financial institutions involved in the credit card payments.
- Liberator: the subcontracted company that takes care of the accounting of MCOL.
- EzGov: the Company that developed the MCOL system.
- DCA: The Department of Constitutional Affairs, which is the host of the service.

The customer connects to the MCOL web server thought the Internet (Internet Explorer, Netscape and Opera). A *Firewall* and an *Intrusion Detection System* have been deployed to enhance the security of the system, and to prevent unwanted activities. The MCOL web server is a single machine that is located at Mitcheldine in the EDS web-hosting centre. The machine runs the UNIX operating system, and more specifically Solaris 8. The FlexFoundation software platform provided by EzGov runs on top of a J2EE Environment, which in turn runs on top of Netscape Enterprise web server software.

The person making a claim is requested to deposit the required fee for starting the claim procedures. The credit card charging facility, part of the

FlexFoundation software, has the capability of taking credit or debit card payments from potential users. In order to acquire authorisation for the transaction, and to give the actual debit order, an interface has been established with an interoperable financial institution.

All the relevant information regarding user accounts, claims, and responses are retrieved and inputted from and to the MCOL database. For security and performance reasons this Oracle database runs on a separate machine. A firewall intercepts communication between the MCOL web server and the MCOL database so that only permitted network activity can be communicated between the two machines. The database's role is to act as the back-end to the MCOL web server, but not to the whole system. The database has a direct both-way write-back to the CCBC system. The role of that interface is multidimensional. Firstly, so that new claims created through the MCOL system can be entered to the CCBC system. Secondly, to get up-to-date information regarding specific claims, and thirdly to make it possible to retrieve information regarding claims that have been initiated by the CCBC and not the MCOL system. This was an enhancement that was implemented during the second phase of the project as described earlier.

The next element within this description of the technical architecture of the system is the CCBC system managed by Northampton Court. The core of the CCBC is the old EDI system, implemented by EDS during the late 1980s. The CCBC can handle claims inputted in three different ways. One is via magnetic tapes; the second is via a dial-up connection, and the third via MCOL. The CCBC system is in essence the central backbone of the entire money claim infrastructure. The CCBC system has a direct interface with the EDS Printing and Posting centre in Washington, County Durham. This is where all the claims, whatever method of input is used, end up for the actual printing and posting of the claim pack to the defendant. Finally, Liberator takes care of the accounting for MCOL charges. These relationships are depicted in Figure 7.3.

User support

The End-User support of MCOL system is organised by introducing three different support lines. The first line of support is run by the Northampton help-desk, which is currently staffed by four people. The Northampton help-desk deals directly with the vast majority of customer issues and problems. If the problem or query is already known and the solution resides in the knowledge base of the support system the Northampton staff will communicate the solution to the customer. However, if the problem seems to

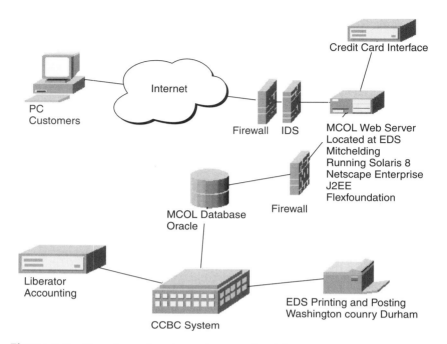

Figure 7.3   Mapping actors to systems and architectures

be persistent and has not yet been documented, the Northampton staff will pass it over to EDS.

EDS is in charge of supporting the CCBC System as well as the MCOL Web server and database. When Northampton contacts EDS regarding a problem, EDS analysts and technicians try to provide the solution. If the problem relates to the operations of the CCBC system, the Printing and Posting system, the Web Server or network connections, then it falls within the scope of the EDS contract and it is accordingly dealt with by EDS, without requesting any help from EzGov. However, if the problem is found to relate to the technical architecture of FlexFoundation, and the EzGov's software, then EDS will address the issue jointly with EzGov.

Issuing and defending money claims – the process in detail

Issuing claims

In order to issue a claim in the judicial system of England and Wales, the key information required is contact details of the defendant and a description of the claim details – which if necessary must be supported by evidence in front of a judge. It is possible to issue different kinds of claims, such as payment of money, return of goods or their value, an order to prevent a person performing an act, damages for personal injuries or housing disrepair (Court Service, 2004). As indicated, MCOL enables claims to be made for a fixed amount of money. These are the only kind of claims that can be dealt with online. Once the claimants have sent the claim form to the court they have to wait for the defendant's response. Depending on this outcome, they can go on to request a judgement order, asking for its enforcement.

Issuing a money claim offline

In the traditional paper-based system, the first step for the claimant is to fill in the form N1. This requires the claimant to state the local county court where the claim will be issued. The defendant's name and residential address in England and Wales are also required. Under the particulars of the claim, the claimant has to state the details and nature of the claim. Finally the claimant needs to give an address for receiving documents, sign a statement of truth and pay the fee of £70 for the claim. This fee covers the entire process, from issuing a claim to requesting a judgement order. When the case ends in a defence (court hearing), there are other court fees, depending on the amount of the claim.

Once delivered in a local county court, a court officer will then issue the claim, give it a case number and prepare the claim pack. The claim and the claim pack are then served to the defendant by first class post. The claim pack comprises the following forms: an acknowledgement of service form, a defence and an admission (forms N9B and N9A).

If the claim pack cannot be served, the Post Office will return it to the court office, and the claim's status will become *not-served*, preventing the claimant from entering judgement. The county court will then send the pack to the claimant for the claimant to attempt service. Once the claimant has served the defendant, s/he must send a certificate of service to the court, and the status will be changed to *served* and updated in the case of the defendant's address having changed.

Issuing a money claim online

The process of issuing a claim online is in its basic structure the same as the offline process in a local county court. There are though certain legal limitations. In the paper-based system it is possible to issue a claim in the High Court, or against individuals under 18 years old, patients conforming with the Mental Health Act or an overseas company. It is also possible to issue a claim for a variable amount of money. These options are not available online, and there are other minor changes like the substitution of the signature by a statement of truth to certify the validity of the information.[1] There are two ways of issuing a claim online, through the CCBC and through MCOL.

As already indicated, CCBC is used for bulk claimants, such as mail-order companies, utilities and credit-card issuers. These send their claims, judgement requests or warrant requests directly to the Northampton offices by tape inputs or by phone. The digital format of these documents must comply with strict requirements in order to be processed by the CCBC system. Bulk claimants have a reduced fee of £63 for issuing a claim.

MCOL is open to any citizen and business although there are certain restrictions on using it.[2] The claimant has to fill out the form online, and once submitted, will receive immediate confirmation of the claim number and have access to check the claim and its status at any moment. Once submitted, claim modifications are not allowed. In contrast to the postal method, in MCOL the users must be registered in order to submit a claim, and for that purpose, personal information as well as credit/debit card details are needed.[3]

The cost of issuing a claim through MCOL is £70, the same as for the traditional method, but the only way of payment is through credit/debit card. It is not possible to request a fee remission or exemption.

Processing the claim online

Once issued, CCBC and MCOL claims are processed the same way by the Northampton Bulk Centre and are issued in the name of Northampton County Court. Once in the Northampton offices, the electronic files of the claims received from MCOL are electronically loaded to the CCBC system (the validation rules for CCBC and MCOL claims are the same, so no modifications are needed). Together, MCOL and CCBC claims are sent to EDS, which will then process all the claims of the day. Thus, the claims will have that day as the 'date of issue'. EDS will then send electronically the day's print file to their Printing and Posting centre in Washington, County Durham.

EDS must print the claims and prepare the claim pack. Under the terms of their contract, they have to post the claim pack to the defendants in no more than 48 hours. So, in the worst-case scenario, the claim is issued on day one, posted on day three by first class post and it is served on day five. This information is sent to the MCOL server and updated every

15 minutes, so the users can know the exact state of the process. Generally, claims submitted and received before 9.00am on a day when the court is open will be processed that day. Where a claim is received after 9.00am it will be processed on the next day that the court is open. The claim will usually be printed and posted to the defendant on the day it is processed.

The claims are not checked at all during the process and nobody signs the claims once received, but that also applies in the case of a local court. In the same way, it is not required for the defendant to sign when the claim is received, it is simply delivered to the address and there is no proof that the right person has received the claim.

The defendant's response

Whenever a claim has been issued electronically in the name of Northampton County Court, it is possible to respond to the court using MCOL. The defendant is already registered in MCOL and can use his/her name and a password, which is on the front of the claim form, to log in and see the details of the claim and the potential courses of action.

The defendant has many possible responses, which range from ignoring the claim to accepting it or defending it. In any case, the defendant has 14 days to respond to the claim. In the case of the paper-based system this 14-day period begins when the defendant is served with the claim pack or with the 'particulars of the claim' – if this is sent separately from the claim pack. In the case of MCOL the 14-day period begins from the date of service – five days from the date the claim is issued. The possible responses include:

- pay the claim in full,
- make a full admission,
- make a part admission,
- file an acknowledgement of service,
- defend the claim/make a counterclaim,
- ignore the claim.

All the responses are free of fees with the exception of a counterclaim. For paying the claim in full or making a full admission the defendant must contact the claimant directly. The part admissions, acknowledgements of service or defences are sent to the bulk centre at Northampton and can be done through MCOL or postal/paper. So, in each step there is the option to go offline and deal with the case in the traditional way.

Paying the claim in full

When the defendant decides to pay the claim in full, including the court fees, s/he must send or make the payment directly to the claimant. The claimant must then inform MCOL, either by e-mail, telephone, fax or post, that the claim has been paid in full. The claimant should also send a receipt or acknowledgement for the money to the defendant.

If the defendant pays in full within 14 days, s/he is not required to contact the court or complete any of the forms. In this situation, the interaction is between the claimant and the defendant and there is no involvement of the court or MCOL.

Making a full admission

Making a full admission refers to the case in which the defendant admits the claim but requests time to pay or some other schedule of payment. In this case, the defendant will complete the admission form N9A and send it directly to the claimant. The claimant has then to decide whether or not to accept the proposal of payment. If the claimant accepts the new proposal, s/he can use MCOL to enter a judgement by admission with respect to the terms offered. If the proposal is rejected, the claimant has to communicate on paper his/her decision and send a copy of the N9A form to the Northampton Bulk Centre. In this case, MCOL will determine how the defendant should pay.

Generally, if the difference between the defendant's outgoings and income is a positive amount, MCOL will make the decision – this is called judgement by determination. But if it is a negative amount, MCOL cannot do this and has to send it to a district judge at Northampton for them to make the decision. This decision is sent to both the defendant and the claimant and if either of them objects to it, MCOL will transfer the claim within 14 days to a district judge for a hearing.

In the case of the defendant admitting the claim but failing to make any offer of repayment, the claimant is entitled to enter judgment against the defendant by default. MCOL will enable this function in the system once the request and the form N9A have been received.

Making a part admission

A part admission is when the defendant agrees that money is owed, but less than is being claimed. The part admission has to be sent to the court, which will send a copy to the claimant. The defendant can make a part admission by completing the forms N9A and N9B or online through MCOL.

MCOL will notify the claimant of the part admission. If the claimant accepts the part admission s/he can enter a judgement by admission through MCOL. If it is not accepted, the case will proceed as a defended claim and will no longer be handled by MCOL.

The claimant has 14 days to contact MCOL if they want to proceed with the original claim (that is rejecting the part admission). If they don't respond in time, they will have to make an application to continue with the claim.

Acknowledgment of service

If the defendant needs longer than 14 days to respond to the claim, s/he can file an acknowledgement of service to extend the total time for filing a response to 28 days from the date of service. The acknowledgement of service has to be sent to the court and can also be used to contest the court's jurisdiction. In the case where the defendant is issuing an acknowledgement of service to contest MCOL's jurisdiction, geographical location cannot be considered as grounds.

The defendant can file an acknowledgement of service using MCOL or by filling out the form in the claim pack. Once an acknowledgement of service has been entered, the MCOL server will be updated, giving the defendant 14 more days to respond. The system will not allow the defendant to enter more than one acknowledgement of service and it is not possible to enter an acknowledgement of service after 28 days have passed, which is the maximum number of days allowed for a response. The system will also prevent the claimant from entering judgement by default after the 28-day limit.

Defending the claim – making a counterclaim

When the defendant wants to dispute the full amount of the claim, s/he has to complete a defence. The defence should be sent to the court and should indicate which allegations in the claim are denied; otherwise it will be considered as an admission.

A counterclaim involves a more complex response and implies that the defendant will produce a claim against the claimant. It is possible to make a counterclaim only if the defendant is filing a defence to all or part of the claim. A counterclaim is also sent to the court and is subject to an additional fee.

To make a defence or a counterclaim the defendant has to complete form N9B or use MCOL. In this case, MCOL will no longer handle the process and will send it to the appropriate county court. The court where the case goes depends on the status of the defendant. If the defendant is an individual, the case will be transferred to the defendant's home court. Where the defendant is not an individual but a formal organisation the case will be transferred to the claimant's (or representative's) home court. MCOL will notify the claimant and defendant of the name and address of the court to which the case has been transferred.

Processing the response

When defendants submit online a part admission, a defence or an acknowledgement of service, they receive a time stamp indicating the date and time when the document was accepted. The status of the new process is actualised and the electronic document sits on the MCOL server. This information is emptied twice a day. The first time is at 9.00am when EDS prints the defences, part admissions or acknowledgements of service of the day and then sends them to the MCOL office. The staff of MCOL receive those requests on paper and enter them in the CCBC system, as well as the part admissions, defences or acknowledgements of service received by post (when the defendant decides not to use MCOL). The other time of the day is 4.00pm, when county courts close in England and Wales, and the deadline for delivering a part admission, a defence or an acknowledgement of service counts from that day. MCOL staff have to enter these requests to the CCBC system that day.

In the case of a defence, MCOL transfers the case to the appropriate court, creates a paper file with the printed documents for the county court, and also sends the data electronically to that county court.

In the case of a part admission, the paper documents are posted to the claimant. The rest of the proceedings are the same as for a defence, except for the 14 day time limit for the claimant's response.

In the case of an acknowledgement of service, the status of the process in the server is actualised, preventing the claimant from entering a judgement by default after 28 days.

If the defendant has not responded within the 14 days (or 28 days in the case that an acknowledgement of service has been entered) the claimant will have the option to request a judgment by default. The option of judgement by default will appear automatically on MCOL after the 14/28 days, but the defendant, once again, has the option to go offline and request it by post.

Entering a judgment order

A judgment order is a decision of the court regarding the outcome of the claim. It will set the terms of the payment decided by the court. There are judgements by admission and judgements by default. The difference between the two is that the latter is on terms specified by the claimant. In this case, the claimant can decide whether s/he wants the defendant to pay by instalments or in one lump sum.

The details of the judgment order will be entered onto the Register of County Court Judgments. Entries usually stay on the Register for six years. Organisations such as banks, building societies and credit companies use the information on the Register when someone applies for credit. Entries on the Register can only be removed by the court and only in very limited circumstances.

Processing a judgement order

In a full or part admission, the claimant can access MCOL at any time and request a judgement by admission, providing the necessary information. MCOL will only allow a judgement by default if the defendant has failed to respond within the 14/28-day limit. In the case of the claimant not entering judgement, the defendant still has time to respond.

When the claimant has requested a judgement, it is sent to the MCOL server. Once again, at 9.00am the judgement requests are sent electronically to the MCOL office. The MCOL judgments and the CCBC judgements are then passed electronically to EDS. EDS then uploads them into the CCBC database that day, but they will not be processed until after 6.00pm. It is an overnight-automated routine, which ensures that if a defence is received on that day prior to 4.00pm, it will take priority over the judgement request.

Thus, during the overnight routine, the system will enter the judgement by default or by admission to the correct case in the terms specified. Once again there is no one checking or verifying the data, and there is no judge making a decision, much like in a local county court. The judgement is entered that night but with the earlier day's date and the new status is updated in the MCOL server. EDS then prints the judgement and posts it to the defendant; the claimant does not receive a copy. At the same time an electronic file goes to the Register of County Court Judgments. In the event that the defendant wants to set the judgement aside, s/he can contact MCOL, but there is no online tool for that service.

If judgement has been entered and the full amount has been paid within a calendar month of the date of entry of judgement, it will be deleted from the Register of County Court Judgments. If it is paid after a month has expired, it will be marked 'satisfied' but it will remain in the Register of County Court Judgments for six years.

Enforcing the judgement order-warrant of execution

There are various types of enforcement methods available to the claimants, such as direct deductions from earnings or the use of bailiffs to seize goods. An enforcement order can be requested if the defendant fails to make payments under the terms of their judgment order (this applies whether the judgment is obtained by default or by admission). In the case of a judgment by default with immediate payment, an enforcement order can be requested immediately.

Processing a warrant of execution

The only method of enforcement available through MCOL is a warrant of execution. Once the claimant has requested a warrant of execution through MCOL and paid the fee, the data goes to the MCOL sever. The server uses a postcode system to identify the county court to which the warrant should be sent. The following morning it is sent to MCOL offices and together with the CCBC warrant requests it is sent electronically to EDS.

Like judgements, the warrant requests are loaded into the CCBC system but not processed until 6.00pm that day. The system will then check that the judgement was entered and update the status in the server. The next morning, the appropriate local county court will electronically import the warrants, confirm the address, accept, print and sign them. The warrants will still be titled in the name of Northampton County Court but the local court will have authority over them.

Analysis and conclusions

The analysis of MCOL and the circumstances under which the service was initially conceived and subsequently developed and implemented suggests a number of interesting findings. *Firstly*, MCOL has emerged out of a system of antecedent technologies and institutional initiatives that formed the necessary, as it were, conditions for the development and setting up of the service. *Secondly*, MCOL was developed against a background of procedural and administrative simplification which shaped the functionalities of the service to a large extent and combined with the installed base to determine the pattern of its implementation. *Thirdly*, MCOL has been essentially supported by an elaborate system of offline arrangements that supplements what can be done through the online service, acting at the same time as a mechanism for offloading complexity onto the traditional system and as a buffer to the reintroduction of complexities into MCOL.

Path dependence and the installed base

As indicated earlier, MCOL has been developed out of a complex web of broader initiatives that sought to increase the provision of online services in justice, overcome their fragmentation and facilitate their execution. These goals were furthermore supported by an even wider governmental initiative for a large, open and interoperable public ICT-based infrastructure that conformed to Internet standards. Governmental support of this sort is often crucial to the outcomes sought by many public institutions and organisations and this holds true for the justice system as well. The governmental quest for the renewal of the public sector in general and justice in particular combined with the spectacular growth of the Internet to establish a discourse (see, for example Civil Justice, 2000; Susskind, 2000; Timms, Plotnikoff and Woolfson, 2003) in which ICT figured as an important vehicle of modernisation. Indeed, MCOL was identified as a possible service against the background of that discourse.

Visions, no doubt, are important guiding principles in laying out roadmaps to the future. Yet, technology-based services like MCOL develop out of the possibilities established by the joint and cumulative game of antecedent technological choices and commitments, hence the notion of path dependence. Prior technological choices can largely determine what can be done at any particular period of time (Ciborra, 2000). The story line of MCOL compiled out of the data collected here suggests that the development of the online service has been heavily influenced by the underlying infrastructure, which MCOL both accommodated and, in some sense, expanded. The EDI infrastructure of the CCBC that was in place for dealing with bulk claims constituted perhaps the most important antecedent to MCOL. The technological options offered by that infrastructure combined with the rapid diffusion of web-based systems and the Internet to enable first the very identification of an interactive (e-filing) service and then its development and implementation.

In other words, crucial elements of the 'mechanics' of the whole process were in place long before the advent of MCOL. By making relatively small adjustments to some parts of that infrastructure, and specifically to the CCBC system, it was possible to add the MCOL service on top of it, expanding and transforming the network in ways that admitted online interaction with citizens. In that process the accommodation of Internet standards, ranging from XML to web browsers, was essential to ensure the viability and openness of the service, while at the same time responding to the government's quest for interoperable services. The same could be said to hold largely true for the organisational and institutional arrangements that were in place to support the processing and settlement of bulk claims. These involved, among other things, the Northampton Court and its administration with the overall responsibility for managing multiple claims submitted electronically, the EDI system and the contract with the EDS and the accounting system for managing the related transactions (see also Lanzara, Chapter 1). Relatively small administrative changes, that is a team and support desk, were necessary to help the existing organisational arrangements to cope with the various tasks that are associated with the smooth functioning of MCOL.

Against the backdrop of these observations, MCOL looks, to a large degree, like an *assembly or collage produced out of the 'ready-mades' of other systems* (Kallinikos, 2006). A significant part of these technological 'ready-mades' were already in place and formed the installed base that accommodated the new service. They combined with the existing organisational and administrative arrangements, governmental policies and the diffusion of the Internet to define the new service. It is true that the service was conceived and developed by the DCA through a process of requirements elicitation and prototype testing. Yet, most of the programming elements or modules that were necessary for transacting with citizens (for example the payment engine, the flex foundation libraries) were brought in from the market and adapted accordingly. In the larger scheme of things, these 'ready-mades' (that is the CCBC, EzGov, government policies on Internet standards, administrative procedures in place) conditioned the very functionality and usability of the service and the ways it was conceived and implemented (see Figure 7.3 and Lanzara in this volume).

Information infrastructures then lay out a system of conditions in which the exercise of choice emerges as a complex navigation among a variety of constraints and possibilities. MCOL was first conceived and identified against the background of possibilities circumscribed by the previous use of ICT-based systems for dealing with multiple money claims and the diffusion of online services coinciding with the increasing economic and organisational involvement of the Internet. By the same token, the development of MCOL had to be made compatible backwards and sideways (Bowker and Star, 1999; Hanseth, 2000, 2004) and accommodate existing technological and administrative structures and established procedures. The empirical data suggests that development of MCOL had to accommodate a polyvalent system of constraints ranging from technical ones (for example CCBC database, the payment engine available to EzGov at the time the service was developed) to governmental policies, civil justice procedures and administrative structures and practices.

Technology as functional simplification

The heavily institutionalised status of judicial practices has often been invoked as an explanatory factor for the low and hesitant ICT involvement in justice (Contini and Fabri, 2003). The code-based regulation of judicial practices and the meticulous rules and procedures they give rise to combine with a strong paper-based and oral culture (for example oral testimonies, court hearings) to make ICT involvement in justice a subtle and intricate venture. Such institutional complexity is further aggravated by the technological conservatism of judges and the legal profession in general (Susskind, 2000; Lanzara and Patriotta, 2001) as well as the procedural and organisational differentiation, often bordering on fragmentation, of the justice system.

The analysis of the case of MCOL suggests an interesting response to the institutional, organisational and procedural complexity that commonly underlies the various domains and jurisdictions of the justice system. At first glance, the multiple character of money claims and the prior existence of CCBC would seem to have played a decisive role in identifying money claims as one possible domain for technological mediation. A closer examination of the functionality of the service nevertheless suggests that the identification and subsequent development of MCOL was crucially shaped by the *judicial and procedural simplicity* of the overwhelming majority of money claims.

Of crucial importance for the *identification* of money claims as a target online service has been the fact that money claims involve straightforward procedures, the large majority of which (up to 95 per cent) are settled without a court hearing. Dealing with money claims had therefore been an object of substantial administrative rationalisation, long before an online service was feasible. The relative simplicity of the established judicial procedures thus combined with the prior administrative streamlining and handling of money claims to make the latter a possible and feasible object of technological mediation. Judicial simplicity and administrative streamlining furthermore formed essential prerequisites for the subsequent *development, implementation* and *gradual diffusion* of MCOL. Online services have to be straightforward and easy to use if they are to have a chance of success, and the domain of money claims clearly conformed to that goal (Timms, Plotnikoff and Woolfson, 2003).

Therefore, the administrative and procedural simplification of the tasks associated with the management of money claims has been crucial to the development and establishment of MCOL. Functional simplification captures the very essence of the service and indicates that the development and successful implementation of technologies crucially depend on the procedural and administrative streamlining of the tasks which these technologies are called upon to regulate (Contini and Fabri, 2003). The spectacular functional abilities of ICT-based systems and artefacts (that is huge processing capacities, transfer and storage of data) very often obscure this essential prerequisite of all successful technological applications, that is, the fact that they presuppose and work successfully in relatively simplified functional environments (Luhmann, 1993, 1995). It is worth stressing that functional simplification does not refer to the simplicity of the technological medium, which in itself can be very complex. It rather indicates that the reduction of the task complexity (procedural, organisational and institutional) within which a particular technology operates is crucial to its successful development and diffusion.

To some degree, the concept of functional simplification seems identical or similar to that of technical standardisation. Standardisation operates, I would say, at a more elementary level than the concept of functional simplification, even though technical standardisation is never purely a technical process (Bowker and Starr, 1999; Hanseth, 2004). The introduction of technical standards responds to the call for interoperability; yet, it inevitably implies a substantial reduction of diversity across settings entailing the negotiation of the social and institutional order within which standardisation takes place (Galison, 1997). In this sense, technical standardisation could be seen as just one specific expression of the wider principle of functional simplification (Luhmann, 1993; Kallinikos, 2005, 2006) upon which all technological regulation is inescapably predicated.

Functional simplification in complex social systems often takes the form of lifting a technological system out of the surrounding institutional and organisational complexity to allow the reconstruction of simplified causal or procedural sequences. Thus simplified, these processes are rendered controllable and thus manageable in relatively smooth and often efficient ways. An essential prerequisite of smooth technological regulation is the decoupling of the operations of the technological system from the wider institutional and social complexity into which it is embedded. When the interaction of the two systems cannot be avoided, then it must be so designed as to take place along controlled pathways (that is a strictly regulated interface between the two systems) that ensure the friction-free functioning of the technological system. Alternatively, accruing and unforeseeable complexity has to be able to be offloaded from the technology back to the institutional system, which can then handle it in traditional ways (Kallinikos, 2006).

Functional simplification has been expressed in the case of MCOL in a variety of ways. Here is a summary of some of these ways:

- As already suggested, the identification of money claims as a possible online service was made on the basis of the simple and straightforward character of money claims. They had already been the object of significant administrative streamlining and rationalisation.
- A number of additional and crucial simplifications were introduced. Variable or unspecified money claims were thought to involve a rather complex set of tasks and their online treatment was thus ruled out. Unspecified money claims often include medical or expert documentation (for example accidents) that lead to complex litigation procedures.
- Some variability associated with local court responses to various money claim issues was discarded and standard responses were built as a way to proceed to technical coding.
- On another plane, a set of legal limitations summarised in *Appendix 1,* were introduced to further simplify the legal-judicial character of the procedures associated with money claims over the Internet.
- Payment modes through credit cards also represent a simplification of the variety of ways fees can be paid in traditional settings.
- The most important form, though, which functional and procedural simplification has taken in the case of MCOL is captured *by the omnipresent possibility of offloading complexity onto the traditional system.* Throughout the process of money claims, a variety of tasks that appear somewhat intricate in functional or juridical terms (for example posting the claims to the defendant, negotiating another payment scheme, asking for additional time, paying the claimant, and so on) are passed onto the offline system, which handles them in the traditional way.
- For legal reasons, MCOL falls under the jurisdiction of the local court of Northampton.

An interesting scenario emerges with respect to the patterns of technological developments in the various domains of contemporary life, in which already established domain-specific modes of conduct are subjected to heavy technological mediation. Overall, the processes described here, with reference to the construct of functional simplification, suggest that online services do not represent a one-to-one mapping of traditional, paper-based processes. Such developments may indeed have far-reaching implications in the medium and long run. What is appearing online is a transformed, indeed lean, version of offline tasks and procedures that are cleansed of cumbersome detours, procedural complexity and decision ambiguity. The cumulative effects of these processes over larger time spans is difficult to predict but it can be conjectured that those parts or procedures of the over-all system that are straightforward or simple may have a greater chance of going online.

This is an interesting observation that recalls some of the premises of technological transcription already recorded in the literature, though in quite different terminology (Zuboff, 1988; Sotto, 1990; Ciborra and Lanzara, 1994). And, accumulated over time, the selection of transac-tional sequences that are simple but perhaps not central in the traditional, offline handling of cases may thus be moved onto the online system. An outcome of this could well be that those complex and recalcitrant, but perhaps essential, offline processes that define a traditional system will fall increasingly out of the jurisdiction of the online arrangements. Accordingly, the development of online arrangements drifts along in a dir-ection that becomes inscribed by the logic of tractability and functional simplification. Overrepresentation of what is possible to be managed may thus become an essential premise of technological objectification. This could in the long run lead to the drift (Ciborra, 2000) towards new, and under particular circumstances distorted, ways of managing the tasks and procedures underlying those domains that are subjected to heavy techno-logical mediation (Mumford, 1952; Kallinikos, 1995). In similar cases, the practices of the old oral and paper-based system and the elaborate network of values which sustain its substantive rationality combat with simplicity and the efficient handling which technological applications seem to enable and promote.

These observations also suggest that the logic of inscription as a form of embodying intentionality (for example Actor Network Theory [ANT]) tends to overlook the premises on which inscription is based (Kallinikos, 1995, 2006). What is inscribed onto and regulated (or delegated) by the technological system is not the offline system in its entirety (money claims in this case) but a lean version of it, simplified along a number of ways. Inscription (as distinct from material embodment) has itself a logic that is driven by the very constitution of the inscribing system (here the algo-rithms and techniques underlying particular software programs) that has been used to produce the various elements of MCOL. Simplicity-based selectivity becomes an additional key premise of inscription. To be sure, simplification is a contested arena that is negotiated by particular actors under particular regimes of power/knowledge, established practices and ways of perceiving and acting upon the world (Galison, 1997). We suggest though, and MCOL presents evidence of it, that the *logic of feasibility and simplification defines an important part of the agenda of negotiations.* Or to put it differently, negotiating reality in similar cases occurs against the background of the widely shared, albeit often tacit, goal of techno-logical objectification and the functional simplification (standardisation) this implies.

Technology is not however a static domain. The forms though which the tasks of particular domains are simplified to accommodate the logic of technological regulation change over time. Placed in such a perspec-tive, technologies and technological applications tend to gradually become more complex, in the sense of being able to accommodate a greater portion of the complexity of those tasks and procedures that they are called upon to regulate. Complexity can thus be reintroduced into the technological system in successive and piecemeal ways that reflect the maturation of a particular technology over time. Nevertheless, such a reintroduction often conforms to the basic logic underlying the function of technology. For instance, in the initial launch MCOL handled only claimants' requests. The defendant's capacity to respond was added later and additional future functionalities may raise the complexity of the service and enlarge the scope of tasks that can be accomplished by relying on the online service. Nothing precludes the gradual re-introduction of complexity but it is cru-cial to understand that such a reintroduction is premised on the very logic (a logic of simplification) upon which the initial online service is predi-cated. Expansion is often introduced in a piecemeal fashion and only after the steps and services concerned have been simplified and streamlined.

A telling example that lends support to the logic of simplification is rep-resented by a new service, which the Department of Constitutional Affairs is contemplating introducing now after the success of MCOL. This ser-vice concerns *Possession Claims Online.* Possession claims are inherently more complex and the procedures for resolving disputes of this sort may involve complex documentation, court hearings and litigation. However, the objective is to develop and use a system capable of dealing with the simpler possession claims. Key actors estimate that even in this judicially more complex field, the majority of cases are relatively straightforward with no complex documentation involved. They could thus be handled by an online service. Complex cases can always be taken offline and resolved accordingly. This could raise significantly the level of service provided by the courts, and at the same time it could reduce documentation costs sub-stantially. The next section considers the complex imbrications and mutual support of online and offline processes.

The observations advanced so far suggest that functional simplification by no means implies that complex tasks will invariably remain outside the regulative aspirations of technology. It does imply, though, that complex tasks will not normally be among the first to be identified as possible objects of technological regulation. As particular technologies mature in terms of expanding functionality they may become involved in the orchestration of increasingly complex tasks (Contini and Fabri, 2003). In the case of justice, ICT was originally used as a means of administrative rationalisation, all the way from databases through case management systems and litigation support. The expanding diffusion of the Internet and web-based systems increasingly makes online transactional services (not just information-based services) both possible and attractive. The further maturation of multimedia technologies makes even the prospect of 'electronic courts' and 'cyber-trials' possible. Vast countries like Australia, in which they are in use, may have considerable gains by using them (Leeuwenburg and Wallace, 2002).[4] These developments cannot be ignored. However, the theory of functional simplification 'predicts' that the expanding functionality of technology will be matched by a corresponding simplification of the tasks and procedures, which will come to be mediated or regulated by technology. Placed in a larger timescale, the exact outcome of these developments and trade-offs may be hard to predict. History suggests though that some institutional simplification will be inevitable (Mumford, 1934, 1952, 1970).

The interlocking of offline and online processes

As already indicated, the most crucial premise of functional and procedural simplification in the case of MCOL is what, at closer scrutiny, emerges as a substantial reliance on the traditional paper-based process. Section 4 suggests that a significant set of procedures must often take an offline route (for example the defendant fully admitting the claim but asking for new terms of payment, or payment arrangements) or that the claimant or the defendant opt at some point to go offline. In other words the online service is predicated on the ever-present option of offloading the dispute onto the traditional paper-based system. Let us consider this argument in some detail.

At one level, the two systems could be said to run parallel to one another. Yet, at every step of the process it is possible to take an offline route. The opposite does not hold true. It is not possible to go online in the middle of an offline process. Since the inception of the service, claimants have had the option to choose between the two services, that is issuing a claim through the traditional post system in the local county court or through MCOL, in the name of Northampton County Court. Once a claim has been issued using MCOL it is possible to go back to an offline process; however, this offline process differs somewhat from the traditional one, because it is not handled in a local county court but by the MCOL staff in the Northampton Court.

As indicated, the offline service covers a broader spectrum of functions than MCOL. Features like changing the details of the claim or requesting the removal of a judgement order are only available through the offline process. In this sense, everything that it is not possible to do online has an offline option. The rationale behind this is to use the online system for the simple cases, leaving more complicated cases to be handled though the traditional, paper-based procedures. Or to put it more strongly and in line with what we claimed in the preceding section, the online service cannot function efficiently, unless it is kept clear from procedural detours and other types of administrative and judicial ambiguity. Thus the offline system runs sometimes in parallel and at other times overlaps with MCOL. For example, if a claim is issued online and the defendant decides to defend the case by post (instead of using MCOL) the systems will be overlapping. If the claimant asks to change the details of the claim, s/he will have to use the offline route. In this case the two systems run in parallel. In other cases the offline system acts as a buffer. Whenever the online processes involve deviations that cannot be handled by the existing functionalities of the MCOL, the process is taken offline.

But MCOL is supported by offline steps in a more straightforward fashion that brings to mind Woolgar's *third* and *fourth rule of virtuality* positing that 'virtual technologies supplement rather than substitute for real activities', leading to the counter-intuitive conclusion of the more virtual the more real (Woolgar, 2002, p. 16–19). For instance, MCOL cannot work without the correct address of the defendant, the printing and physical posting of the claims entered into the online system, the acknowledgement of service and paper receipt of payments. The same holds true for the offline service but online services often cultivate the illusion of purely electronic, non-physical processes and this overstatement must be rectified. Overall, the parallel running of the two systems, the overlaps and the essential dependence of MCOL on offline arrangements suggest a complex interlocking of offline and online processes that warrant further examination. It is also important to point out that the imbrications of the virtual with the real, and the online with the offline in this case are amply demonstrated by the ultimate anchoring of MCOL in the Northampton Court. The virtual 'everywhere' or 'nowhere' need and implicate the 'somewhere'.

There are though a series of other less visible yet highly relevant cultural characteristics that support MCOL. Crucial among them seems to be the level of trust present in British society, which has a direct bearing on what is often conceived as the straightforward simplicity of money claims. Money claims can always become a complex issue and may end in a court hearing if the parties so choose. We suggest that immediate or quasi-immediate acceptance of money claims by defendants either presupposes a high level of social trust or some sort of compliance to the legitimate order. Indeed, without this crucial presupposition, money claims might have been a significantly less straightforward enterprise and MCOL perhaps less successful. These implicit cultural requirements have to be seriously contemplated when the notion of transferring MCOL to Mediterranean Europe is considered. There are other institutional and cultural factors (from the reliability of the postal service to the simplicity of court procedures in England and Wales) that have to enter the picture when MCOL is evaluated from an international perspective. Cultural and institutional arrangements thus play a crucial role in sustaining online services. The pervasive character of these arrangements, however, makes them easy to overlook.

Appendix 1

Who can use MCOL

MCOL can be used by individuals, solicitors, government departments; or businesses if they are:

1. issuing a claim for a fixed amount of money;
2. and where the claim has been issued online they can also:
3. enter the judgment;
4. apply for a warrant of execution.

It is not possible to use MCOL if the user is:

- a child (a person under 18 years of age);
- a patient as described in the Mental Health Act 1983;
- a legally assisted person within the meaning of the Legal Aid Act;
- a vexatious litigant (a person who has been forbidden by a high court judge to issue proceedings in any county court in England and Wales without permission).

It is not possible to issue a claim using MCOL against:

- a child or patient;
- the Crown, including Ministers of the Crown in their official capacities and government departments.

Other conditions:

- the claim must be for a fixed amount of money which is less than £100,000;
- the claim is against no more than two people;
- the address of the person(s) is within England and Wales; and
- the user needs to have a valid credit or debit card.

Information needed for MCOL

Before starting a claim the following information is needed:

- the full name and address of the defendant(s);
- the exact amount of the claim including any contractual or statutory interest;
- particulars of the claim – for example: dates, details of goods or services provided, events, invoice numbers;
- credit/debit card details – that is card number, card type, expiry date, cardholders name; and
- an e-mail address.

The particulars of the claim must be stated in no more than 1,080 characters (including spaces and punctuation): this is a technical limitation within the system.

Statement of truth

A statement of truth normally has to be signed by the person providing the information on the claim or defence form. In order to sign a statement of truth on MCOL, the user has to type in his/her name and, where appropriate, the position or office held if signing on behalf of a company or firm.

By completing a statement of truth, the user certifies that the information provided is true. A person who completes a statement of truth without an honest belief in the truth of the given information is liable to be subject to proceedings for contempt of court.

Notes

1. See Appendix 1 for more details on 'statement of truth'.
2. See Appendix 1 for the list of restrictions on using MCOL.
3. See Appendix 1 for more details on the requirements for using MCOL.
4. Elements of electronic courts such as electronic systems to display evidence, information screens outside each courtroom and information kiosks for court information have been introduced in Britain too. See UK Court Service (2001), 'First Hi-Tech Crown Court Unveiled Today', http://www.courtservice.gov.uk/notices/crown/kingdemo_press.htm; visited 6 February 2006.

References

Bowker, G. and S.L. Star (1999), *Sorting Things Out: Classification and Its Consequences*. Cambridge, MA: The MIT Press.

Ciborra, C. (2000) (ed.), *From Control to Drift: The Dynamics of Corporate Information Infrastructures*. Oxford: Oxford University Press.

Ciborra, C. and G.F. Lanzara (1994), 'Formative Contexts and Information Technology'. *Accounting, Management and Information Technologies*, 4, 611–626.

Civil Justice (2000), 'A Vision of the Civil Justice System in the Information Age'. *Civil.Justice.2000*. Retrieved from www.dca.gov.uk/cj2000/cj2000fr.htm. Visited 6 February 2006.

Contini, F. and M. Fabri (2003), 'Judicial Electronic Data Interchange in Europe'. In Fabri, M. and F. Contini (eds), *Judicial Electronic Data Interchange in Europe: Applications, Policies and Trends*. Bologna: Lo Scarabeo.

Court Service (1998), *Modernising the Civil Courts, Modernising Justice*. White Paper Cm 4155, London.

Court Service (2001), 'First Hi-Tech Crown Court Unveiled Today'. Retrieved from www.courtservice.gov.uk/notices/crown/kingdemo_press.htm; visited 6 February 2006.

Court Service (2004), 'Forms and Guidance'. Retrieved from www.courtservice.gov.uk/cms/forms.htm. Visited 6 February 2006.

EzGov (2003), 'Money Claim Online, the Court Service UK'. *Flex Foundation, EzGov*. Retrieved from www.ezgov.com/pdfs/EMEA_SUCCES_MCOCS.pdf. Visited 6 February 2006.

Fabri, M. and F. Contini (2003) (eds), *Judicial Electronic Data Interchange in Europe: Applications, Policies and Trends*. Bologna: Scarabeo.

Galison, P. (1997), *Image and Logic: Material Culture of Microphysics*. Chicago: The University of Chicago Press.

Hanseth, O. (2000), 'The Economics of Standards'. In Ciborra, C. (ed.), *From Control to Drift: the Dynamics of Corporate Information Infrastructures*. Oxford: Oxford University Press.

Hanseth, O. (2004), 'Knowledge as infrastructure'. In Avgerou, C., Ciborra, C. and F. Land (eds), *The Social Study of Information and Communication Technology*. Oxford: Oxford University Press.

Kallinikos, J. (1995), 'The Architecture of the Invisible: Technology is Representation'. *Organization*, 2 (1), 117–140.

Kallinikos, J. (2005), 'The Order of Technology: Complexity and Control in a Connected World'. *Information and Organization*, 15 (2), 185–202.

Kallinikos, J. (2006), *The Consequences of Information: Institutional Implications of Technological Change*. Cheltenham: Elgar.

Lanzara, G.F. and G. Patriotta (2001), 'Technology and the Courtroom. An Inquiry into Knowledge Making in Organizations'. *Journal of Management Studies*, 38 (7), 943–971.

Leenwenburg, J. and A. Wallace (2002), *Technology for Justice 2002 Report*. Melbourne: The Australian Institute of Judicial Administration.

Luhmann, N. (1993), *The Sociology of Risk*. Berlin: de Gruyter.

Luhmann, N. (1995), *Social Systems*. Stanford, CA: Stanford University Press.

Luhmann, N. (1998), *Observations on Modernity*. Stanford, CA: Stanford University Press.

Mumford, L. (1934), *Technics and Civilization*. London: Harvest/HBJ.

Mumford, L. (1952), *Arts and Technics*. New York: Columbia University Press.

Mumford, L. (1970), *The Myth of the Machine*. Two Volumes. New York: Columbia University Press.

Plotnikoff, J., Woolfson, R. and S. Lyons (2001), 'The Technological Challenge of a Fragmented Justice System: ICT in England and Wales'. In Fabri, M. and F. Contini (eds), *Justice and Technology in Europe: How ICT is Changing the Judicial Business*. Dodrecht: Kluwer Law International.

Sotto, R. (1990), *Man without Knowledge: Actors and Spectators in Organizations*. PhD Thesis, Stockholm: School of Business, Stockholm University.

Susskind, R. (2000), 'Transforming the Law: Essays on Technology, Justice and the Legal Marketplace'. New York: Oxford University Press.

Timms, P., Plotnikoff, J. and R. Woolfson (2003), 'Judicial Electronic Data Interchange in England and Wales'. In Fabri, M. and F. Contini (eds), *Judicial Electronic Data Interchange in Europe: Applications, Policies and Trends.* Bologna: Scarabeo.

Woolgar, S. (2002) (ed.), *Virtual Society? Technology, Hyperbole, Reality.* Oxford: Oxford University Press.

Zuboff, S. (1988), In the Age of the Smart Machine: The Future of Work and Power. New York: Basic Books.

CHAPTER 8

Assemblage-in-the-making: developing the e-services for the justice of the peace office in Italy

Marco Velicogna and Francesco Contini

Introduction

This chapter tells the story of an ICT project that was set up within the context of the Italian judiciary and of the dynamics involved in the implementation of the project. As the description demonstrates, viable solutions adopted during the running of the project could not be determined *ex-ante*. They had to be constructed through the interaction of a multiplicity of actors attempting to shape, assemble and tune technological, normative and organisational elements.

We try to focus on technological development 'in action' in order to emphasise the fact that technology design, or rather the activity of assembling technological and institutional components (Lanzara, Chapter 1), can be better understood through its practice and not as an abstract, disembodied phenomenon (Brown and Duguid, 1991; Lave and Wenger, 1991; Blackler, 1995). The concept of assemblage-in-the-making seems to capture, in a distinctive manner, the dynamics observed in this case. It stresses the idea of 'becoming' while pointing to the controversial, ephemeral, and experimental character of both cognitive and practical activities underlying the creation of the assemblage (Lanzara and Patriotta, 2001, p. 967).

Many case studies have based the reconstruction of innovation processes on the description provided *ex-post* by informants. The problem with these studies is that much of the extemporaneous improvisations, discontinuities, and the apparently random and erratic wanderings that characterise design in action (Lanzara, 1999) are lost in such representations. This is because 'modern organizing [...] takes place in a net of fragmented, multiple contexts, through multitudes of kaleidoscopic movements' (Czarniawska, 2004, p. 786). We are not simply describing a process once it is finished: we are trying to follow its enactment (Weick, 1988).

The position of the authors within the project – as observers and as reflective interventionists (Lanzara, 1999) during four years of activity – allows them to provide a detailed description of the interaction that took place between actors, norms, interests and artefacts. In addition to the data collected from this vantage point, other data were gathered through qualitative interviews and analysis of all the project documentation. Formal and informal interviews with the main actors and selected informants (Platt, 2001, p. 49) were conducted during the project. The interviews allowed the collection of data on the perceptions and grounded opinions of the participants regarding the dynamics involved and the reiterative processes of design, development and practical experimentation that took place during the project.

The project

The purpose of the project was on the one hand to experiment with the potential of e-services for the Italian judiciary in the context of courts with limited jurisdiction. On the other hand, it was an attempt by researchers to study ICT design and adoption processes. An organisation like the judiciary, where such processes have often been characterised by great difficulties resulting from the conflicting interplay between deep and formalistic normative layers and the new technological requirements (Contini, 1999), provided what the researchers thought would be a challenging field for research and experimentation.

The e-services development process was supported by previous knowledge regarding the methodologies to be used to support innovation in a normatively dense institutional environment, as is the Italian judiciary (Fabri and Contini, 2001; Fabri and Contini, 2003). The traditional approach followed by the Italian Ministry of Justice *'based on the assumption that organizations and information systems are distinct entities, which* [in one way or the other] *will adapt to each other'* (Contini and Cordella, 2007, p. 50), has led to unsatisfactory results (Carnevali, Contini, Fabri and Velicogna, 2006, 2007). Instead, the researchers wanted the development of e-services to be based on and to take advantage of the existing technical and institutional installed base supporting the organisation chosen for the experimentation (Hanseth, 1996; Ciborra, 2000). From this perspective, e-services would act as a web-based interface to the already existing information resources of the office.[1] Furthermore, the e-services were conceived as a new channel of communication to be added to the pre-existing ones. Another important aspect to be considered was how to support accessibility for potential users[2] with only basic technological infrastructures such as PCs and slow Internet connections.

One of the challenges at the heart of the project was how to interpret the complex regulative layer in such a way as to avoid building techno-juridical barriers between the judicial office and the users in the exchange of data and documents in judicial proceedings. The aim of this approach was to facilitate the reaching of a critical mass of users as soon as possible. This is considered to be a key step for the healthy growth of an information infrastructure (Hanseth, 2002; Hanseth and Aanestad, 2003).

Another idea was to use the experience of the users of the application to improve its functionalities. The plan was therefore to give the users an initial version of the application as quickly as possible. The rapid introduction of the initial version would enable the in-depth monitoring of its use. The rationale was to gather feedback from the users and to use it for fine-tuning the application and for the development of new and better versions. In this way we put in place a design-in-action strategy (Bødker and Grønbæk, 1992; Lanzara, 1993), an incremental process in which the development of the application is closely related to the observation of its day-by-day use and involves an on-going dialogue with its users.

This approach, rooted in the concept of information infrastructure (Ciborra, 2000), with its evolutionary dynamics and using the concept of cultivation (Dahlbom and Mathiassen, 1993) of the installed base, was not new *per se*. It was nevertheless radically innovative within the judicial context. In such a context, ICT was – and still is – regarded simply as a tool for automation and the development process is still based on old-fashioned structured methodologies (Dennis and Wixom, 2000).

The main actors

Four project partners were involved in the development and practical experimenting of e-services: CESROG, a research centre of the University of Bologna and IRSIG, a research institute of the Italian National Research Council, two publicly funded but independent research units working on the development of practical and theoretical knowledge on the functioning of judiciaries;[3] Cineca, an Interuniversity Consortium for the development and managing of ICT;[4] and DGSIA, the ICT Department of the Italian Ministry of Justice.[5]

The e-services were developed at a Justice Of the Peace office (JOP), a court of limited jurisdiction composed exclusively of 'honorary judges', which deals with a large workload of small claims and settles a wide range of minor disputes using simplified procedures. It is the only court where pro se litigation is allowed[6] and in which the public has direct contact with the justice system without the mediation of a lawyer.[7]

The JOP selected for the project is of medium-large dimensions. Thanks to the skills and the initiative of the Court Administrator, the office had, in previous research studies, shown a record of good efficiency and sound organisation (Contini and Fabri, 2003). These factors influenced the choice of this office.

Prequel

Choosing a beginning for a story can be a very tricky exercise (Czarniawska and Wolff, 1998). We decided to start our story from the initial attempts to analyse the installed base and to develop the first prototype. Nevertheless, some reference must be made to the initial objectives, discussions that took place and choices that were made prior to the assemblage effort but which at the same time created the initial window of opportunity for it.

The objective of the project – the expected result for which funds had been granted – was to develop and *'experiment a web platform capable of supplying a set of electronic services to the users of judicial offices'* (IRSIG–CNR, 2001). Which offices and which services, though, had still to be decided.

In the preliminary meetings held to better define the activities to be carried out within the e-services project, the decision was taken to select a court of limited jurisdiction, the Justice Of the Peace (JOP) for conducting the research. This would reduce security issues, provide an organisation that was eager to participate, as the JOP had up to that moment been neglected by the innovation efforts of the Ministry and at the same time it would allow research to be conducted, but would avoid potential conflicts with other ICT projects within the Ministry of Justice.

As far as the web platform and e-services were concerned, IRSIG-CESROG proposed to experiment with *inCounter*, an open source e-filing system available for free (McMillan and Carlson, 2002). The idea was, as with MCOL and other similar European and US projects, to use simple technologies and simplified procedures in order to experiment the exchange of documents between parties and the court. As the JOP deals with very small claims, the researchers considered it a very low risk environment.

DGSIA, though, made it clear that regulations on the electronic exchange of data and documents already existed and the research project had to observe them. Since the technical implements required by the normative framework were not available at the time, and would have never been made available to the general public, the researchers made several attempts to persuade DGSIA to try the system at least as a research experiment before writing it off. Unfortunately, these attempts were of no use. What could be tried out was simply a system to allow access to court data. As the direction of the project was similarly oriented, the e-services assemblage effort could begin (Table 8.1).

The beginning: assessing the installed base

As the original idea was to develop the e-services building upon the existing technical and institutional installed base, the first logical step was to conduct an assessment of the court office chosen for the experimentation. This assessment was oriented towards studying the organisation with its

Table 8.1 Justice of the peace e-services timetable

Time	Key events
March 2003–October 2003	Installed base assessment
April 2003–November 2003	The official website of the JOP is designed and put online
April 2003–September 2003	The first prototype of e-services is developed (applications: *ContenziosoCivile* and *Rubrica*)
July 2003–December 2004	Problem of the database mirror creation and update
July 2003–January 2004	Problem of the users' access to the database mirror and to the e-services
March 2005	Experimentation start-up meeting
March 2005–April 2005	A new application is developed (*RichiestaCopie*)
April 2005–September 2005	First experimentation phase (*ContenziosoCivile* and *RichiestaCopie*)
April 2005–June 2005	A new application is developed and experimented (*PrimaUdienza*)
June 2005–September 2005	New applications are developed (*InfoByMail*, *CalendarioUdienza* and *ProssimaUdienza*)
January 2006–March 2006	Network breakdown
March 2006–December 2006	Second experimentation phase (*ContenziosoCivile*, *RichiestaCopie*, *PrimaUdienza*, *InfoByMail*, *CalendarioUdienza* and *ProssimaUdienza*)
March 2006–November 2006	Problem of adapting the e-services to the new CMS (SIGP)
December 2006–February 2007	Modification of *ProssimaUdienza* in order to make it available to the general public
April 2008	The e-services are still online

settings and functioning, and also to note users' expectations and evaluations of the office, the technological installed base, and the normative framework. The assessment had three main aims. Firstly, to identify one or more typologies of services that could be provided to court users through the Internet; secondly, to develop knowledge which would allow an evaluation of the utility and feasibility of the various services; and finally to assess potential problems that might arise in the development, implementation and subsequent phases.

The organisation

Even though the project team conducted a detailed study of both formal and informal organisation, norms and practices of the JOP and of its interactions with its users (Lanzara, 2003), here we will only consider those elements that are more relevant for communication exchange and for e-services.

First of all, the case folders and the case management system were considered. The case folder is one of the main coordination mechanisms for court operations. It gathers all the information relevant to the case and keeps track of any events that are pertinent to the case. Furthermore, all the main steps taken in a judicial proceeding have to be tracked in an automated Case Management System (CMS).[8]

Another element is information exchange. Exchange of information, both between JOP personnel and between the JOP and the court users, showed particular complexity from an e-services development perspective. The presence of a variety of highly specific and contextual elements indeed posed more than a small concern (Lanzara, 2003). An example of this specificity is the type of medium in which the information is recorded. To have an authenticated copy of a ruling, the court user needs a photocopy of the original, hand-signed and certified by a court clerk. Other examples are the rules that govern specific operations. To file a case, the filing petition document must be delivered by hand to a court clerk. Another element that increases the complexity in the case of e-services targeted not only at professional users but also at the general public is the gap between everyday language and juridical language and terminology. E-services of this type face the problem of providing an alternative to the instant translation and procedural information constantly provided by court personnel working in the front-office.

Another important factor is the skills of the court personnel and their attitude towards the project and ICT innovation. First of all, the Court Administrator was a supporter of the concept of ICT innovation and organisational change as a way of increasing efficiency and quality of service. As an example of these attitudes and skills, with her support, a technician had created two software applications to allow lawyers, with a user-name and a password but only from public terminals within the office, to consult some of the registries of the CMS. The personnel, albeit not formally trained in the use of computer technologies, showed interest and a positive attitude towards the use of computers and new technologies.

The users

Two main groups of users were identified: the general public and the professional users.[9] As field research and interviews conducted in the first phase of the project showed, the general public typically consults the office for information regarding the possibility of taking someone to court and, if they decide to go ahead, the procedures to be followed (naming, blaming, claiming) (Felstiner, Abel and others, 1980/1981). Some of their questions might be cleared up through a standardised answer in a web portal but in general they are seeking a personalised, 'human mediated' response.

Professional user information needs were studied through semi-structured interviews that were conducted between August and October 2003. Professional users expressed the need to obtain specific information (or certified information/documents) from the case folder or from the CMS.

In general, the professional users appeared to possess a sound knowledge of well-established court procedures and practices, which allowed them to easily access the necessary information through traditional means.[10] Furthermore, professional users and court personnel shared a specific legal/technical jargon that enabled the professional user to decode the 'raw' data provided by the court. And last but not least, professional users had in general used the 'homemade applications' developed by the court technician, and some had experience with an e-services platform in use by the local court of general jurisdiction (Polis web). These three elements provided a sound basis for developing e-services for accessing data and a system of data codification that, replicating the ones already in use, could be easily understood by the professional users (Sapignoli, 2003).

The technologies

The Cineca personnel acquired data on the office servers, LAN and Internet connections. The issues of where to position the e-services server, how to provide the data and how to connect the server to the Internet were noted, but their solution was deferred to the future. Given that the ICT department of the Ministry of Justice was among the project partners, these issues did not seem to be particularly problematic. They then focused their attention on the CMS and on the two above-mentioned 'homemade' applications. The CMS application is based on an Oracle Database that stores the mandatory records of the office. Despite the lack of formal training, the CMS was actively used, and the care devoted to data entry accuracy and promptness was particularly high compared to the general standard of Italian courts. The application also allows personnel to add notes with additional information on case or file status. The software can manage the civil proceedings of the office, from the filing of the lawsuit, through the preliminary proceedings, to the settlement of the dispute in the decision phase, thus collecting all the key data of civil procedures.

Another element was an unofficial JOP website developed by the Court Administrator and hosted on her server *'at home'*. The website provided a number of forms, information on regulations and procedures, and useful examples for pro se litigants and lawyers. It also provided an e-mail contact for both users and personnel of other JOPs, which the Court Administrator used for answering specific questions.

The norms

In the Italian judicial system, where the judge is still seen in many cases as *la bouche de la loi*, formal rules are all too often thought of as being unambiguous artefacts void of interpretative ambiguities. All procedures are strictly regulated by codes of procedure (set out in legislation) and detailed regulations issued by the Ministry of Justice, and other public agencies. These procedural and technical rules (Joerges and Czarniawska, 1998) describe and prescribe in detail when, what and how a certain action can be taken by a party. They prescribe the 'technical' features of each working tool. Each step recorded on a paper docket, even its size, is formally prescribed by regulations, as is the specific data that has to be entered. Finally all the regulations that describe in detail the functioning of judicial organisations are binding *erga omnes*, – that is for all judicial actors, and for every judicial office – and are enforced in several ways (the appeal process, inspections, internal hierarchy and various sanctions) (Contini and Cordella, 2007).

Accordingly, at least in theory, everything that can be done and how it can be done in the area of ICT and of e-services is strictly regulated and clearly defined. But reality is far less simple, especially in a context where even the institutions that should foster consistency in the interpretation of the norms seem to be incapable of achieving acceptable results (Taruffo, 1991). As the case study showed, how norms should be interpreted and enacted is something that is open to discussion. The privacy code, the norms on the management of the CMS, on electronic documents and on the right to access data are but some of the regulations that create the complex normative landscape on which, from which, and also against which, the e-services were assembled.

Summing-up

From an organisational perspective, the personnel of the JOP were well disposed towards the project, and the organisation seemed capable of providing adequate support for the development and implementation of e-services. The installed base seemed to offer a fertile ground on which to cultivate the new e-services. As far as the users are concerned, the professional users showed both interest in the e-services and the ability to use the tools. On the other hand, providing e-services to the general public seemed more problematic both because of their more complex needs, the language barrier and general inexperience in using similar tools. Furthermore, the complex interconnection of norms and the generally formalistic and restrictive interpretation that was traditionally given by the Ministry of Justice seemed as if it might present a potential source of trouble. The idea that this was a research project, though, was perceived by at least some of the project partners (IRSIG-CESROG) as an opportunity to create a liminal space (Czarniawska and Mazza, 2003) where new things outside the normal rules could be tried out.

Developing the system

A start was made on the software development of the official portal[11] and of the first e-services prototype while the assessments of the JOP installed base were still being carried out. This decision was taken by the project team and the JOP in order to speed up the project schedule and so that practical experimentation could begin as soon as possible. Changes and new features were then going to be added to the prototype as data from the surveys and from the experimentation was collected and analysed.[12]

The writing of the software code was carried out by Cineca. Suggestions put forward by IRSIG-CESROG experts and by the Court Administrator aided the choice as to the contents and services supplied by this initial proto-type. At the same time, the first results of the technological installed base assessment provided insights on how to give substance to the suggestions (Lanzara, 2003).

The Portal

The developers based the design of the portal on the pre-existing contents and structure of the unofficial website. The contents were placed at their disposal by the Court Administrator. The first step was to create a set of new graphic interfaces and to add a section which allowed access to the e-services. Some suggestions put forward by the Court Administrator and her staff were then integrated. These suggestions mainly related to the image of the JOP that the official website was going to portray: '*Some orange* [colour] *might help! Like this* [the website] *is too grey and shallow! We are not a court of general jurisdiction ... people also come to the JOP because they see it as an institution which is close to the people. This will turn them away! ... and we also need a better logo – something which represents the office, its role, and its proximity to the people*'. In November 2003 the website was put on line on a Cineca server.[13] It pro-vided both general information on the court and its procedures (opening hours, telephone numbers, printable forms and so on) and a link to the e-services. Since then it has been available on the Internet. Statistics on website visits and contacts shows a consistently positive trend of growth.

The portal, conceived as a gate to the e-services (the real core of the pro-ject), was ready in a few weeks. All in all, its development went smoothly and no problems arose.

The e-services

As with creation of the portal, the creation of the first prototype of e-services features, functionalities and applications presented no particular difficulty for the *Cineca* programmers and took place in a short space of time. The prototype consisted of two applications, *ContenziosoCivile* and *Rubrica*, which could be accessed through a still rudimentary interface. They were created as improved and web-oriented applications of those already in use at the office. For security reasons, it was decided that the e-services were not going to use the data from the CMS database but from a database mir-ror.[14] *ContenziosoCivile* was developed with the professional user in mind and it allows the user, after being identified by the system, to access the data of the CMS relating to the user's lawsuits. For privacy reasons, only the parties involved in the lawsuit were going to be allowed to access such data. To make this data available to them alone, it was necessary to verify the identity of the user and to transmit the data through secure means. *Rubrica,* on the other hand, was developed both for the professional user and for the general public, and in consideration of the existence of rights other than those regarding privacy in the provision of justice, which deserve to be protected. In line with this interpretation, the project team thought it reasonable to allow open access to a more limited amount of information[15] on lawsuits filed at the court (Dodaro, Bacchelli and Recchia, 2004).

The presentation of the applications to the Court Administrator, her staff and to the IRSIG-CESROG won the praise of those present. The need for minor changes, and a more user-friendly interface before starting with the experimentation was noted, but did not seem to pose any real problems. Furthermore, some unforeseen potential statistical and managerial uses for *ContenziosoCivile* came to the mind of the Court Administrator during the presentation. *'It would really help us if we could access the data in this way and elaborate it instead of having to collect it on paper as we do now... If we could just slightly change this* [pointing at the interface] *to...'* The prototype was beginning to work as a reflective tool, stimulating new ideas and proposing new uses. Such feedback, suggesting development options that had not been foreseen,[16] instead of being conceived as a problem or as a limit, was exploited to develop the system.

The project team asked the software developers to work on the interface of the e-services prototype to provide easier and more intuitive access to the contents. Only minor adjustments seemed to be needed before running the experiment. The graphic interface was going to be designed to take into account the newer, more colourful version of the court's web page.

Up to this point everything seemed to be proceeding in a very straightforward, linear manner. The problems, however, were just around the corner.

The Internet Access Problem: issues of security and privacy

As everything seemed to speed up in the direction of the e-services prototype experimentation by a real, albeit small group of professional users, the problem of how to make the services available through the Internet emerged. There were two aspects to this problem: first, how to create and update a mirror (that is a copy) of the CMS database on a server connected to the Internet and on which the e-services applications could run (see

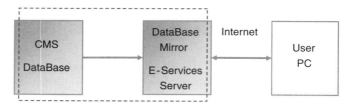

Figure 8.1   From the case management system to the database mirror

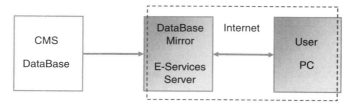

Figure 8.2   From the database mirror to user's PC

Figure 8.1); second, how to select and control access to the sensitive data contained in the database mirror (see Figure 8.2).

What follows is a summary of the main actions and events that took place in the subsequent two years in the attempt to solve these two problems. This simplified yet still cumbersome narrative should provide the reader with the flavour of the magnitude of the effort needed to unravel multiple techno-juridical Gordian knots in the making of an assemblage.

Assembling the database mirror

During the initial development stages, the e-services server and the database mirror were located at Cineca. In order to update the data on the server, Cineca and JOP personnel suggested daily transmission from the JOP to Cineca through a secure connection.[17] The office of the JOP was connected to the virtual private network of the Ministry of Justice (RUG) and, through the RUG firewall, to the Internet. In order to allow the transfer of data through the firewall the activation of a 'security policy' was required. On July 15 2003 the JOP had sent a request to the local DGSIA office for the activation of a 'security policy' requiring authorisation for data transmission from the JOP to the Cineca e-services server through the Internet.

After three months, during which attention had been focused on other techno-juridical issues (see next paragraph), and during which period no reply had been forthcoming from the local DGSIA office, IRSIG-CESROG researchers started to press for the activation of the 'security policy'. Initial attempts in October and November were made with the local DGSIA office. As a first response, on 13 October 2003 the local DGSIA office director replied that the procedure was not safe enough and that at least an additional firewall would be needed. Two options were proposed by Cineca to the local DGSIA office: 1) to provide the JOP with a firewall in order to allow it to transmit the data directly to Cineca, or 2) to send the data through the RUG to the local court of general jurisdiction and to configure the firewall policy of the court of general jurisdiction in order to allow the JOP to send the data through it. No clear reply was received regarding the proposals. Given the lack of any reaction, in December 2003, IRSIG-CESROG asked for the intervention of a DGSIA Deputy Director who was following the project. In mid January 2004 a one page report, which briefly analysed the two options, was sent from the local DGSIA office to all the parties involved. The report informed them that both options were feasible but that the request had to be submitted to the Firewall Control Center in Naples. Furthermore, the Net Office of DGSIA had to authorise the changes in the security policies of the local court of general jurisdiction's firewall if such a firewall was going to be used. At this point, it was clear that the decision to develop the e-services was bringing a growing number of actors onto the scene. The use of specific technical components and infrastructures in the assemblage required the involvement of new actors.

The Chief of the Net Office of DGSIA, to whom the report had also been sent, pointed out a RUG security issue and a problem with the bandwidth that the transmission would use. She nevertheless agreed to contact the local DGSIA office directly to try to sort out the problem. At the end of January the local DGSIA office asked the JOP to re-submit the request for the activation of a 'security policy', signed not by the Court Administrator but by the office's Chief Judge. The JOP submitted the request on the same day but then nothing seemed to happen. In mid February IRSIG-CESROG again sought the help of the DGSIA Deputy Director to put some pressure on the DGSIA Net Office and local DGSIA office personnel involved in the project. On 4 March 2004 the Deputy Director personally paid a visit to the Chief of the Net Office. The same day, the Chief of the Net Office and the Cineca developers discussed the problem. It was becoming rapidly obvious to the technicians that the proposition of transmitting the data from the JOP to Cineca through an Internet connection was not acceptable to the Chief of the Net Office.

The problem was discussed at a general coordination meeting with all the project partners on 23 April 2004, but no solution was found. On 26 April, IRSIG-CESROG sent a detailed e-mail to the DGSIA Director, summarising the history of the data transmission problem and stating that it was now up to her and to the manager of Cineca in charge of the project to find a solution.

In order to avoid further waste of time and resources, Cineca asked DGSIA to provide indications of what would be acceptable. The result of this request was the beginning of a joint effort on the part of Cineca and the local DGSIA office to find possible solutions to the problem. It was one of the very few active efforts made by the local office. The local DGSIA office played the role of mediator in an attempt to identify an assemblage configuration which would be not only technologically feasible but also institutionally compatible. As a result of this collaboration, a document with four main options was drafted between May and June 2004. By the end of October 2004, one of the options had been selected. Instead of sending the data through the Internet to Cineca as had been previously envisaged, a server within the court of general jurisdiction would be used. In this way, the transmission of data would take place through the RUG. The new configuration (which included new technical components 'discovered' during the collaboration) was compatible with the policies of the Ministry's Net Office, the real 'owner' of the RUG. Furthermore, the server was already situated in a so-called 'demilitarised zone' protected by firewalls. It already hosted the Ianus Authentication Station of another application, Polis Web,[18] and its specifications and Internet connectivity were adequate, at least for experimentation of the e-services with a limited number of users. The JOP could send a copy of the data extracted from the CMS database through the RUG. The users would be able to access this server through the Internet without compromising RUG security.

Looking into the mirror

The second problem came up during a dispute over the techno-juridical modalities to be used to make the data on the e-services server (that is the contents of the database mirror) available to the users (see Figure 8.2). The problem emerged during the presentation of the two applications in July 2003. During the meeting the Cineca personnel requested authorisation from the JOP for processing the data for the e-services. Authorisation – as provided for by the privacy code – was required to allow the storage, processing and communication of personal data in compliance with

obligations imposed by EU legislation, national laws and technical regulations. Furthermore, Cineca wanted to use the Ianus Technology,[19] *'in order
to ensure proper access to the data'*, to identify the *ContenziosoCivile*
users, in accordance with the requirements of the new personal data protection code (Legislative decree nr. 196 of 2003). Ianus was only one of the
possible technologies used in those years by the judicial offices to ensure
secure access to data. It was, however, the technology selected for Polis
web, the official e-services application for the courts of general jurisdiction, developed by the Ministry of Justice.

IRSIG-CESROG researchers feared that the use of such proprietary
technology might create a barrier for users. Such a barrier could hinder
the creation of a 'self-reinforcing process of growth' (Hanseth, 2002) once
the system was available to all the JOP's users. Furthermore, the inclusion
of this technology was seen as a 'death sentence' for the aim of allowing
general users to access the system. As far as the application *Rubrica* was
concerned, as it provided access only to a limited set of data, the use of ID
and password was considered sufficient by Cineca too.

The issues relating to the use of Ianus were discussed in a project meeting
in September 2003 without any visible results. At the end of September, in
a smaller coordination meeting with IRSIG-CESROG and JOP representatives, the manager of Cineca in charge of the project clearly stated that
they wanted to use IanusGate and that the DGSIA Director (previously
contacted by him) thought it was the only technology at their disposal with
a sufficient security guarantee. And it was *'the solution already adopted
by the Ministry for Polis web!'*

The attempt made by IRSIG-CESROG researchers (contrary to normal Ministry of Justice practice) to use simple technologies and simplified procedures in the e-services assemblage and to have them legitimated
through use and diffusion to a critical mass of users was nipped in the bud.
In the end it was only possible to experiment with an assemblage that was
more *'in harmony with the institutional background in which it operated –
locally and translocally'* (Czarniawska and Wolff, 1998, p. 52).

Authorisations and authorising to authorise

At the beginning of October 2003, Cineca submitted to the JOP a draft of
the authorisation they wanted the Court Administrator to sign. This draft
provided for the use of IanusGate to allow lawyers access to *Contenzioso-
Civile*, and for open access to *Rubrica*. Questioned on the subject a few
days later by IRSIG-CESROG researchers and by the Court Administrator

in a last-ditch attempt to avoid the use of Ianus, the DGSIA Director stated that the decision was not up to her because it concerned on the one hand the Court Administrator, who was responsible for the data, and on the other hand, it related to the relationship between Cineca (the e-services provider) and the lawyers (the users). It was then up to Cineca and the lawyers to define the issue on their own. Strangely enough, while the Net Office had clear jurisdiction over the RUG, DGSIA decided to avoid taking a position over the choice of the identification technology to be used to secure access to the e-services. This response, though, changed the JOP Court Administrator's attitude towards the data protection issue. She was now unwilling to sign the authorisation for the treatment of the data without previous 'authorisation to authorise' from the DGSIA Director as a guarantee of the ability of Ianus to ensure the security level needed. The DGSIA Director agreed that the JOP could send an official letter asking for authorisation concerning the access procedures required. At the same time, Cineca suggested that for the duration of the experimentation, IanusGate could be provided to the small group of selected users for free. On 13 October 2003, the JOP sent the request to the DGSIA Director. As no reply came to the request, on 19 December 2003, IRSIG-CESROG researchers sent an e-mail to the DGSIA Deputy Director. The DGSIA Director signed the authorisation a few days later. The authorisation explicitly referred to the Ianus technology as 'adequate' for the needs of the experimentation. In January 2004, just after the Christmas break, the JOP authorised Cineca to process the data using the Ianus technology.

If for *ContenziosoCivile* everything was resolved, a new issue had emerged concerning *Rubrica*. Given the extreme caution shown by the Ministry of Justice, the Court Administrator decided that *Rubrica* provided too much personal information to be made available on the net without any restrictions. The confrontation between IRSIG-CESROG and Cineca on the privacy issue and on normative interpretation had radically increased the sensitivity of both the Ministry of Justice and of the Court Administrator. The Ministry of Justice's formal position on the privacy issue had been taken and Court Administrator bureaucratic defences had been activated. The original choice to allow open access to *Rubrica* was no longer available and this e-service was abandoned.

Experimenting with the prototypes: at long last!

After 20 months spent finding a configuration of technological and institutional components compatible with the interpretation of the normative framework and with the interests of the actors involved, the experimentation could finally begin.

The experimentation was however limited to the *ContenziosoCivile* application. A group of ten users was selected by the JOP. Two main criteria were used: firstly, the user needed to have a significant number of cases; secondly the user needed to show interest in participating in the experimentation.

On 23 March 2005, a start-up meeting was organised at the JOP to present the e-services project to the potential users and to demonstrate the application. The meeting was thus the moment for the 'investiture' of the project before the users (Czarniawska and Mazza, 2003, p. 273). The presentation was conducted by IRSIG-CESROG and Cineca personnel, and involved the participation of the local DGSIA Director. The presentation itself was an occasion for initial feedback from the professional users. It also allowed some constructive discussion between the lawyers, the local DGSIA Director and the other project partners. As a result, the idea for an application much-requested by lawyers, *PrimaUdienza,* was elaborated. Strange as it may seem, in Italian civil proceedings, the defendant is not necessarily notified when the claimant has actually filed the case and a hearing date has been set. This information need called for an application similar to *Rubrica*, with access restricted to identified users, that would exclude a random search but which nevertheless would allow the user to verify this information. As the defendant knows the name of the claimant, it was this information that was requested in order to access the data. A similar mechanism was used by other judicial offices in other experimental trials and was, *de facto*, endorsed by the Ministry. The decision was also taken to develop a new functionality of *ContenziosoCivile*, *RichiestaCopie*, before the beginning of the experimentation. *RichiestaCopie* allows the users to submit the request for a copy of a ruling of one of their cases from their office. To be implemented, this e-service required some changes in the working procedures and in the usage of the CMS.

On 7 April 2005, the experimentation of *ContenziosoCivile* and *Richiesta-Copie* started. More than 18 months had elapsed since *ContenziosoCivile* had been ready for testing by the users.

Support and a user-guide were provided both for the installation of IanusGate and for the use of the e-services application but very few problems emerged. Users easily integrated the e-services in their working practices. When, on 20 June 2005, *PrimaUdienza* was added to the e-services package, the users readily adopted it too. In-depth interviewing conducted in the period between May and June combined with the analysis of the logs and of the users' diaries provided on the one hand a clear picture of the different ways in which the applications were being used and, on the other hand, they provided suggestions for improving the applications in use and ideas for developing new applications. The more easily adopted suggestions were implemented during the course of the experimentation. More complex suggestions and emerging ideas were selected for the creation of a second version of the e-services to be piloted in a second phase. The experimentation of the first version of the e-services was concluded on 26 September 2005, but the users were allowed to continue using the tool. Analysis of the experimentation was conducted and at the same time the second version of the e-services was developed, including three new e-services (*InfoByMail*,[20] *CalendarioUdienza*[21] and *ProssimaUdienza*[22]) as well as new functions for *ContenziosoCivile*[23] and *PrimaUdienza*.

The presentation of the results of the first phase of experimentation and of the new version of e-services was planned for October but was delayed until February 2006 because of the need to complete the data analysis. The new e-services were presented to the lawyers on 7 February. Ideas for further developments emerging from the more recent analysis were also discussed. There was only one small problem before starting the new phase of experimentation and development: there was no longer a connection between the e-services server and the Internet.

The Breakdown

In the days following the breakdown in the connection, Cineca first contacted the local court of general jurisdiction and then the local DGSIA office to find out what had happened and what solutions could be adopted. The answer to what had happened was quite simple. As previously mentioned, the JOP e-services were using the same server and the same Internet connection used by Polis web of the local court of general jurisdiction. In January 2006, the connection service of Polis web of the local court of general jurisdiction to the net was centralised. As a consequence, the connection used by the JOP e-services, supplied by a private provider (FastWeb) was terminated. The obvious consequence was that, on 10 January 2006, the e-services suddenly disappeared from the net. The complex assemblage that had been put together with so much effort, painstakingly trying to mediate between the various requirements and interests to make the prototype work, was rendered useless by the unexpected failure of one of its components. The ghost of the problem that had stalled the experimentation from July 2003 to October 2004 had suddenly reappeared.

The local DGSIA office did not have the economic resources to sign a new contract for the provision of Internet services so that straightforward solution was out of the question. Instead, a totally different configuration was suggested. As Cineca had been hosting the Ministry of Justice website, an access point to the RUG had been in existence for years. This meant the server could be moved to Cineca and that the data could be transmitted from the JOP to Cineca through the RUG.[24] The suggestion was rapidly adopted and the server was moved to its new location. A path for the data transmission that had been available since 2003 but which had not even been considered at the time by Cineca and DGSIA, suddenly became the course to take.

On 7 February 2006, pending the reactivation of the e-services, but hoping for a prompt solution to the problem, IRSIG-CESROG and Cineca organised a meeting with the professional users, the Court Administrator and the chief of the local DGSIA office at the JOP. The purpose was to present the results of the first experimentation phase and to introduce the new version of the applications and the new services to be trialled in the next phase. The users showed interest in the new services, stressed the importance of having the e-services back and showed some concern regarding what would happen once the project was concluded. On that occasion, the Cineca technician pointed out that the reactivation of the e-services was not a problem which would be technically complex to solve. When asked about a date, the Director of the local DGSIA office assured those present that, if there were no unforeseen complications, the e-services would be online again at the beginning of March. The meeting was also a chance for IRSIG-CESROG researchers, the Court Administrator and users to engage the Ministry in the task of ensuring the e-services would continue after the end of the project.

A technical problem relating to the RUG connection of the JOP and the need for activation of a 'security policy' slowed down the reactivation process, but not by much. Thanks also to the more wholehearted support of the DGSIA Deputy Director, and the understanding of aspects of the RUG (and how not to upset the RUG guardians of the Net Office) that had matured during the development of the project, the problems were solved in less than three months. The time before, it had taken 18 months to solve the same problems.

On 23 March 2006, Cineca finally communicated that they were ready, although not everything was perfect yet. Some bricolage was still required to make the assemblage work. The following day e-mails were sent to the users informing them that the second trial phase would start on 27 March 2006.

A new CMS

As the second experimentation phase began,[25] the project team started to discuss the next step. The main points were the possibility of new e-services and how to move from the experimentation of the pilot stage to the diffusion of the e-services and their systematic utilisation by court users. Soon enough though, the focus of attention shifted to a new issue. The Court Administrator informed the group that the Ministry was developing a new case management system, SIGP. It was planned that the JOP of Bologna would start using SIGP from summer 2006. This would disrupt the e-services provision. Cineca technicians pointed out that adapting the e-services to the new system was not going to be a problem. On the other hand it would require resources. The group would have to decide whether to have new e-services or to adapt the system.

The adaptation would allow the use of the e-services after the end of the project. In the other eventuality it seemed probable that the e-services would remain just an interesting research experiment. Furthermore, the Court Administrator pointed out that SIGP was not going to allow lawyers to access the data through workstations within the JOP as the old system did. The office was consequently looking at an increase in front office activities. Enabling the e-services that had already been developed to work with the new CMS would clearly help to solve this problem. For these reasons, instead of developing new e-services as initially planned, it was decided to focus on adapting the e-services to enable them to work with the new CMS.

Unfortunately, the development of SIGP did not proceed as smoothly as predicted by the Ministry of Justice. Cineca kept holding the work back waiting for a definitive version of the SIGP database structure and possibly a working database. Finally, between 17 and 24 November 2006, the JOP database of the old CMS was migrated. The migration was considered 'technically' successful as it had taken place in accordance with the terms stipulated in the contract with the Ministry. In reality, though, this was far from the case. A large portion of the data that was much needed by the office had not been migrated as the terms of the contract had not provided for it. Given the amount of resources that manual data entry would require, the Court Administrator and the Chief Judge decided that the office could not use SIGP and had to continue to work with the old CMS.

Changing priorities

Just as the project was nearing its formal end, it became clear that it was not realistic to expect SIGP to work within a reasonable timescale. In the meantime, there had been a change in the case load of the JOP. A new automatic system for traffic control had started to issue fines and hence substantially increased the number of appeals against administrative proceedings. A large number of citizens were approaching the office in order to have information concerning the procedure to follow to bring a case before a judge. More importantly, after filing the case, all of them needed to know if the hearing date had been fixed and when it was. The office was clearly overloaded. Although the answer to procedural issues could be provided through the website and information leaflets, it was possible to make the hearing date available on line only by developing a new e-service open to everybody.

Starting from these new premises, and when the project deadline had almost been reached, the project team decided to proceed with a modification of *ProssimaUdienza* in order to make it available to the general public. A simple user guide was also produced.

Even if it was not a 'silver bullet' (Brooks, 1987), the service is still online and certainly helps the office by reducing the number of users who have to go to the court office to get the information they need and thus allows the office to provide a better service.

Analysis and appraisal

Reflecting on the JOP e-services story, a number of points drew our attention. In the first place, it is a story describing the emergence of an assemblage involving people, organisations, technologies and norms. The assemblage 'is created by individual interactions within a social context' (Czarniawska and Wolff, 1998, p. 35). It is in actual encounters between people, technology and norms that assembling takes place. Starting from the initial concept of e-services, Cineca software developers wrote the code for the first prototype. In order to connect the prototype to the Internet, the local and Central DGSIA offices were involved. The use of the RUG was then decided. This in turn led to the involvement of the Net Office and of the Firewall office. At the same time, given the structure of the RUG, the local court of general jurisdiction and Polis web (including the contract for the provision of Internet services) were involved. In order to provide secure access to the e-services, Cineca introduced Ianus technology, which initiated a chain of events that in the end led to the use of Ianus Gate for accessing the e-services and also to the abandoning of the e-service *Rubrica*. And so on...

One of the results of this process is that the outcome of the assembling activity, '*accumulated over time, is by no means an ordered and coherent world*' (Lanzara and Patriotta, 2001, p. 963). It is the result of *ibi et tunc* decisions,[26] local 'fixes' and solutions that are patched together and accumulate over time, providing a temporary functioning configuration (*ibidem*).

Secondly, the development activity which made the assemblage (and the e-services delivery) possible was carried out by a plurality of actors, each one with multiple interests, priorities and objectives. As Weick (1979, p. 91) pointed out, '*partners in a collective structure* [in-the-making] *share space, time and energy, but they need not share visions, aspirations or intentions*'. In our case, the partners in the assemblage activities each had multiple visions, aspirations and intentions. As an example, in the course of the project, Cineca seemed to pursue at least three different objectives with varying intensity. The first and most obvious one was that of ensuring that the e-services were developed. This was important, if nothing else, because this was the reason for its participation in the project. A second important objective was to avoid DGSIA objections as far as technological choices were concerned. The e-services were only a marginal project compared to other activities Cineca carries out for the Ministry of Justice. Another objective was to stay in the (potential) market for technologies used to secure electronic transactions by the Ministry of Justice. On the other hand, short term material gains were not the only driving force. The e-services are still running on the Cineca server long after the end of the project, free of charge.

The Office of the Justice of the Peace clearly stated from the beginning that it was taking part in the project with the aim of improving service delivery and in the hope of reducing its workload. At the same time, defensive stances such as the request for an authorisation to authorise taken during the four years demonstrated a desire to avoid potential problems with the Ministry of Justice.

As far as IRSIG-CESROG is concerned, the researchers often seemed to be more interested in developing knowledge and in the experimentation of 'new' ideas, rather than project management and maximisation of service delivery within the existing normative framework interpretation. If the effort was towards developing a system that actually did something to improve the delivery of justice and did not just look good on paper (as the team leader stated on more than one occasion), at the same time there was the belief that the project had a role to play in promoting a new view of ICT development and innovation in the judicial administration.

DGSIA's attitude can be considered to be one of benevolent indifference. The e-services project was of limited importance to DGSIA, which at the time was devoting more and more resources to the development of the Trial OnLine Project (see Fabri, Chapter 5). DGSIA preferred to follow the well-trodden path and minimise the risks of new problems arising (Ianus technology was already used for a similar application). The security of the RUG and data protection were top priorities for DGSIA. The implementation of e-services (for example the improvement of the services the JOP offers to its users) was clearly just a secondary goal. Another interest of the DGSIA (and of the Ministry of Justice) was to use the RUG, and more generally ICT applications (Contini and Cordella, 2007), as a means of strengthening its control over courts in order to standardise organisational behaviour. In pursuing this goal the Network office at the DGSIA is in a key position because of its control over RUG. From its viewpoint, technology is conceived mainly as a controlling, standardising and centralising device. The DGSIA's unwillingness to create an *ad hoc* 'security policy' for JOP e-services was consistent with this. Networks (firewalls and routers) are thus powerful centralisation tools in the hands of the Ministry of Justice in the face of the tendency of courts and judges' to move towards loose coupling organising (Contini and Cordella, 2008).

The DGSIA position was even more fragmented. Its Deputy Director for example clearly took a more active stance when he became directly involved. At the same time, the efforts of the local DGSIA office were mainly aimed at avoiding any potential problems and any involvement whenever possible. No real interest in the e-services was ever shown. Finally, the Net office efforts were clearly oriented towards protecting the RUG. Ensuring functional closure (see Kallinikos, Chapter 3) of the net to keep it safe from potential threats obviously came before any possible interest in assisting the project team and the court in providing the e-services. This multiplicity of interests, priorities and objectives was at the root of the complex interplay that took place in controlling and influencing the unfolding of events.

Thirdly, and adding to the general complexity, the assembling activity was influenced by the presence of two different logics that needed to be followed: a technological logic and a bureaucratic-normative one. On its own, the technological component looked relatively simple. Developing technological components and assembling them in configurations to allow the provision of e-services did not pose any real technical problem. What was technically feasible, given the installed base of the JOP and the resources available for the project, was already quite clear after the first preliminary surveys. The development of the first prototype (version 1 of the e-services) was simple and unproblematic, rapid, and relatively inexpensive. Both the development of the prototype and its adoption were positive: the goal of allowing users to experiment with them was achieved; new e-services were quickly identified and developed; the existing ones were fine-tuned; ideas for new e-services came from external and internal users, as well as from the researchers. The technological abilities of the JOP and lawyers proved to be sufficient for a smooth and unproblematic development and adoption of the e-services.

If understanding what was technically feasible was simple, understanding what could actually be done was another matter. What emerged during the assemblage effort was that the decision on which configuration was to be used depended on the bureaucratic position and normative interpretation of a multiplicity of actors whose jurisdiction and power could not be easily established *ex-ante*. These actors, given their different experience, interests and priorities, interpreted the normative framework and the technological components differently.

The question of the Internet access first and the breakdown of the Internet connection later, clearly show that the use of ICT changes the landscape of the traditional forms of information exchange between the JOP and its users. In order to provide the e-services, it was necessary to include new actors in the service provision. These actors brought with them new interests and priorities that had to be taken into account and which in some cases set the agenda. We are thus talking about a system that is enabled by the imbrications of technological and institutional elements (rules, jurisdictions and so on). At the same time, the assemblage is a mediation between these elements.

The e-services were developed from existing technologies and norms which are deeply ingrained in practices, taken for granted and visible only in their effects (the CMS usages, the regulations for allowing access to data, the privacy code and so on), and these suddenly came to the fore. New actors, technological components and forgotten norms were re-discovered. Boundaries were moved and at the same time the exchange of information took place across different boundaries. The service provision was 'dislocated' (Lanzara, Chapter 1) outside the traditional organisation boundaries. In particular, the owners (with their interests and priorities) of the infrastructure used to provide the e-services became central to the process of providing the service. In a way, the mediation between what could or could not be done in the given framework moved away from the place where the services are provided. The decision was no longer taken by the office or by the clerk at the front desk. Mediation involved actors with veto power in Rome.

In a bureaucratic and normative field which consists of great many (and often only approximately interconnected) norms, the interpretation of 'what can be done and how' may diverge quite a bit. Accordingly, opportunities and restraints emerged from difficulties in understanding the complex and cumbersome layer of formal rules regulating the electronic exchange of data and document in courts. While mediation and interpretation took place, it is important to bear in mind that normative and technological components are not 'infinitely malleable' (Orlikowski, 2000, p. 409). '*Saying that* [their interpretation and uses are ...] *situated and not confined to predefined options does not mean that* [they are] *totally open to any and all possibilities* [...inscription and] *physical properties of artefacts ensure that there are always boundary conditions on how we use them*' (*ibidem* p. 409). Much of the assembling activity pivoted around the problem of interpreting what it was possible to do, what was certainly prohibited and what, maybe, could be done. On the one hand it was a typical problem of legal interpretation and legal arguments. On the other hand, ability in building legal arguments was not sufficient *per se*. There was also a problem of authority and power: the interpretation of the rules arrived at by a top official of the Ministry of Justice proved to be certainly more authoritative than that arrived at by a Court Administrator of the local court.

At the same time, it was only when the assembling activity took place that what could be done and what could not was actually defined. In this process, the actors enacted '*strategies for the construction of alternative versions of reality*' (Lanzara, 1993; Lanzara and Patriotta, 2001, p. 960), consistent with their beliefs, values and objectives. Intensive negotiations and attempts at reaching consensus took place; compromises had to be made between the initial ideas and what was acceptable to the new actors, and ideas had to be adjusted to fit in with existing institutional patterns that were discovered on the way. In order to create a working assemblage, research, negotiations and mediations were necessary in order to reach an interpretation which was shared by or would be acceptable to all the actors involved. In some cases, the actors did not have a particular interpretation until they were required by the assembling effort to produce one. At the same time, their agreement was necessary in order for the assemblage to work (for example the Net Office of DGSIA). In a way, the various actors discovered technologies, norms, other actors and their interpretations in the interaction generated by the assembling effort. As the story of the project shows, '*rather than neat conversion processes, we have multiple transactions and trade-offs, through which actors try to reconcile divergent views and interests into a shared body of legitimate* [options]' (Lanzara and Patriotta, 2001, p. 967). On more than one occasion, this process was eased by anchoring the new solution to already accepted pre-existing practices. This is what took place when *Rubrica,* was reshaped into *PrimaUdienza.* The new solution was not in line with the normative interpretation given by

DGSIA. However, a similar mechanism had already been endorsed by the Ministry and had thus been legitimised in practice. This, more than any other element, led to DGSIA accepting the solution.

Finding solutions did not always require a complete understanding of the component to be included in the assemblage, but simply required an understanding of what could be done with it and how it could be included. During the development of the project the RUG map was not clear, either to Cineca or to various technicians, managers and officials of the Ministry of Justice. The discovery of its technical features (for example point to point connections, the exact location of firewalls, the security policies, the person with the authority to enact a change in these policies, or the person that can technically implement these changes in a specific firewall) required a kind of research-in-action. In the end, despite the efforts made by researchers, the RUG remains a black box with many undisclosed secrets. What was important, though, was the understanding of what was acceptable from the Net-office perspective in order to allow the data to flow through it.

The emerging objective was to find a good enough interpretation of the components that were going to be used to make the assemblage work. To a certain extent, this process at least partially undermined the initial goals of the project. However, it was only when the (new) interpretations had been accepted by the actors involved that the working assemblage could come into being. In this way, the technological assemblage was legitimated from a normative point of view (technical choices are driven by normative interpretations). When the assemblage was complete and activated, by repeatedly performing its task successfully it quickly stabilised and seemed to be 'organised-for-good' (Czarniawska and Wolff, 1998, p. 35; Czarniawska, 2007, p. 146). Functionally and pragmatically legitimised, most of its components soon became invisible.

This though was just a temporary state because 'an assemblage [...] is the outcome of controversy and bricolage, resilient as a whole but subject to local disputes, experiments and reassembling' (Lanzara and Patriotta, 2001, p. 964). The components of the assemblage were not and could not be frozen. The life of the assemblage was linked to that of its components. This was the case with the introduction of the new CMS, SIGP, which still hangs over the last surviving e-services like a sword of Damocles. Even though it was foreseeable to a certain extent, the project also experienced unexpected breakdowns and elements had to be dismantled. On these occasions, on the one hand, as a result of the disconnection (failure) of certain components and the breakdown of the e-services, the assemblage became suddenly visible again in all its multiple elements. On the other hand, much of the understanding about 'what could be done and how' was already in place, ready to be re-used to re-assemble the system. For example, when the Internet connection of the local court of general jurisdiction was cut, finding a new path turned out to be much easier than it had been the first time round. Another source of change originated from the change in actors' priorities and interests, which in turn reshaped what was feasible. This led to adaptation of the system in the attempt to meet the new needs. The decision to open *ProssimaUdienza* to the general public is a clear example of this. It is in this way that the assemblage evolves (which does not necessarily mean improve) 'in the face of the changing environment' (Lanzara, Chapter 1).

Conclusions: Assemblage as negotiated order

The results of this study highlight the need to move from a concept of technological development as an issue of linear design, subject to drifts and shifts (Ciborra, 2000), to acknowledging that it is a more complex nature of inquiry and a dispute-based process (Lanzara and Patriotta, 2001). These elements might not be visible in the final product, the up and running assemblage, but can only be appreciated through the 'in-the-making' of the assemblage. Moving on from the ideas of Lanzara and Patriotta (2001) on organisational knowledge to the field of technology design, the way to understand complex technological systems is to forget about the end product and look at technology development 'in the making', as opposed to 'ready-made'. As pointed out by Latour (1987, p. 21), *'we go from final products to production, from "cold" stable objects to "warm" and unstable ones'*. Assembling activity relies on transient constructs, makeshift artefacts and patchwork (Lanzara and Patriotta, 2001, p. 964), mediation between technological and normative layers and negotiation between actors with different interests, understanding and perspectives on the issues at stake. Revisions, improvements and breakdowns are part of the process. Assemblage inevitably seems to require inquiry into the relationships (but also the creation of relationships) among the artefacts, the actors and the broader institutional context (Lanzara and Patriotta, 2001, p. 967).

We think that this perspective offers useful inputs to researchers and academics who wish to study projects such as e-government, which are both institutional and technological at the same time. It also offers a useful input to those who are trying to assemble complex ICT systems within the public sector and in other organisations outside the public sector. This case study demonstrates the way in which many of the critical skills and capabilities required are indeed quite different from those traditionally expected, as the researchers had plenty of occasions to find out.[27] What is needed are, on the one hand, skills in inquiry and experimentation, and on the other hand, bargaining and combinational skills (Strauss, Schatzman, Ehrlich, Bucher and Sabslin, 1963).

Inquiry and experimentation is what drives the exploration of the 'known' installed base, the discovery and reflection of its features, and the discovery of unknown installed base components which are important in the assemblage. The discovery and activation of the installed base components leads to – and is at the same time led by – the emergence and activity of new actors, areas of authority, and the multiple constraints and opportunities hidden in the existing technological infrastructure (Hanseth, 2002) as well as in the institutional setting.

Dealing with all these elements requires the ability to gather people around and create connections between them right from the start. This is necessary not just in order to develop and implement the technology, but also, to make it possible to 'design' the technological and institutional components of the assemblage. Design can be here conceived as the result of multiple negotiations about what can be done and how, and of the dealing with the many misunderstandings and incomprehension that emerge. What is important is the ability to find combinations that are feasible and acceptable in the 'here and now' of the negotiation. In this, it is important to be able to deal with (and to take advantage of) the sudden drifts, changes of direction and breakdowns that occur when assembling a system by patching together objects and procedures that already exist in established practices, where they still perform their tasks. Also, the need to integrate potentially conflicting interests and values requires the ability of building shared meaning through a mix of consensus, coercion and negotiation.

Order, though, is not negotiated once and for all. In time, changes in rules, ways of understanding, goals and interpretations take place. Also, an added-on component may break down sooner or later. When any of this happens, 'what can be done and how' is once again subject to discussion. Assemblages are thus more than just stabilised negotiated orders. They can be conceived as negotiated orders constantly under threat of falling apart, continually in need of care and renegotiation, and always in-the-making.

Notes

While this chapter is the result of a joint effort of the two authors, individual sections may be attributed as follows: Francesco Contini, Sections 1–4; Marco Velicogna, Sections 5–11.

1. In particular, the database of the automated case management system in use in the office was considered to be an excellent starting point.
2. Court users, parties and the general public.
3. In the project, thanks to a long tradition of cooperation, CESROG and IRSIG acted as a single organisational actor, even though some specific tasks were accomplished by just one of the two organisations. Their goals in the project were identifying and diffusing new methodologies for the support of innovations in the administration of justice (IRSIG-CNR, 2001). The project was co-financed by a grant from the Italian Ministry of Universities and Research (FIRB, RBNE01KJTP). As we will see more in detail, they were responsible for a number of different aspects: overall coordination, the organisational analysis of the JOP and of the users of its services, the identification of the application to be developed and of the general developmental approach, the analysis of the practical experimentation of the new application, and so on.
4. Cineca can be considered a twofold organisation. On the one hand it has research interests and participates in large-scale research efforts; on the other hand, it is a private organisation working in the market on infrastructures, high-end applications and services for public institutions and private enterprise. Its main tasks in the project were to plan and develop the web platform (e-services) to write the applications and to offer the technological infrastructures required by the implementation of the new services.
5. Its role within the project, in the persons of its Director and of a Deputy Director, was to support and direct design, development and experimentation of the e-services. Apart from this, three other offices of DGSIA were involved in the project. The local branch of DGSIA, operating in the judicial district of the JOP where the project was conducted, had the formal role of facilitating and supporting the project at a more local level. The other two offices are the Net Office of DGSIA and the Firewall Control Center of Naples.
6. There are some very limited exceptions (e.g., industrial disputes up to €129 before the Court of First Instance with General Jurisdiction).
7. Even though pro se litigation is allowed only for disputes in which the sum of money disputed does not exceed a certain amount, the number of such cases is considerable.
8. The CMS has replaced most of the paper dockets previously in use in the office.
9. This second group consisted mainly of lawyers, public administration staff and firms.

10. That is walking to the court office and presenting a request for specific information in a codified way.
11. This portal would take the place of the unofficial web site developed by the court administrator.
12. The prototype was seen as a transient construct Lanzara, G.F. (1999).
13. www.giudicedipace.bologna.it/; visited 4 March 2008.
14. A database mirror is a dynamically updated copy of a (primary) database. It is often used as a back-up source in case the primary database fails. In the JOP case, allowing external users to have access only to a database mirror and not the primary database was a way to keep the primary database safe from potential intrusions from the Internet.
15. With a search for name and surname of one of the parties, it provided the General Register Number, the name of the judge in charge the proceedings, and the date and time of the next hearing.
16. This is what Barbara Czarniawska in Chapter 2 refers to as an 'arc of reciprocation'.
17. The use of SSH2 protocol was proposed to allow 'secure' connections.
18. The e-services project of the court of general jurisdiction.
19. A 'set of products developed at Cineca to ensure the security and control of information flows.' http://pah.cineca.org/Cineca_AMR_security.pdf p. 5. Visited 4 March 2008.
20. This application sends e-mails to users who subscribe to the service. The e-mails keep them up to date on the general progress of their proceedings.
21. This provides the user with a calendar of the hearings for the week (General Register Number and name of the judge).
22. It allows the user, who keys in the General Register Number, to find out the status of the case. If the case is still open, it provides name of the judge and date and time of the next hearing. This application does not make any reference to the names of lawyers and parties and is intended to be accessible not just to professional users but also to the general public.
23. Such as the possibility of downloading the user data in .txt, .csv or .html format and a more powerful research mask.
24. This solution was similar to one of the four options that had initially been suggested in the period between May and June 2004.
25. The abilities of the users of the assemblage were also used to test out some tools that were of no particular interest to them personally but which, given the experience they had gained, were especially suited to testing and evaluation by them. *InfoByMail*, for example, while of no particular interest to the users, who had access to *ContenziosoCivile*,

was going to be very useful to those that did not have IanusGate or who only dealt with a limited number of cases.

26. Decision made 'then and there'.

27. The mix of these two layers of complexity (technological and normative), and of the (legitimate) interplay between actors, made the integration activities of IRSIG-CESROG as frustrating an exercise as trying to catch waves with bare hands.

References

Blackler, F. (1995), 'Knowledge, Knowledge Work and Organizations: an Overview and Interpretation'. *Organization Studies,* 16 (6), 1021–1046.

Bødker, S. and K. Grønbæk (1992), 'Design in Action: from Prototyping by Demonstration to Cooperative Prototyping'. In Greenbaum, J. and M. Kyng (eds), *Design at Work: Cooperative Design of Computer Systems.* Mahwah, NJ: Lawrence Erlbaum Associates, Inc., (197–218).

Brooks, F.P. (1987), 'No Silver Bullet: Essence and Accident in Software Engineering'. *Computer,* 20 (4), 10–19.

Brown, J.S. and P. Duguid (1991), 'Organizational Learning and Communities of Practice: toward a Unified View of Working, Learning and Innovation'. *Organization Science,* 2 (1), 40–57.

Carnevali, D., Contini, F. and M. Fabri (2006), *Tecnologie per la giustizia: I successi e le false promesse dell'e-justice.* Milano: Giuffrè.

Carnevali, D., Contini, F., Fabri, M. and M. Velicogna (2007), 'Technologies for the Prosecution Offices in Italy: the Tension between Legacy and Creativity'. In Fabri, M. (ed.), *Information and Communication Technologies for the Public Prosecutor's Office.* Bologna: Clueb (229–281).

Ciborra, C. (2000), *From Control to Drift: the Dynamics of Corporate Information Infrastructures.* Oxford: Oxford University Press.

Contini, F. (1999), 'Processi di innovazione e context making: L'adozione della tecnologia dell'informazione negli uffici giudiziari'. In Ciborra C. and G.F. Lanzara (eds), *Labirinti dell'innovazione.* Milano: Etas (163–204).

Contini, F. and A. Cordella (2007), 'Information System and Information Infrastructure Deployment: the Challenge of the Italian E-Justice Approach'. *The Electronic Journal of e-Government,* 5 (1), 43–52.

Contini, F. and A. Cordella (2008), 'Italian Justice System and ICT: Matches and Mismatches between Technology and Organisation'. In

Cerrillio, A. and P. Fabra (eds), *e-Justice*. Hershey, PA: Information Science Reference (an imprint of IGI Global) (117–134).

Contini, F. and M. Fabri (2003), *Formazione interattiva a distanza (FID) – Ministero della Giustizia: Relazione sulla sperimentazione del prototipo FID 2*. Bologna: IRSIG–CNR.

Czarniawska, B. (2004), 'On Time, Space, and Action Nets'. *Organization Studies,* 11 (6), 773–791.

Czarniawska, B. (2007), 'Complex Organizations Still Complex'. *International Public Management Journal,* 10 (2), 137–151.

Czarniawska, B. and C. Mazza (2003), 'Consulting as a Liminal Space'. *Human Relations,* 56 (3), 267–290.

Czarniawska, B. and R. Wolff (1998), 'Constructing New Identities in Established Organization Fields: Young Universities in Old Europe'. *International Studies of Management and Organization,* 28 (3), 32–56.

Dahlbom, B. and L. Mathiassen (1993), *Computers in Context: the Philosophy and Practice of Systems Design*. Cambridge, MA: Blackwell Publishing.

Dennis, A. and B.H. Wixom (2000), *Systems Analysis and Design*. New York, NY and Chichester, UK: Wiley.

Dodaro, C., Bacchelli, R. and P. Recchia (2004), '*Portale dell'ufficio del giudice di pace di Bologna: Studio per lo sviluppo degli e-services*'. Bologna: Cineca.

Fabri, M. and F. Contini (2001), *Justice and Technology in Europe: How ICT Is Changing the Judicial Business*. The Hague: Kluwer Law International.

Fabri, M. and F. Contini (2003), *Judicial Electronic Data Interchange in Europe: Applications, Policies and Trends*. Bologna: Lo Scarabeo.

Felstiner, W.L.F., Abel, R.L. and A. Sarat (1980–1981), 'The Emergence and Transformation of Disputes: Naming, Blaming, Claiming ...'. *Law & Society Review,* 15 (3/4), Special Issue on Dispute Processing and Civil Litigation, 631–654.

Hanseth, O. (1996), *Information Technology as Infrastructure*. Goteborg: Department of Informatics, School of Economics and Commercial Law, Goteborg University.

Hanseth, O. (2002), 'From Systems and Tools to Networks and Infrastructures: from Design to Cultivation. Towards a Theory of ICT Solutions and Its Design Methodology Implications'. Retrieved from Heim.Ifi.Uio.No/~Oleha/Publications/Ib_ISR_3rd_Resubm2.Html. Visited 4 March 2008.

Hanseth, O. and M. Aanestad (2003), 'Design as Bootstrapping: on the Evolution of ICT Networks in Health Care'. *Methods of Information in Medicine,* 42 (4), 385–391.

IRSIG–CNR (2001), *Information and Communication Technology for Justice: FIRB Research Project*. Bologna: IRSIG–CNR.

Joerges, B. and B. Czarniawska (1998), 'The Question Of Technology, Or How Organizations Inscribe The World'. *Organization Studies*, 19 (3), 363–385.

Lanzara, G.F. (1993), *Capacità negativa. Competenza progettuale e modelli di intervento nelle organizzazioni*. Bologna: Il Mulino.

Lanzara, G.F. (1999), 'Between Transient Constructs and Persistent Structures: Designing Systems in Action'. *Journal of Strategic Information Systems*, 8 (4), 331–349.

Lanzara, G.F. (2003), 'Relazione di sintesi'. In Lanzara, G.F. (ed.), *Relazione annuale progetto FIRB: Tecnologie per la giustizia. Unità di ricerca CESROG-DOSP e IRSIG-CNR*. Bologna: IRSIG–CNR.

Lanzara, G.F. and G. Patriotta (2001), 'Technology and the Courtroom: an Inquiry into Knowledge Making in Organizations'. *Journal of Management Studies*, 38 (7), 943–971.

Latour, B. (1987), *Science in Action*. Cambridge, MA: Harvard University Press.

Lave, J. and E. Wenger (1991) (eds), *Situated Learning: Legitimate Peripheral Participation*. Cambridge: Cambridge University Press.

McMillan, J. and T. Carlson (2002), *Incounter: an Open-Source Electronic Filing Demonstration Project*. Williamsburg, VA: National Center for State Courts.

Orlikowski, W.J. (2000), 'Using Technology And Constituting Structures: A Practice Lens For Studying Technology In Organizations'. *Organization Science*, 11 (4), 404–428.

Platt, J. (2001), 'History of the Interview'. In Gubrium, J.F. and J.A. Holstein (eds), *Handbook Of Interview Research*, London: Sage (33–54).

Sapignoli, M. (2003), *La rilevazione delle opinioni di utenti dell'Ufficio del Giudice di pace di Bologna riguardo a servizi telematici da avviare: una prima analisi delle informazioni raccolte*. Bologna: DOSP, University of Bologna.

Strauss, A.L., Schatzman, L., Ehrlich, D., Bucher, R. and M. Sabslin (1963), 'The Hospital And Its Negotiated Order'. In Friedson E. (ed.), *The Hospital in Modern Society*. New York, NY: Free Press.

Taruffo, M. (1991), *Il vertice ambiguo: Saggi sulla Cassazione civile*. Bologna: Il Mulino.

Weick, K.E. (1979), *The Social Psychology of Organizing* (Second edition), New York, NY: McGraw-Hill.

Weick, K.E. (1988), 'Enacted Sensemaking in Crisis Situations'. *Journal of Management Studies*, 25 (4), 305–317.

CHAPTER 9

ICT, assemblages and institutional contexts: understanding multiple development paths

Francesco Contini

Introduction

This chapter presents a comparative analysis of the case studies explored in the book, using some of the theoretical perspectives discussed in the first part. This heuristic exercise is not intended as a systematic comparison of the different projects. Rather, we will go back and forth between the case studies, drawing out similarities and differences and discussing key features of various e-government projects and some of the dynamics underpinning their development.[1] The chapter also represents an empirical test of the heuristic value of the concept of assemblage. Lanzara introduced this concept to capture the distinctive character of e-services and more generally of e-government and of the 'digital institutions' emerging from the development of these projects (Chapter 1). He argues that assemblages are 'collections' of institutional and technological components which tend to maintain their specificity. These components are connected in different ways to various actors such as public agencies (courts), administrative and technical authorities, as well as the software and hardware companies that shape the new technology-enabled 'service domain' which provides the e-services to the users. The chapter explores the different components of the assemblages, their relations and the mediations occurring between actors and between technological and institutional components. We will look both at the process of design of e-services, and at the context of use in which assemblages emerge.

Before going on, it is however necessary to introduce some specific features of the justice systems that may have a bearing on our argument and findings. To understand changes brought by e-government projects, we have to consider the technological and normative installed base of justice systems prior to the introduction of ICT. Despite some national differences that will be discussed in the following sections, the basic institutional and organisational setting was roughly the same in most of the cases considered in this book. Any action was strictly formalised, and regulated by procedural codes and other rules enacted by different bodies (ministries, judicial councils, courts). This regulative layer was and still is justified by various arguments, among which is the constitutional requirement of assuring an equal treatment of citizens before the law in 'judicial proceedings' (Damaska, 1986). Such proceedings, from an information systems perspective, can be conceived as a set of rule-driven tasks (mainly procedures of an administrative nature) required to present the relevant information to the decision maker, that is the judge. Also, the key judicial artefacts, such as dockets and folders, were set up according to legal provisions. Information and document exchange was mainly based on face to face relations (at the counter or during the hearing) and by the use of standard mail services or bailiffs for official communications. Thus, as with most public agencies, judicial institutions were self-contained bureaucratic organisations, operating in a given legal framework with technologies developed in-house and firmly under the control of key actors such as clerks and judges (Contini, 2000). For this reason, the service was delivered by a single agency (the court) and an annexed institution (bailiffs). Market-like relations with technology providers were in practice non-existent.

However, despite the efforts of the regulative bodies (parliaments, ministries, etc.), and the enactment of the above mentioned institutional and technical machinery, the functioning of the judicial system was still subject to significant local adaptations. The bottom line is that, despite efforts towards standardisation and control, a significant degree of discretionality was left to the individual operator performing a specific action such as the identification of a lawyer at the counter or an update to the paper docket in the back office. The institutional and technological installed base left room for local adaptations which were necessary to match the general rules with local settings and specificities and to guarantee the workability of the systems.

From a juridical perspective the possibility of playing around with the rules was understood as a limit of the system, a problem to solve in order to enforce the general principle of equal application of the law. Here ICT, with its greater powers of inscription and delegation (Czarniawska, 2004), emerged in many cases like a Trojan horse which would solve the problem by increasing standardisation and thus ensuring equal application of the law (Kujanen and Sarvilinna, 2001; Langbroek and Tjaden, 2007).

The inscription of a significant body of rules and tasks into the systems was therefore consistent with this long-term effort and with the related constitutional and institutional expectations.

The public administration and the specificities of the judiciary

Standardisation and rule-based behaviour (March and Olsen, 1989) are organisational features shared by the public sector at large to protect key values such as fairness and equality. In this shared framework, however, justice systems show two specific features which – since they affect innovation processes – have to be assessed: the particular *role of judges* (Guarnieri and Pederzoli, 2002; Di Federico, 2005) and the thickness of the regulative layer. Given these specificities of the judiciary, some caveats have to be made from the point of view of assessment, if our observations and analysis are to be transferable to the public sector at large.

First, judges enjoy a high degree of institutional and organisational independence in order to guarantee impartial judgements and, more generally, the principle of equality of citizens before the law (Cappelletti, 1989). This independence has a profound effect on the dynamics and the results of any innovation (technological, organisational or procedural). Judges enjoy a degree of freedom in adopting (or ignoring) a given innovation which is not comparable with the situation other public officials find themselves in, and which hampers the dynamics of innovation (Fabri and Contini, 2001; Contini and Cordella, 2007). However, it must be noted that judges are not directly involved in the processes of innovation described in the case studies in this book. It is always the administrative staff (clerks, officials and so on) that take care of data and information exchange, whether it be paper-based or electronic. So, the staff take care of the innovation, buffering the judges, who continue to operate in the old manner. Therefore, this critical specificity of the judiciary does not directly affect the development of e-services.

Second, the degree of formalisation and regulation is higher in justice systems than in many other institutions delivering public services. In addition, the dispute between the parties makes more visible (and critical) the interplay between ICT innovation and the normative installed base. Within the framework of each proceeding, each individual party can in principle contest the use of any technological artefact on the grounds that it is illegitimate. Thus a party can ask the judge to assess if a given information system is operating according to the established normative framework (procedural and technical regulations, and so on). In this hypothesis an ICT-enabled procedural step (such as an electronic summons) can be nullified, with ramifications on the outcome of the trial itself.

This example serves to emphasise how the question of the legitimation of technology (Lessig, 1999, 2007) might be magnified in judicial systems. Therefore, the making of assemblages is not just a progressive and linear deployment of a technological layer upon the pre-existing institutional one. Rather, assemblages are the result of conflicts, mediations and accommodations between formal rules, institutional components, technology and people. We will analyse the collection of case studies first from a design perspective. Then, we will change the focus to look at the use of the systems. In doing this, we will consider some key design issues such as the selection of a given e-service from among the wider set of procedures and services delivered by justice systems, and the critical issues of access and identification of users of the e-services are concerned. Then, we will explore the consequences of such design choices on the 'context of use',[2] looking first at the technological and institutional architecture of the assemblage, and then at the mediations between actors and between technological and institutional components that shape the assemblages.

The design issues: selection, functional simplification, legitimation

Given the technological and institutional features of the installed base, the procedures and the services delivered, each project faced the question of the selection of which kind of e-service ought to be developed. In the case studies the answers to this question have been partially different. We will look at this issue first by considering different areas in which functional simplification has taken place. Then we will consider the mediations and adaptations between the existing regulative regime and the technological innovation from the point of view of questions of access and identification.

The construction of a functionally simplified order: operations, procedures and structures

Kallinikos (2001, p. 22) defines functional simplification as the '*identification and selection (hence the reduction of complexity) of sets of operations that are thereby instrumented as strict cause-effect couplings in which a particular cause is expected to lead to its specific effects'*. E-services, however, are not self-contained technologies, and the *'construction of a simplified functional order'* calls for simplification not only at the level of operations. The selection of the actors and organisations to be involved in the project, the judicial procedures to be put online, and the interlocking between online and offline procedures are just a first set of design issues emerging from the case studies.

As illustrated in the MCOL case study (Chapter 7, pp. 199–204), functional simplification operates as a design principle in multiple areas. The first of these is the *selection of the judicial procedures* to be handled electronically. In each country, judicial systems handle cases of different levels of complexity, as is the case in any other public sector agency. This is true not only from a judicial decision-making perspective (which is not immediately relevant to our case), but also from a procedural and administrative perspective: the kind of data and documents to be managed and exchanged or the procedural steps to be taken (number and types of hearings, legal briefs, and so on) vary. Despite the specificities of each justice system, some of these proceedings may be extremely complex (large-scale fraud or bankruptcy or a multi-faceted breach of contract case), while others are fairly simple. This is the case of the so-called debt recovery proceedings, also known as *money claims*. All these cases involve regulated exchanges of documents in which a plaintiff asks for a court order declaring that a given amount of money is owed by a defendant. Money claims are therefore highly standardised cases, and represent a large proportion of the cases dealt with by each court system. In the cases of ELC and *Santra* in the nineties and of MCOL ten years later, the development of e-services started with this kind of simplified procedure.

However, the selection of an 'already simplified' judicial procedure is just a first step. In MCOL, functional simplification also operates by the selection of *sub-types* and *segments of procedure,* thus facilitating the isolation of a simplified functional order. So MCOL can only handle cases with a 'fixed value' (a sub-type of the procedure) and not those with a value to be specified by the judge (requiring more complex proceedings). In addition, MCOL handles the procedure from the filing to the payment of the sum or to a court order based mainly on quasi-automatic decisions such as a default judgment, or judgments by determinations, (Chapter 7, p. 192), while other procedural 'segments' have to be dealt with in the traditional way.

The joint effect of these two simplifications reduces the decisional, procedural and the institutional complexity dealt with by MCOL. The involvement of judges in MCOL procedures is minimal, since the value of the case is fixed,[3] and if the defendant does file a counterclaim, the file is sent to the county court concerned. Therefore, in this specific sub-type of procedure, the whole procedural segment from filing to court order by 'default judgement' can be handled without the direct involvement of the judge. The substantial detachment of judges from the MCOL procedure and the innovation process is a major source of complexity reduction at the decisional, institutional and organisational levels. But, as pointed out by Kallinikos (Chapter 7, p. 204), MCOL demonstrates another strategy of functional simplification: the *interlocking* of online and offline procedures. MCOL procedures are clear-cut and as soon as the case cannot be handled online there is an automatic switch to offline procedures.

Without entering into details, it is worth mentioning that similar design choices have also been made in the case of ELC and of *Santra*. However, comparison of these cases highlights a peculiarity of MCOL. It is the only case study that does not entail the adoption of the technology by all the courts in the country. MCOL is managed by a single centralised unit (the CCBC in Northampton), under the jurisdiction of the Northampton County Court. For all the other county courts, MCOL remains somehow invisible. Only if the claim is not manageable by MCOL does the county court concerned receive the file, which has to be dealt with using the traditional procedure.

The choice of organising the management of the service within a single organisation (Northampton County Court and CCBC) allows a radical simplification. On the one hand it reduces the number of actors involved, and any specific procedural and organisational features of each individual court. Consequently it radically simplifies decision-making. On the other, by concentrating design and implementation within a single organisation, it facilitates institutional and organisational change.[4]

As anticipated, money claims proceedings were a fertile ground for cultivating e-services. However, once a simplified functional order was sealed into a smoothly running technology, and the technology was satisfactorily adopted, it became a piece of the installed base upon which new and more complex e-services could be developed.

Just to give some examples, over time, new procedural segments have been added to MCOL. More recently, the Possession Claim Online Project, a spin-off of MCOL, was launched to manage claims for possession of residential property and for non-payment of rent or mortgage.[5] Both ELC and *Santra* experimented with a progressive increase in terms of kinds of procedures and documents (forms) handled by the systems (see Chapter 5, p. 120 and Chapter 6, pp. 165–166). The increasing number of different functionalities and procedural segments inscribed into these systems indicates how functional simplification is not just a sort of 'unconditioned' design principle, capable of identifying once and for all the procedures that can be handled online.

Rather, once an ICT-enabled, functionally simplified order has been effectively rolled out and adopted by users, it becomes a fertile ground for identifying new e-services and technological developments. This is affected by two groups of factors. First of all, once these systems have been rolled out, they may offer a functioning solution to *'techno-juridical'* knots such as access and identification of users. Second, from an *information infrastructure* perspective (Hanseth, 1996; Ciborra, 2000), the successful deployment of these systems may attract a critical mass of users, thus affecting the growth, and ultimately the effectiveness of e-services. Both issues will be discussed in the next two sections.

Techno-juridical knots: the access to court systems and the issue of identification

As has been seen, the decision to establish the opening of an electronic channel of communication between courts and users poses the problem of the limited transferability of practices and procedures from offline to online. Only 'carefully selected' procedural segments will fit the requirements of online procedures, and this is not just a consequence of functional simplification. A second dynamic emerges as the result of the interplay between technology and formal rules. We have cases where statutory and regulative changes have created a framework in which technology can be easily hosted (Ciborra, 1999, 2002), while other cases are more demanding for reasons that will be explored in the following pages.

In administrative and judicial procedures, the right to be informed regarding a specific case, as well as the information accessible or exchangeable by a party and the court, depend on establishing the *identities* of the actors. As a general rule, at the office counter identification is based on the presentation of ID cards and also on contextual and personal knowledge. In many cases, the court staff know the lawyers personally, and thus the formal procedure based on the checking of ID cards is not required.

We can observe that identification in the traditional public service environment is accomplished by tools and means specific to the environment such as ID cards, face-to-face communication, and personal acquaintance which has developed over time. Moving the identification into the electronic environment, face-to-face communication and personal acquaintance disappear and a new set of institutionalised practices based on remote regulative digital technologies has to be set up. Exactly the same happens for the hand signature on paper documents (Aalberts and van der Hof, 2000).

The problem is how to extend the conditions of confidentiality of the communication to e-services, together with the integrity, authenticity, non-repudiability of the data and documents exchanged, which were granted in the paper-based environment by the identification procedures and the hand signature. The solutions demonstrate different possible mediations between legal frameworks and technological alternatives which have repercussions on the development process.

In most of the case studies, the aim was to set up automatic and self-contained identification and signature procedures, thus inscribing the whole process of identification, access and signature into the new technological system. However, the case studies also offer an alternative approach, which exploits the interlocking between online and offline procedures. In this case identification, access and signature are mediated by human intervention.

As we will see in the following, the solutions found to these techno-juridical knots shape the assemblages. They set up the normative framework in which the e-service will operate and identify the key technological components of the assemblage. Therefore, the analysis casts some light on the mediations between the two regulative regimes, as well as on architectural choices.

Closed network technologies: ELC and Santra

In a first group of cases, the Ministries of Justice set up a system based on *closed networks* and *ad hoc technologies* which were regarded as an extension of the justice networks already in place.

The Austrian government has successfully exploited the fact that the delivery of justice is generally mediated by lawyers. From the early nineties, the Austrian Ministry of Justice developed a closed network accessible only to lawyers and to limited groups of users. The architecture of ELC is simple: authorised users, a gateway run by a private company to grant access to the justice network, and the Federal Computing Center, which checks users, procedures and data, and forwards everything to the centralised court data base.

In the same period, a similar solution was adopted in Finland with *Santra*. Here, as Fabri points out (Chapter 5, pp. 120–121), the Ministry of Justice adopted a closed-network architecture to allow data interchange between courts and authorised users.

In the ELC case, access and identification is based on the correspondence between the personal identity of the users (lawyers and so on) and personal identification codes established during the registration process by the systems (Velicogna, 2007, p. 419). *Santra* applies a similar system. Finnish law (nr. 594 of 1993) states that the Ministry of Justice can give an applicant permission to transmit information regarding a claim to the court's EDP-system.

The problem of signature has been got round using two stratagems. First, the closed network technology certifies the identity of senders and receivers. Second, the assumption is that EDP systems of courts and authorised users, through *Santra* or ELC, are simply exchanging data and not documents (as would happen using traditional procedures).

Both cases illustrate how *ad hoc* technologies can be used to identify well established groups of users (lawyers, notaries, debt recovery companies and so on) and control their access to ministerial systems. The legitimation of technologies is based on formal regulations enacted by authorised institutions which state that the chosen technology can be used by a pre-established group of users for a given set of operations.

Incidentally, we can observe in these cases that networked technologies, instead of acting to *disintermediate* access to public services, ended up by increasing the asymmetries of access to the services. However, these systems were developed in the first half of the nineties (ELC and *Santra*), when the Internet was not yet widely used. In addition closed networks, with their embedded security strategies, guarantee the protection of the system from misuse, fraudulent access and other risks that have to be faced when the Internet technology is adopted. Last but not least, this architecture is consistent with the logic of unilateral control displayed and practised by many public institutions.

E-mail and 'human-gateways' in Finnish civil proceedings

Another strategy for avoiding the problems of access, identification and signature can be seen in a second project of the Finnish Ministry of Justice. In 1993, the Finnish Parliament, suitably inspired by the Ministry of Justice, endorsed the option of filing civil cases by mail, fax and e-mail. This 'low tech' solution leaves the question of identification and signature open. The statutory provision already quoted states that *'the document does not have to be signed as long as there is sufficient information on the message to enable the court to contact the sender if it doubts the originality of the message'* (Laukkanen, 2000). If the clerk or the defendant has doubts regarding the identity of a plaintiff, the data required to check it are available. If identity has not been correctly provided and cannot be ascertained, the case is not filed. So, *in this case the solution* has been found more at the level of legal changes rather than at the level of technological developments (Kujanen and Sarvilinna, 2001, p. 35).

In comparison with the other case studies, this option does not allow automatic data interchange (and the related improvement in court efficiency[6]). There is still an operator who enters the data into the case management system, acting as a 'human-gateway' that interfaces the two systems. But on the other hand, it is an extremely effective way of exploiting ready to hand technologies (such as e-mail) to improve access to a public service.

Like MCOL – and perhaps in an even more radical way – this system is based on a smart interlocking between actions and procedures inscribed into ICT and traditional paper-based human-mediated procedures. If doubts arise, the civil procedure still provides many points at which authorised actors can question, check and decide. To guarantee the certainty of the identity of the users *ex-ante* by technological and automatic means would have been too complex and expensive and would have led to the closure of the system to the general public, as has been the case in other case studies. A judicial process is always partially human mediated, and apart from judicial decision-making, the question of what to leave to humans and what to machines is always open. The cases of E-mail (Finland) and MCOL clarify how statutory changes and appropriate interlocking mechanisms between online and offline procedures can facilitate the accommodation of ICT even in formalised institutions such as justice systems.

Unlike the other cases, where the question of identification has been inscribed into the system to much higher degrees, in Finland (in the case of e-mail, fax etc) it is human agency that takes care of this. This brings in the point that formal procedures within public organisations are – even if to different degrees – human-mediated and paper-based. Hence, system-to-system architectures with corollaries of gateways, networks and so on are not technological necessities, but rather choices made at the design stage.

PKI and digital signature: TOL

Almost ten years after the first implementation of ELC, *Santra* and E-mail, the Trial OnLine (TOL) project leaders in Italy decided that the 'access and identification' question should be solved by a state of the art solution. The Ministry of Justice argued that a public key infrastructure (PKI) and digital signature were required to guarantee the identity of the parties, check their eligibility to file a case in court, and sign electronic documents. These technological implements would be developed according to specifications established by an EU directive and by Italian law. This would allow court staff, judges and lawyers to digitally sign each document and certify each individual connection with court data bases while observing all the provisions of the code of procedures and other relevant statutes (Chapter 5, pp. 134–137).

The first consequence of this decision is that the access to court systems, electronic data and document interchange and the signature of electronic document are regulated by a massive body of statutes and technical rules. Among other things, this regulative framework prescribes the use of smart cards supporting PKI-based digital signatures to access the Ministry of Justice network, while a second smart card is required to digitally sign the documents exchanged with courts. It also provides each lawyers' association with the option of setting up its own 'access point' to the Ministry network, an access point that will grant access solely to members of the lawyers' association.

This architectural framework is based on the widely accepted belief that PKI- based digital signatures (also called 'strong digital signatures') are technological and juridical state of the art solutions for guaranteeing confidentiality and the integrity of the message along with authenticity and the non-repudiability of signatures and document interchange. Therefore, where a hand-written signature is required for a paper document, a strong digital signature is required for the digital one. Where the identification of an actor has to be provided with ID cards, a digital identity has to be provided by smart cards and so on.

The basic idea is that once this new technological layer (PKI, smart cards, digital signature and access points) had been set up, it would be easy to use this secure communication infrastructure for the full data and document interchanges required by all the different procedures set out in the civil code.

So, whereas the other projects revolved around the search for 'simple' judicial procedures in order to move online, and smart solutions for getting round the techno-juridical knot, the TOL attempted to set up an electronic communication system to move all civil procedures online. The joined-up ideas of state of the art technology and full inscription of the code of civil procedure into the ICT systems is the hallmark of TOL. It appears to be a shortcut, capable of legitimising technology from both functional and normative points of view: technology is just a means through which the code of procedure can be literally transplanted from the traditional environment to the new digital one.

Technology is legitimised by technocrats (PKI and digital signature are cutting edge), and by various bodies enacting a huge *corpus* of regulations (the EU Parliament, the Italian Parliament, the Ministry of Justice, and ICT authorities) establishing in great detail what each technology and system can and should do. The code of procedure remains the same institution already legitimised by statutes, practices and Supreme Court decisions. The code of procedures is 'simply' transposed into the digital environment bringing in all the formal requirements (signatures, identifications are just exemplifications) that are rooted in the old service domain.

Unfortunately, the results of this seven year-effort have been negligible. In 2006, the ICT Department of the Ministry (DGSIA) made a dramatic about-turn and – pushed by lawyers – decided to deliver (in one court only) a first version of TOL limited to the money order procedure. It is something very similar to MCOL, which, we must remember, was rolled out in the space of six months.

The techno-juridical framework and the JOP

The techno-juridical framework developed for TOL also had ramifications for the development of the JOP case and other Italian projects not discussed in this book (Velicogna and Ng, 2006, p. 380). As we have seen, the vast number of technical regulations introduced to enable the setting up of TOL suggests that the only way to exchange data and document with courts is through the complex technological framework we have shortly described.

This set of techno-juridical requirements, difficult, complex and expensive to implement, and above all requiring a PKI infrastructure which is not yet available to users, forced the research and development team of the JOP to give up on the idea of developing e-filing and document and data interchange.

The JOP project team made several attempts to convince the Ministry (DGSIA) to accept a simpler technology and a simplified procedure. The argument was that the JOP office deals with very small claims and pro se litigation is more common there than in ordinary courts. Nevertheless, the DGSIA did not change their mind and rejected any alternative proposals. It was therefore impossible (or even prohibited) to roll out a project supporting document and data interchange as happened in the other case studies. For these reasons, the JOP project leaders rolled out a drastically functionally simplified project. Instead of developing e-filing and document interchange by adopting open source software already available (McMillan and Carlson, 2002), as had originally been planned, they simply developed a system to allow access to court CMS data. In this case, digital signatures were not required. Besides, the questions of access and identification were solved thanks to a technology already used for similar purposes in another Ministry of Justice project.[7] In passing, we can observe that this solution was made possible since technical rules did not specify the kind of technology to be used in any given case: the technology used was not legitimated normatively but functionally since it had worked satisfactorily in previous experiments.

These few data allow us to focus on the drawbacks of a normative framework which imposes complex information infrastructures based on components not already shared by potential users. Such a normative framework, by determining in advance that only one specific technology can be used has the effect of getting rid of competing technologies before real experimentation can take place. Here, the tensions between the different regulative regimes – the code of law and the software code – become more visible, but we will return to this topic later.

Smart mediations at MCOL

To conclude the analysis of the different mediations found for the questions concerning access to the system, identification, signature of electronic documents, etc, we would like to cite MCOL as an example, once again, of finding a smart mediation between different requirements. As mentioned by Kallinikos in his analysis (Chapter 7, p. 177), one of the institutional goals of MCOL was to improve access to justice. Closed networks were not suitable for this goal. PKI and smart cards, not being in common use among the general public, were also inappropriate.

On the other hand, some means of automatic control of the identities of the parties was desirable, as were automatic payment procedures for court fees. Based on these design requirements the solution was twofold: first registration in the system, carried out independently by the parties and where privacy was protected by technological means such as case sensitive passwords and encryptions,[8] and second the use of debit and credit cards for paying court fees and checking the identities of the parties. In the case of doubt or contestation, there was always the option of switching from the online to the offline procedure.

Here, unlike the case of E-mail in Finland, the identification procedure is inscribed into the system. But as in the Finnish case, the system exploits features of the installed base. First it takes advantage of the organisation of judicial proceedings in which defendants have many procedural alternatives for ascertaining the identity of claimants. Second the system is built on technological components which are already available such as the systems of the CCBC as well as the web, e-mail, and credit or debit cards as far as potential users are concerned. Once again, we notice how viable solutions require smart interlockings and mediations between online and offline procedures, and between workable technological solutions and legal requirements.

The context of use: architectures, governance and users

In the previous sections we have mainly discussed design issues and the mediation used to unravel the techno-juridical knots. We have seen that the design of an e-service requires first its careful selection from within the plethora of data, processes and services of an administration. Systems must be developed (by the Ministry, by contracted companies or by purchasing systems available on the 'market') and the law amended to facilitate the integration and the hosting of the technology within the institutions.

When we look at the consequences of these actions and decisions we move from the context of design to the context of use (Chapter 2, pp. 61–62). We can look at this context from two different perspectives. First, design decisions previously discussed lead inevitably to the marketization of the 'service domain' with the involvement of companies providing technologies, services and infrastructures (Chapter 4). Second, these decisions, shaping the institutional and technological architectures (Table 9.1), have a significant effect on the dynamics and growth of the information infrastructure required for delivering e-services. Once the technological and regulative infrastructure has been set up, potential users are expected to connect up and exploit the e-services. But the case studies tell us a different story. The results, in terms of access and usage of these systems, have not always come up to the expectations of the project leaders. It is important to understand why. As we have seen, the technologies selected to unravel the techno-juridical knot shape a 'service domain' in which a growing number of actors are involved. The technologies are highly specific assets and thus call for long-term bilateral transactions between the providers and the public sector agencies. In addition, as will be clear in a while, there may also be problems in the development (or in the costs) of the technologies to be used by lawyers to access the e-services.

Judicial procedures are formalised systems regulating and supporting the information exchange required to present relevant case-related information to a judge. Hence, these procedures (ICT enabled or not) are shared

Table 9.1   Basic architectures of the case studies

	E-mail	Santra	ELC	MCOL	TOL	JOP
Court or Ministry of Justice systems	Court CMS	Court CMS	Court CMS	CCBC CMS	Court CMS	Court CMS mirror
	Court mail boxes	*Santra*		MCOL System	TOL System	e-services
Intermediate agencies and technologies			Federal Computing Center systems		PKI access point	
			Datakom–Telekom systems	Debt card system	PKI for digital signature	Cineca's Systems Ianus gate
Communication infrastructure	Internet	Closed network	Closed network	Internet	Internet	Internet
Users systems	Users' mail box	*Ad hoc systems*	*Ad hoc systems*	Users web	*Ad hoc systems (form writer)*	Users web

resources put in place and employed by courts and parties for information exchange. In other words, it is an information infrastructure (Hanseth, 1996; Ciborra, 2000). Among the many features of information infrastructures, their evolutionary dynamics are critical to our analysis.

Since they are shared among large groups of users, information infrastructures do not change through the smooth replacement of old components with new ones (as in the case of simpler technological systems shared by small groups of users such as CMS). Rather they evolve through slow processes in which new elements (for example a new e-service) are added to the existing information infrastructure, while other elements (for example the customary filing systems) become obsolete and are abandoned by users. Besides, since they are shared communication systems, their value for the users depends on how many people make use of them (Hanseth, 2003, p. 385). Apart from the functionalities it offers, an e-service has little value if the majority of potential users still follow the 'old' paper-based procedures. In this case, the e-service is simply a cost for both the agency that rolled out the system and for the parties that decided to buy (or develop) the technological implements required for connecting to the infrastructure.

Hence a sharp and rapid increase in the number of users and transactions is a critical goal in each of our case studies. Therefore, it is crucial to identify the conditions which will facilitate the growth (in terms of users) of the information infrastructures.

The more users adopt the new systems, the more the value of e-services as a means of communication is built up, and new users will find them attractive. With these self-reinforcing cycles, the e-service loses its experimental glaze and becomes a constitutive part of the overall information infrastructure. Once this has taken place, e-services are legitimated not just from a legal perspective (as seen above), but also in practice.

Following Hanseth and Lyytinen (2006) we can single out two principles that should enable a rapid growth of e-services and a self-reinforcement of the installed base. The first one is 'users before features'. This can be achieved by *'focussing on the needs of specific users groups to whom the infrastructure can add significant value even though the number of users is small'* and by keeping the infrastructure *'as simple as possible [...] cheap to develop and adopt, and easy to change'* (2006, p. 3). The second principle is to *'avoid lock-in by the installed base'*. In highly institutionalised systems, where backward compatibility has to be guaranteed, a *'revolutionary strategy for sweeping transformation'* is very unlikely, while an evolutionary strategy is possible. It can be pursued by modularising the infrastructure and using gateways and *'clean interfaces'* connecting the different modules of the infrastructures so that they may evolve independently (2006, pp. 25–26).

Moving from this analytical framework we can now reconsider the case studies. Even if most of them mainly focus on the contexts of design, they provide examples and data which are useful for exploring the context of use.

Robustness versus fragility of the assemblage: the JOP case

One of the original goals of the JOP project was to roll out e-services fully based on web technologies already available to court users. This would allow the speeding up of self-reinforcing cycles. As the case study pointed out, however, the ICT Department of the Ministry and one of the research partners pressed for a more closed and secure architecture. This was achieved thanks to a proprietary technology already used to grant the privacy and transaction security in similar projects. As it was only an experimental project, this third party technology was offered free of charge to the participants during the experimentation (Chapter 8, pp. 225–226). However, the need for such technological tools prevented a wide take-up of the e-services. This further step would have required an agreement between the court, the local lawyers' association and the provider of the third party technology. But for the court it was not appropriate to press the lawyers' association to use that or another proprietary technology.

While 'users before features' was a ubiquitous guideline in the JOP case, pressure from the Ministry of Justice and the provider of the technology forced the use of a technological tool that made the growth of the information infrastructure much more problematic. Once the experimentation was over, the lack of a critical mass of professional users made it difficult to keep the e-service online. Users thought they had just taken part in an 'interesting' experiment, and the game was over. For the JOP, to have a few lawyers (out of several hundred) with online access to their system was not a solution to the long queues at the counter. It was more important to keep online the e-services that were open to all users and which were accessed frequently.

This case is also interesting in terms of *governance*. 'Proprietary technology', with its specificities and costs, modifies the traditional relationship between the court and the lawyers which, as a rule, is not mediated by any technology or institution. The problem is only apparently trivial. This 'proprietary technology', placed between court and user systems, falls into a kind of 'no-man's land', in an area in which nobody has clear jurisdiction. Is it appropriate for the court to impose on the lawyers' association and the lawyers the use of a given technology provided on the market by a third party? Is the lawyers' association supposed to decide (impose) which technology must be used to access the systems of the Ministry? Is a joint decision required between these actors? In a highly regulated institutional framework with areas of competence and duties formally set out in law, the need to take this kind of decision can soon turn a smoothly running project into a never-ending problem-solving exercise and sometimes into a nightmare.

The case also shows the divergent values, interests and points of view of those who control the network (the ICT Department), those who provide the services (courts) and the public (lawyers and private individuals etc). While courts and users were really interested in the development and use of electronic channels of information exchange, the Ministry seemed more concerned with the security of the network.

This case is just one example of the growing power of those that provide or control the technologies and who have the authority to filter information and services (Benkler, 2006, pp. 75–80). The paradox is that e-government, instead of facilitating and enabling information exchange between the court and the users, makes it more complex and subject to decisions and jurisdictions of other agencies.

However, this technological and institutional complexity made e-services vulnerable to changes in the service domain. The replacement of the network provider of the Ministry and the subsequent adaptation of security and network policies suddenly posed a threat to the assemblage. The court administrator implemented a strategy to keep the e-services running and freely accessible to users. This was easier from technological and institutional points of view, since proprietary technologies were not required as they were for the other e-services which were accessible for lawyers. It was also more important from a JOP perspective given the larger number of users. However this episode of the JOP case study is not over yet.

Costs of access and growth of information infrastructure: E-mail and *Santra*

The use of e-mail in Finnish courts is an illuminating example of how amendments to the regulative layer can radically reduce the complexity of the technological architecture required and related problems. Here the architecture, in terms of actors and technologies involved, is very simple: the user's mail system, through the Internet, sends a message to a dedicated mail address in the court. This means that all the technologies required were in principle available to the potential users. The drawbacks are clear. Automation is much lower than in all the other cases. Clerks, operating as human gateways, still have the job of checking the identity of the applicant and, if it is in doubt, can carry out a specific procedure. Also, data entry into the courts' CMS is performed manually by entering the data provided by the claimants via e-mail or fax. So, continuous human supervision (to check and enter the data) is required. This is exactly what ELC, MCOL, and *Santra* attempted to inscribe into the system, and what made them more complex and difficult to roll out.

The Finnish e-mail case epitomises the exploitation of the design principle of 'users before features', since e-mail and fax are (and were also back in the nineties) widely available to court users even if their features (functionalities) were poor in comparison to any other electronic communication technology. Furthermore, this option allows a great deal of flexibility: moving from this technological and institutional installed base, it is easy to improve the system as is the case with the recent development of a secure e-mail system for the Finnish lawyers' association (Chapter 5, p. 120). Finally, this solution also works from a governance perspective. The Ministry, as well as the courts and the users, does not need to develop technologies with a high degree of specificity or to involve third parties in long-term bilateral contractual relationships, which is what happened in most of the case studies.

The other Finnish project, *Santra*, tells a different story. The Ministry of Justice (without the involvement of other actors) 'offers' users the option of connecting up to the Ministerial Network through *Santra* and exchanging data with the courts' CMS (*Tuomas*). To do this, however, the users have to procure (develop or buy) an *ad hoc* system designed to exchange data with *Santra*. The expectation of the Ministry had been that lawyers would adopt this technology widely, but in the event just a few large debt recovery companies, handling a large number of small claims in courts, bought or developed the systems required to exchange data through *Santra* (Laukkanen, 2000). As we have seen, practising lawyers preferred to use other channels to file cases such as fax, e-mail or the traditional ones. While *Santra* has more functions than e-mail (data interchange, automatic notifications and so on), it is more rigid, more expensive and less suitable for the lawyers with a small number of cases in court. While email and the web are already available and are free of charge, *Santra* is more demanding and hence suits the needs of a more limited group of users.

Austria's ELC and the statutory minimal technological requirements

In comparison with the cases discussed so far, ELC has a more complex architecture. Two distinct organisations are placed between users' and courts' systems to grant access and secure data interchange (Datakom and the Federal Computing Center). While *Santra* was developed and is managed by a unit of the Ministry of Justice, in the Austrian case, the Ministry of Justice has left the management of some of these components to external organisations (Datakom and the Federal Computing Center, and IBM), thus increasing institutional complexity. The transactions with these organisations are governed through long-term agreements, and no problems have been mentioned, even if such transactions may incur high transaction costs. This could lead to heavy dependence on the providers and this could also compromise further development of the project (see Cordella e Willkocks, Chapter 4, p. 95).

As in the other case studies, one of the key problems is the development of the systems to be used by lawyers to connect up to Ministry of Justice systems. Unlike the case of *Santra*, in Austria systems are offered by different companies to lawyers with pay per use contracts as well. The strategy of the Ministry has been clear-cut and successful. All the technical specifications of ELC necessary for software developers were published from the start. Once a year, the ICT Department of the Ministry of Justice organises a meeting which is open to all software developers to discuss problems and to present any planned developments of the system. It is also important to note that the Austrian Ministry of Justice does not impose a specific technology. Rather, it establishes the technological standards required to connect up to their systems and disseminates the information necessary for an efficient functioning of the development of the market of such applications (Chapter 6, pp. 162–167).

However, it should be noted that the use of ELC for filing cases was fairly limited until 1995. Since then, a faster growth of the number of transactions can be explained by the use of the systems by banks and insurance companies (users with bulk and highly standardised cases), and also by the use of ELC for enforcement proceedings.[9] The statutory changes brought in 1999 are even more important, since they required that lawyers had at their disposal the use of a minimal technological platform. Since then, lawyers have been obliged to install the technical systems required for using ELC. In addition, the court can send documents to lawyers electronically without the lawyers' agreement. These changes led to a further boost in the number of transactions.

Building the last mile from scratch: TOL

As usual, TOL is the most complex case of all. The architecture designed by the Ministry of Justice requires the setting up of access points to the Ministry's network based on the verification of the identity of lawyers certified through a smart card and PKI. A second digital signature – also supported by a smart card – must be used to sign electronic documents. A third technology must be developed for drafting the electronic documents to be sent to the court. So, in comparison with the other cases, the architecture of TOL has a deeper layer of technological tools and actors between the courts and the users. In addition, it is important to highlight that these technologies are neither developed by the Ministry nor by a company contracted by the Ministry of Justice. Rather, the development of the technological tools required to link the Ministry systems to those of potential users (that is the last mile) has been left up to the users and their organisations (the lawyers' associations), as was the case for *Santra* and ELC. However TOL is more demanding because of the complexity of the architecture. This requires the development and integration of different technologies (PKI, access points, lawyers' CMS) by different actors with different interests. Therefore, the governance of the service domain also becomes a tricky issue.

At present TOL is facing the problem of development and deployment of the different pieces of infrastructure still needed to link the lawyers to the systems of the Ministry. The local lawyers' associations suddenly discovered that there were only a few companies in the market, and the costs for setting up and maintaining the systems to link up with the Ministry systems were unreasonably high, as were the costs for integrating the lawyers' CMS with the technical standards of TOL.

Other problems were with the Ministry of Justice. The Ministry did not share promptly and fully the TOL technical specifications required for developing the software (as was done by the Austrian Ministry), nor did they make a prototype available to allow software developers to check 'live' the integration of their systems with those of the Ministry.

This decision gave rise to a huge number of practical and technical problems. One of these was, and still is, that many components of information infrastructures (such as smart cards and access points) were not available or in common use. Another problem is that the Ministry has not played much part in promoting or pressing lawyers' associations and lawyers to develop or buy these expensive infrastructures. At the time of writing, almost eight years since the launch of the project, the Ministry has stated that their systems are ready (as far as money claim procedures are concerned), while they blame lawyers and lawyers' associations for not having set up their systems yet.

Building the last mile from the installed base: MCOL

The difficulties to be faced for developing information infrastructures from scratch, (that is requiring components which are not available and not shared by potential users) are clear, as well as the reasons for the faster track of projects based on components already to hand as with the Finnish E-mail system (discussed above), and with MCOL.

In comparison with the other case studies, the main difference is the way in which the techno-juridical knots of user's access and identification have been unravelled. Instead of building closed networks (ELC and *Tuomas-Santra*) or new components of information infrastructures starting from scratch (TOL), in MCOL identification and the payment of court fees have been delegated to the systems of debit and credit cards. Therefore, MCOL's architecture is fully based on technologies which are already part of the technological installed base of potential users. While other projects were facing the challenge of building new components of the information infrastructure, such as closed networks or PKI, the rapid development and deployment of MCOL was based on existing pieces of software and infrastructures. Users do not need to use specific technologies, since the system is web-based. Transactions are carried out through the Internet and are supported by external infrastructural elements already in place (debit or credit cards), used for the payment of court fees, for curbing the misuse of the systems, and checking the identity of the plaintiffs. 'Users first' is clearly the key guideline.

Mediations and the making of assemblages

The pervasive deployment of ICT in highly regulated institutions poses key questions of the legitimation of technology (Lessig, 1999, 2007) and of its regulative power (Chapter 3). While in the traditional paper-based environment the legitimation of operations and working practices is rooted in well established procedures and authority, the question is still open in the domain of ICT. In the public sector (and foremost in judicial systems), technology cannot be legitimated just because 'it works', that is from a functional or pragmatic point of view. In each case study, the technology has also been legitimated – even if in different ways – by law. Statutory changes may ease the hosting (Ciborra, 2002) of technological innovation in an organisation or institution. They may also state that a given technology is compatible with, appropriate or even mandatory for, a particular set of operations. But as the TOL case demonstrates, even the most detailed regulative effort may fail to make e-services work. Therefore the question is how to legitimate the ICT both functionally and normatively.

The simple model of developing technology first, making it work and then, only at a later stage, provide it with normative legitimacy generates the problem of leaving (for some time) doors open to technologies which have not been authorised by the authority concerned. This may hamper the fairness of proceedings.

On the other hand, a development based on an *ex-ante* normative legitimation of technology, followed by an attempt at making it work (functional legitimation) is not any easier. One of the reasons is bounded rationality, and the consequent difficulties in regulating such a complex system *ex-ante*. Other reasons are related to the growing inscription of formal procedures[10] into technological systems to curb the discretionality of organisational actors (TOL and ELC above all). This happens with the automation of a growing number of tasks and the centralisation of the management of systems. Systems are increasingly designed and run at centralised level and local adaptations are in many cases not allowed. This does not mean that technology is not malleable in a given context (Chapter 3, p. 70). Rather, it means that the Ministries of Justice are carrying out a strategy to reduce such malleability and to increase their control over operations. As a consequence, the mediations that usually occur between the multiple logics, requirements and expectations affecting the service domain are moved from the context of use (such as the counter of the court) to the context of design.

The need for mediation between different and sometime conflicting logics becomes clear when we consider the huge number of practices and procedures situated in the traditional context (paper- and rule-based) which for different reasons have not been able to 'travel' from the old to the new technology-enabled setting, from the old to the new medium.

The translation model (Callon, 1986; Czarniawska and Sevón, 1996) offers an appropriate metaphor for re-considering the changes we have observed. From this point of view, the e-services running in our case study are the result of a translation of artefacts, codes and practices from a traditional context (based on face-to-face relations, and supported by paper) to a new one (mediated, enabled and supported by ICT). The translation has been characterised by *'displacement, drift, invention, mediation, creation of new links that did not exist before'* (Latour, 1993, p. 6 quoted in Czarniawska and Sevón, 1996). In these dynamics while some issues have been successfully translated, many others have been 'lost in translation' as a result of decisions taken at the design stage, or as a consequence of problems emerging during the development or piloting stages.

In most cases, the design of e-services is aimed at the identification of the pieces of the old system that can be translated (and adapted) into the new one. These pieces of the old system have two key features: they respond to and are consistent with the requirements of both the regulative and the technological layers. As illustrated by the case studies, the design of successful e-services has been achieved with selection and simplification operating at multiple levels and in different areas.

1) Identification of the *services* (document interchange, public access to court data bases), that can be reasonably handled online, as when the JOP project was aimed only at providing access to court data and not to e-filing.

2) Identification of simple *procedures*, such as money claims (MCOL, *Santra*, ELC), which can be functionally simplified.

3) Selection of *sub-types of procedures* (money claims for fixed amounts) and of *segments* of *procedures* (form filing to default judgement) that can be easily translated into strict cause and effect, streamlined and inscribed into the system, as in the case of MCOL.

4) Selection of appropriate *gateways* and *interlocking* mechanisms between online and offline procedures (MCOL; ELC, *Santra*, E-mail), to

support the smooth flow of judicial procedures even when they go beyond the limits of online proceedings, or when it is appropriate to switch from offline to online or vice-versa for any reason;

5) Identification of the *organisations* involved in the innovation process, for example MCOL in which just the CCBC and the Northampton County Court are actively involved, while other county courts have not been directly affected by the innovation.

However, a careful and precise selection process is not enough to provide for acceptable mediations. *Statutory changes* have been introduced to ease the translation of judicial practices into the new media and the accommodation of the new technological artefacts into the pre-existing institutional context. Illuminating examples are the reduction in signature requirements (Finland), the replacement of hand signatures with ready to hand functional equivalents (MCOL), or the abolition of the requirements to present the original copy of the evidence to court at the filing stage or when the claim is not contested (Finland, ELC and MCOL). The joint effect is a new judicial procedure where documents are not signed, and evidence is not produced unless absolutely essential. So, after selection, functional simplification, and statutory changes, some of the building blocks of traditional judicial proceedings remain in the old context. These blocks have been 'lost in translation', without apparently altering the principles and the fairness of judicial proceedings.

To be 'lost in translation' is not necessarily a consequence of mistakes. Rather, it is a consequence of the multiple mediations (Sassen, 2004, p. 88) that occur in the development and use of e-services. To focus on this last point, it is worth looking at TOL again. In this case study, the original problem was not the selection of which features to translate into the digital environment and the accommodation of statutes and codes of procedures to facilitate the adoption of the system. Rather, the design process was aimed at the identification of the technologies required to translate the entire code of civil procedure into the new media. As Fabri notes, technology has been used to 'enable' the existing code of civil procedure, and enforce its correct application. This approach led to the identification of a technology fully capable of managing digital signatures and electronic documents, and to the enactment of a huge body of technical rules regulating the functioning of technological tools. Nevertheless, this huge undertaking has not been sufficient to translate (totally or in part) the Civil Trial OnLine.

The selection of functionally simplified procedures (money orders in this case as well) was arrived at several years after the launch of the project. Lost in translation, in this case, appears more the result of a change in the original strategy: a change which was motivated by the impossibility of assembling the technological and institutional components as originally planned.

The comparison of the different case studies shows that the assemblages call for an adaptation of the pre-existing normative layer to ease the accommodation and the hosting of the new services enabled by technology. More generally it requires mediation between the specific requirements of software and legal codes. Mediation poses a challenge and, in one way or another, many constitutive elements of the existing set-up will be lost in translation. On the other hand, certain technologies may not be acceptable for legal codes (or to policy makers with the powers to amend them).

Last but not least, mediation also occurs between the different actors involved in the development and use of the e-services. The development of an information infrastructure shared by multiple independent agencies and actors requires an approach which is different from approaches traditionally followed for simpler automation projects. As clearly emerges in the JOP case, the Ministry of Justice, the courts, the users and the providers of the technology have different perspectives, interests and goals. Mediations are so important in the making of assemblages, that new skills are probably required for the development of e-government projects. While jurists, engineers, lawyers, systems developers, and office staff look at the development of these systems from their technical and selectively specific perspective, the assemblage of elements that are composite and have only limited compatibility requires the skills of mediators. As with any mediator, their role is to facilitate communication between the parties, to assist them in focusing on the limited compatibility between the elements to be assembled and in unravelling the techno-juridical knots in a workable way and, as a consequence, to design and set up robust assemblages.

Notes

1. For this reason, I will focus the analysis on the systems developed to offer e-services to citizens (G2C) and in particular Money Claims Online (England and Wales), Civil Trials Online and Justice of the Peace e-services (Italy), Electronic Legal Communication (Austria), and Santra and e-mail (Finland).

2. In Chapter 2 Barbara Czarniawska emphasises that '*the arc of reciprocation is always wider than the arc of projection*'. Following this line of argument, we change our focus (from design to use of the systems) to reveal some of dynamics of the context of use, which tends to pose problems that go beyond the projections of the designers.

3. Hence does not have to be ascertained by judges.
4. The JOP case also focused on just one court, but this is because it was a research project promoted by a research team and not a typical project launched by the Ministry of Justice.
5. www.hmcourts-service.gov.uk/onlineservices/index.htm. Last visited 10 April 2008.
6. Considering the time and costs involved in developing highly integrated and automated systems, this last comment is however open to question.
7. The technology allows precise identification of every single computer connected to the Ministry of Justice network, and therefore reproduces the closed network approach of *Santra* and ELC.
8. www.hmcourts-service.gov.uk/onlineservices/mcol/userguide/claimant/secure.htm. Last visited 4 March 2008.
9. Peter Kritz, E-Justice – Datahighway to Austrian Courts, Judicial Electronic Data Interchange, presentation at the Conference Judicial Electronic Data Interchange (JEDI), Bologna, 11–12 October 2002.
10. By these terms I mean procedures set up following the minutiae of the provisions of the law in the books. This approach does not consider the specificities and local adaptations that in most cases are required to transform the law in the books into accepted working practices.

References

Aalberts, B. and S. van der Hof (2000), *Digital Signature Blindness. Analysis of Legislative Approaches toward Electronic Authentication.* The Hague: Kluwer.

Benkler, Y. (2006), *The Wealth of Networks. How Social Production Transforms Markets and Freedom.* New Haven, NJ: Yale University Press.

Callon, M. (1986), 'Some Elements of Sociology of Translation: Domestication of the Scallops and the Fishermen'. In Law, J. (ed.), *Power, Action and Belief: A New Sociology of Knowledge*, London: Routledge and Kegan Paul, (196–233).

Cappelletti, M. (1989), *The Judicial Process in Comparative Perspective.* Oxford: Clarendon press.

Ciborra, C. (1999), 'Hospitality and IT'. In Ljungberg, F. (ed.), *Informatics in the Next Millennium*, Lund, Sweden: Studentlitteratur, (161–176).

Ciborra, C. (2000) (ed.), *From Control to Drift.* Oxford: Oxford University Press.

Ciborra, C. (2002), *The Labyrints of Information. Challanging the Wisdom of the System*. Oxford: Oxford University Press.

Contini, F. (2000), 'Reinventing the Docket, Discovering the Data Base: The Divergent Adoption of IT in the Italian Judicial Offices'. In Fabri, M. and P.M. Langbroek (eds), *The Challange of Change for Judicial System*. Amsterdam, The Netherlands: IOS Press.

Contini, F. and A. Cordella (2007), 'Information System and Information Infrastructure Deployment: the Challenge of the Italian e-Justice Approach'. *The Electronic Journal of e-Government,* 5 (1), 43–52.

Czarniawska, B. (2004), 'On Time, Space, And Action Nets'. *Organization Studies,* 11 (6), 773–791.

Czarniawska, B. and Sevón, G. (1996), *Translating Organizational Change*. Berlin: Walter de Gruyter.

Damaska, M.R. (1986), *The Faces of Justice and the State Authority. a Comparative Approach to the Legal Process*. New Haven: Yale University Press.

Di Federico, G. (2005), 'Independence and Accountability of the Judiciary in Italy. the Experience of a Former Transitional Country in a Comparative Perspective'. In AA.VV. (eds), *Institutional Independence and Integrity*. Budapest: Central European University.

Fabri, M. and F. Contini (eds), (2001), *Justice and Technology in Europe: How ICT is Changing Judicial Business*. The Hague, The Netherlands: Kluwer Law International.

Guarnieri, C. and P. Pederzoli (2002), *The Power of Judges: a Comparative Study of Courts and Democracy*. Oxford: Oxford University Press.

Hanseth, O. (1996), Information Technology as Infrastructure. Unpublished PhD Thesis, Goteborg: School of Economics and Commercial Law, Goteborg University.

Hanseth, O. (2003), 'Design as Bootstrapping. On the Evolution of ICT Networks in Health Care'. *Methods of Information in Medicine,* 42 (4), 385–391.

Hanseth, O. and K. Lyytinen (2006), 'Theorizing about the Design of Information Infrastructures: Design Kernel Theories and Principles'. Retrieved from Heim.Ifi.Uio.No/~Oleha/Publications/ Isrinfrastructurefinal05–12-05.Pdf. Visited 10 April 2008.

Kallinikos, J. (2006), *The Consequences of Information*. Cheltenham: Edward Elgar Publishing Company.

Kujanen, K. and S. Sarvilinna (2001), 'Approaching Integration: ICT in the Finnish Judicial System'. In Fabri, M. and F. Contini (eds), *Justice and Technology in Europe: How ICT is Changing Judicial Business*. The Hague, The Netherlands: Kluwer Law International.

Langbroek, P.M. and M. Tjaden (2007), 'Developing Information and Communication Technology in the Dutch Criminal Justice Chain: between Central Control and Diversity in Decentralised Agencies'. In Fabri, M. (ed.), *Information and Comunication Technology for the Public Prosecutor's Office*, Bologna: Clueb.

Latour, B. (1993), *Messanger talks*. Lund: The Institute of Economic Research Working Paper No. 9.

Laukkanen, S. (2000), *The Challenge of Information Society: Application of Advanced technologies in Civil Litigation and other procedures, National Report of Finland*. Retrieved from ruessmann.jura.uni-sb.de/grotius/Reports/Finnland.htm#<4T. Visited 18 April 2008.

Lessig, L. (1999), *Code and Other Laws of Cyberspace*. New York: Basic Books.

Lessig, L. (2007), *Code and Other Laws of Cyberspace. Version 2.0*. New York: Basic Books.

March, J.G. and J.P. Olsen (1989), *Rediscovering Institutions: the Organizational Basis of Politics*. New York: Free Press.

McMillan, J. and T. Carlson (2002), *Incounter. An Open-Source Electronic Filing Demonstration Project*. Williamsburg, VA: National Center for State Courts.

Sassen, S. (2004), Towards a Sociology of Information Technology. In C. Avgerou, Ciborra, C. and F. Land (eds), *The Social Study of Information and Communication Technology*. Oxford: Oxford University Press.

Velicogna, M. (2007), 'Il processo telematico in Europa'. *Informatica e diritto,* 16 (1–2).

Velicogna, M. and G.Y. Ng (2006), 'Legitimacy and Internet in the Judiciary: A Lesson from the Italian Courts' Websites Experience'. *International Journal of Law and Information Technology,* 14 (3), 370–389.

INDEX